L.M. MONTGOMERY
AND WAR

L.M. MONTGOMERY
AND WAR

Edited by

Andrea McKenzie and Jane Ledwell

McGill-Queen's University Press

Montreal & Kingston • London • Chicago

© McGill-Queen's University Press 2017

ISBN 978-0-7735-4980-7 (cloth)
ISBN 978-0-7735-4981-4 (paper)
ISBN 978-0-7735-4982-1 (ePDF)
ISBN 978-0-7735-4983-8 (ePUB)

Legal deposit second quarter 2017
Bibliothèque nationale du Québec

Printed in Canada on acid-free paper

This book has been published with the help of a grant from the
Canadian Federation for the Humanities and Social Sciences, through
the Awards to Scholarly Publications Program, using funds provided
by the Social Sciences and Humanities Research Council of Canada.
Funding was also received from the L.M. Montgomery Institute
at the University of Prince Edward Island, through a SSHRC
Connection grant.

McGill-Queen's University Press acknowledges the support of the
Canada Council for the Arts for our publishing program. We also
acknowledge the financial support of the Government of Canada
through the Canada Book Fund for our publishing activities.

Library and Archives Canada Cataloguing in Publication

L.M. Montgomery and war / edited by Andrea McKenzie and Jane
Ledwell.

Includes bibliographical references and index.
Issued in print and electronic formats.
ISBN 978-0-7735-4980-7 (cloth).– ISBN 978-0-7735-4981-4 (paper).
– ISBN 978-0-7735-4982-1 (ePDF).– ISBN 978-0-7735-4983-8 (ePUB)

1. Montgomery, L. M. (Lucy Maud), 1874–1942 – Criticism and
interpretation. 2. War and literature – Canada. I. McKenzie, Andrea,
author, editor II. Ledwell, Jane, 1972–, editor

PS8526.O55Z757 2017   C813'.52   C2016-907733-0
                                                C2016-907734-9

Contents

Figures

Acknowledgments

We are grateful to the Social Sciences and Humanities Research Council of Canada for assisting with the publication of this book through a Connections grant. We are equally grateful to York University and the University of Prince Edward Island for additional funding for research assistants. We would also like to thank the L.M. Montgomery Institute for funding a Visiting Scholarship for 2013–15, which greatly aided in our collaboration.

The journey through L.M. Montgomery's war has been challenging. We would like to thank the L.M. Montgomery Institute for its whole-hearted support of our work, including the chairs of the LMMI Committee, Mark Leggott and Philip Smith, LMMI founder Elizabeth Epperly, who encouraged us throughout the process, 2014 conference co-chair Benjamin Lefebvre, and conference coordinator Elizabeth DeBlois. We are also grateful to the Heirs of L.M. Montgomery and to their representative, Sally Keefe Cohen, for their support. The staff of the Robertson Library at the University of Prince Edward Island was always helpful, including Simon Lloyd in Special Collections and Pauline MacPherson, administrator extraordinaire. Our research assistants, Anastasiya Ivanova at York University and Mark John Cousins at the University of Prince Edward Island, performed excellent work, and we are grateful for their dedication.

Our colleagues in the L.M. Montgomery world have contributed greatly to the final work. We would like to thank the contributors to this volume for their collaboration. Among other colleagues, we are grateful to Benjamin Lefebvre for contributing his outstanding knowledge of Montgomery's works, scholarship, and resources; Carolyn Strom

Collins for her expertise on Montgomery's publications during the war; and Sarah Glassford for deepening our knowledge of Montgomery's war work as a minister's wife and head of women's organizations.

This book would not have come to fruition without acquisitions editor Mark Abley at McGill-Queen's University Press, whose expertise helped at every stage of the process. We are grateful to the competent and professional team at the press.

In the personal world, Andrea would like to thank her partner in all things, Ro Sheffe, for his constant, unflagging support; he, too, has journeyed through the war and lived to tell the tale. And thanks, too, to her mom, who has quietly contributed many books to Andrea's collection of L.M. Montgomery's early editions across the decades, and whose ideas are invariably fruitful.

Jane would like to thank her partner, Stephen B. MacInnis, and their children, Anna and Sam, for their patience. She is grateful to her colleagues at the PEI Advisory Council on the Status of Women and to friends at the University of Prince Edward Island, particularly to Montgomery co-conspirator Jean Mitchell, and to Laurie Brinklow and Joan Sinclair, colleagues at Island Studies Press, for deepening understanding of island(s) history and culture.

L.M. Montgomery, Emily of New Moon, The Story Girl, and *Blue Castle* are trademarks of Heirs of L.M. Montgomery Inc. *Anne of Green Gables* and other indicia of "Anne" are trademarks and/or Canadian official marks of the Anne of Green Gables Licensing Authority Inc.

L.M. MONTGOMERY
AND WAR

Introduction

Andrea McKenzie and Jane Ledwell

In March 1885, when Métis under Louis Riel clashed with the North-West Mounted Police and volunteer militia in the territory that would become Saskatchewan, nine of the volunteer soldiers from the nearby town of Prince Albert were killed.[1] Two thousand miles away, in far-off Cavendish, Prince Edward Island, an eleven-year-old girl waited to hear from her father, who was one of the volunteers from Prince Albert. Many years later, she would write, "communication between [Prince Albert] and the outside world was cut for months. During all that time I had no word from father and it was not known if he were living or dead ... How glad I was when at last a letter came from father."[2]

The young girl was L.M. Montgomery, and the North-West Resistance, organized to try to obtain rights for the Métis people from the Canadian government, was her first encounter with war and conflict. At eleven years of age, Montgomery experienced the suspense of not knowing whether her soldier father, Hugh John Montgomery, was alive or dead in battle. Many years later she would parlay that emotion into her best-known novel about war, *Rilla of Ingleside*, in which its teenaged heroine, Rilla Blythe, her mother, Anne Shirley Blythe, and other characters suffer the agony of suspense about the fate of family members and friends fighting overseas during the First World War.[3]

Although Montgomery is usually linked with the First World War through her published writing, she experienced four major conflicts during her lifetime. Born in 1874, she lived during the North-West Resistance (1885), the South African War (1899–1902), the First World

War (1914–18), and the first part of the Second World War (1939–45), dying in 1942 in the midst of this last conflict. Her father fought in the North-West Resistance; her half-brother, Carl Montgomery, in the First World War; and her son Stuart (after she died) in the Second World War.[4] Her attitudes and emotions about war would shift throughout her lifetime, from childhood naïveté in the 1880s to horror at Hitler's rise in the 1930s and the prospect of another global war.[5] Yet her education and her status as a member of an elite Presbyterian clan, including a grandfather in the Canadian Senate, led to her unquestioning stance on the side of the government in the North-West Resistance and on the side of the British Empire in the South African War and the First World War.[6]

In 1899, the twenty-five-year-old Montgomery regarded the South African War, then known as the Boer War, very differently from the North-West Resistance. She was spared the personal suspense she suffered throughout the resistance, because no one close to her was involved. She wrote about the South African War as "stirring and exciting and tingling," causing "red-hot excitement" across Canada, even in "this quiet little Island thousands of miles from the seat of war."[7] When she met soldiers who had fought in South Africa, she invested them with an "aura of romance and interest" or a "halo of romance," even when she found their personalities and speech uninteresting.[8] Major battles and assaults, tales of daring and courage, still held the allure of the conflicts she had read about in Victorian novels and poetry, as Holly Pike describes in chapter 3. Tellingly, although Montgomery found the set battles of the first part of the South African War to be exciting, she characterized the "bush-whacking" tactics of the war's later stages as "tedious."[9]

But the South African War was a distant combat that affected Canada only because it sent its first contingents overseas to fight, including its first twelve military nurses (one of them from Prince Edward Island).[10] Canada's status and territory were not threatened; the issues and the fighting were confined to South Africa. When Britain was drawn into the First World War, the thirty-nine-year-old Montgomery, whose excitement over the outbreak of the Boer War had been palpable, had a very different reaction: "I sat down weak and unnerved ... dumbly trying to realize ... that our Empire was at war.

And such a war!"[11] Her response to the South African War is comparable to British author Vera Brittain's response to the First World War. Brittain, twenty years old in 1914, saw the prospect of war as "thrilling" and urged her eighteen-year-old brother to "join the army," showing him "an appeal for young unmarried men."[12] Like Montgomery, Brittain's attitude towards war would change. In 1933, in her renowned autobiography, *Testament of Youth*, she attempted to explain the "glamour" of war for youth: "The causes of war are always falsely represented: its honour is dishonest and its glory meretricious, but the challenge to spiritual endurance, the intense sharpening of all the senses, the vitalising consciousness of common peril for a common end, remain to allure those boys and girls who have just reached the age when love and friendship and adventure call more persistently than at any later time."[13] Brittain wrote these words with hindsight, fifteen years after her fiancé, her brother, and two close friends had been killed in the First World War: grief and her sense of disillusionment about the war's merit wrought her change in attitude.[14] Montgomery's change in perspective was not caused by grief at relatives or friends being killed, but by maturity and motherhood. The years between 1899 and 1914 saw great changes in Montgomery's circumstances. By 1914, war was no longer the exciting adventure that it was to Brittain, but a conflict that would bring heartbreak, death, and change, especially to the women who watched their sons, brothers, fathers, and sweethearts go overseas.

In 1899, Montgomery earned $96.88 by publishing her writing, and in 1901, she earned $5.00 per week as a proofreader for a Halifax newspaper.[15] By August 1914, she was an internationally renowned author with a number of novels to her credit. In 1908, she published her bestselling first novel, *Anne of Green Gables*, about a spirited, imaginative red-haired orphan, Anne Shirley, who finds a home and love on a Prince Edward Island farm. *Anne of Avonlea* (1909) wittily describes Anne's brief teaching career; it was followed by *Kilmeny of the Orchard* (1910), a romance about a beautiful young woman with a disability. *The Story Girl* (1911) and *The Golden Road* (1913) tell of the King family children and their friends, exalting the art of storytelling on many levels. All of these novels were set in Prince Edward Island, and all became bestsellers.

In 1899, too, Montgomery was a single woman who had only recently given up a teaching career to move back to Cavendish to care for her grandmother. In 1911, when her grandmother died, Montgomery married the Reverend Ewan Macdonald and moved from Cavendish, PEI, to Leaskdale, Ontario, combining her writing work with the busy life of a Presbyterian minister's wife. In 1912, their first son, Chester, was born. When Britain declared war on Germany on 4 August 1914, Montgomery was expecting their second son. Tragedy struck mere days after the war began when she bore a stillborn child, Hugh. Their third and last child, Stuart, was born in 1915. Despite the claims on her time of motherhood, writing, and her work in the parish, Montgomery rapidly became an active war worker, serving as president of the local Red Cross chapter, reciting poems at recruiting meetings, and, perhaps hardest to bear, comforting local parishioners when their sons, brothers, and sweethearts were wounded or killed overseas.[16] Montgomery kept a "khaki row" of photographs in her home, one for each young man she knew who went overseas.[17]

Throughout the war, Montgomery continued to write. Carolyn Strom Collins quotes a letter that Montgomery wrote to her penfriend Ephraim Weber in 1916: "It seems to me that I cannot settle down to real work as long as the war lasts – in its critical stage at least. The nervous strain is too great."[18] Yet Collins's scholarship reveals that Montgomery's output contradicted her claim to Weber.[19] From July 1914 through November 1918, Montgomery finished one novel, *Anne of the Island* (1915), about Anne's years at college, and wrote another two, *Anne's House of Dreams* (1917), which covers Anne's marriage to Gilbert Blythe, and *Rainbow Valley* (1919), which focuses on Anne's children and their friends. She published *The Watchman* (1916), a volume of poems; wrote and published at least six new stories; published her autobiography as a serial in *Every Woman's World*; and wrote two essays. In addition, she corresponded throughout the war with her penfriends Ephraim Weber and George Boyd MacMillan and wrote copiously in her private journals, pouring out her anguish about the war, the agonizing wait for the newspaper each day, and her horrific imaginings about the young men being killed, wounded, and gassed overseas. In her fiction, writing became an escape from the war; in her journals, an immersion in it.

Montgomery's love for her sons and the anguish of enduring her second son's death gave her empathy for the mothers who suffered during the First World War. The importance of the mother is apparent in Montgomery's two wartime novels: in *Anne's House of Dreams*, Montgomery transfers her own heartbreak over losing her second son to Anne Blythe, when her fictional character's first child, Joy, dies on the same day she is born. Elizabeth Epperly calls this novel "a passionate celebration of home and love," claiming that "Montgomery is writing against the ravages of war."[20] The anguish of loss brings Anne to acknowledge the tragedy of heartbreak, yet the novel affirms that "love is an active force that can defeat evil."[21] *Rainbow Valley*, written during the war, celebrates the "childhood faith and chivalry of Canada's embryonic soldiers and wartime workers."[22] This novel focuses on the Meredith children, motherless and being brought up by an elderly aunt and a dreamy father, and the Blythe children, secure in the love of their parents, Anne and Gilbert Blythe. The importance of the mother is shown through the Meredith children's neglect: their clothes wear out, they eat tasteless food, their house is dirty, and their attempts to bring themselves up are disastrous. Throughout the novel, Anne Blythe's sympathy and love serve to highlight the emotional and physical emptiness of the Merediths' motherless lives.

The Meredith and Blythe children, chivalrous and courageous, become emblematic of one of the popular justifications for the First World War: that it was a fight for children, to ensure that their futures were free and untrammelled by tyranny. Yet Montgomery also foreshadows the Ingleside children's future as soldiers, showing Jem as fearless and patriotic, and Walter as loathing war but ready to fight for justice.[23] In this closing scene, Montgomery again reminds us of the cost of motherhood during wartime: "Jem was to be a soldier and see a greater battle than had ever been fought in the world; but that was as yet far in the future; and the mother, whose first-born son he was, was wont to look on her boys and thank God that ... never would it be necessary for the sons of Canada to ride forth to battle 'for the ashes of their fathers and the temples of their gods.'"[24] Montgomery's rhetoric about "the mother" is infused with high language and poetry, while her talk of soldiers "rid[ing] forth to battle" recalls former wars with cavalry, rather than the mechanistic trench warfare that characterized the Western Front during the First World War. Montgomery reminds us that the cost of war – the loss of soldier sons – is the grief of mothers, couched in elegiac terms, which is thus made equal to the soldier's sacrifice.

The First World War ended on 11 November 1918. At the time, Montgomery was at Park Corner, PEI, helping her cousin, Frederica Campbell Macfarlane, nurse family members during an epidemic of influenza. "The Great War is over," Montgomery wrote. "The world's agony has ended. *What has been born?* The next generation may be able to answer that. *We* can never fully know."[25] For her, as a child is born from a mother's pain, some beneficial blessing would ensue from the war's anguish.

In January 1919, Montgomery suffered perhaps the greatest loss of her life when her beloved cousin Frederica died in the influenza epidemic.[26] More anxiety followed when Ewan Macdonald, grieving over Frederica's death and perhaps worn out by and conflicted about his own war work, became deeply depressed with "religious melancholia," an illness poorly understood at the time, with no effective treatment available.[27] Frederica became Montgomery's war casualty; her grief at her cousin's loss would haunt her for the rest of her life.

Despite her husband's illness and her own grief, Montgomery began work on her new novel, intended to be the last of the *Anne* series.[28] *Rilla of Ingleside* depicts a Canadian community during the First World War.[29] Its heroine is Anne's daughter Rilla, fifteen when the war begins, and nineteen when it ends. For Rilla, war serves as a crucible: the terrible suffering she undergoes burns away shallow frivolity, creating a mature, strong woman who is ready to help shape the postwar world and Canada's future.[30] Although *Rilla* underscores women's anguish during wartime, the novel also rings with humour and wit: the sentimentality of a war wedding is undercut by a dog's fit, and Rilla's romantic farewell to a soldier-lover turns to hilarity when an oblivious Susan Baker, the Blythes' servant, takes over the entertainment.[31] Women are the focus of the novel, actively working alongside men as part of the war effort, although, as Benjamin Lefebvre and Andrea McKenzie note, the work they perform tends to be what Montgomery considered suitable: running Red Cross chapters, volunteering as nurses, mothering motherless babies, taking men's places in stores, and organizing fund-raising concerts.[32] Susan Baker may work in the fields at harvest, but Rilla does not, and radically non-traditional forms of work – in munitions factories, for instance – are not mentioned.

Montgomery translated her terrible grief at her cousin Frederica's death into *Rilla*, vividly depicting the impact of wartime losses on women of the time. Grief, for many women during the war, was "glamorised": by "elevating" women's sacrifice of their loved ones, women could be "persuaded" that they were "participat[ing] equally in the mythology of [their] country."[33] Part of the prescribed "script" for women was being stoic – hiding their grief – and expressing pride in the loved one's sacrifice.[34] Montgomery does conform to this script in the character of Rilla; after collapsing when news of Walter's death arrives, Rilla rises to stoically run the household and "keep faith" with the war effort.[35] But as Andrea McKenzie observes in chapter 9, Montgomery disrupts the prescribed pattern for women's grief by her graphic portrayal of the cost of loss: Anne, for instance, is prostrated for weeks, and her son's death will mark her for life, while Gertrude Oliver, a teacher boarding with the Blythes who has believed her fiancé dead, cries wrenchingly throughout the night when she discovers that he is alive. More than a decade before Brittain's elegiac *Testament of Youth* was published, Montgomery revealed the cost of war for women through their grief, and as Caroline Jones demonstrates in chapter 8, grief and darkness would continue to haunt Montgomery's postwar and Second World War works.

Montgomery's journal reveals the horror and suspense she felt throughout the war at the loss of young men overseas and the sufferings the war caused children and other civilians overseas. Although her life choices and her morals were heavily influenced by Presbyterianism – her family was Presbyterian and she was a Presbyterian minister's wife – her attitude towards religion remained unorthodox in her private writings.[36] But during the First World War, she adhered to the precept that, "without shedding of blood, there is no remission of sins," a belief she expressed in her journals and gave to John Meredith, the Presbyterian minister in *Rilla,* to underscore its importance.[37] As Reverend Meredith explains, the war's bloodshed "is the price humanity must pay for some blessing ... which *we* may not live to see but which our children's children will inherit."[38] In Montgomery's thoughts, then, the soldiers who died became Christ, sacrificing their lives for the good of humanity's future. Montgomery was not alone in using this (British) myth to justify the human cost of the war.[39] Jonathan Vance observes that this myth "was central to Canada's memory of the Great War ... Through his death in battle, the individual soldier sacrificed his life to atone for the sins of the world."[40] For women, such a belief gave meaning to their grief and their sacrifice of loved ones; without this consolation, the sacrifice would become "not only horrible, but also meaningless."[41] Montgomery, then, foregrounded grief in her novels but also gave grieving women hope in the midst of their pain and despair.

For these and many other reasons, Montgomery's story of a community at war rang true with Canadian reviewers of the time.[42] Though American reviewers tended to gloss over Montgomery's depiction of war,[43] a reviewer in Toronto's *Globe* wrote that *Rilla* "is a story that might be written of a thousand communities in Canada, where the quiet life was suddenly upset by the European explosion,"[44] and *Saturday Night*'s review commented that "most Canadians lived and felt ... the fifty-odd months of war ... much as did the Blythe family and their friends."[45] The *Manitoba Free Press* went as far as to say that, "a hundred years hence, *Rilla of Ingleside* will be useful to historians for a picture of Canadian home life during the Great War."[46] Montgomery herself wrote: "In my latest story, 'Rilla of Ingleside,' I have tried, as far as in me lies, to depict the fine and splendid way in which the girls of Canada reacted to the Great War – their bravery, patience and self-sacrifice. The book is theirs in a sense in which none of my other books have been: for my other books were written for anyone who might like to read them: but 'Rilla' was written for the girls of the great young land I love, whose destiny it will be their duty and privilege to shape and share."[47] *Rilla* was Montgomery's immediate postwar novel, one that is still acknowledged to reflect the way that Canadians thought and felt about the war.[48]

Once *Rilla* was launched, Montgomery created a new and enchanting heroine, the developing writer Emily Byrd Starr, in a trilogy of works – *Emily of New Moon* (1923), *Emily Climbs* (1925), and

Emily's Quest (1927) – that would inspire newer generations of Canadian female writers such as Jane Urquhart and Alice Munro.[49] Compared to Anne Shirley's Avonlea, orphan Emily's world is darker, more complex, and sharper edged.[50] Although the war is never mentioned, Montgomery's writing has a harsher ring than it had in her earlier books. War is waged within the household when Emily's Aunt Elizabeth tyrannizes over its members and tries to force Emily to stop writing. But Emily's passion cannot be denied. Montgomery depicts writing as an unstoppable and integral force that overcomes all challenges.

Other new heroines followed in the 1920s: Valancy Stirling, who becomes a rebel within her highly conventional family when she is diagnosed with a heart ailment and decides to live with joy and without fear in *The Blue Castle* (1926); and Marigold Lesley, a delightfully imaginative younger child, in *Magic for Marigold* (1929). In 1931, Montgomery completed her witty novel for adults, *A Tangled Web*. Throughout this time period, nature was solace to Montgomery: though war touched her works, Ewan's health was an ongoing concern, and a long-running lawsuit with the Page publishing company troubled her greatly, the beauty of the natural world remained an enticing escape from household issues and problems.

In 1926, the Macdonalds moved from Leaskdale to Norval, Ontario. Although the move was a wrench for Montgomery, Ewan's new position meant that Toronto, a major city, was in reach by car or by radial railway, allowing Montgomery to escape parish duties, attend more social activities, and give lectures and readings in nearby communities. But by the early 1930s, Montgomery was beset by personal and financial problems. Her older son, Chester, secretly married a parishioner's daughter because she was pregnant, a major scandal for a minister's family, and Ewan's mental condition worsened.[51] The worldwide financial depression affected Montgomery's investments, and, for the first time in decades, she felt pressured to write to earn money. *Pat of Silver Bush* (1933) and *Mistress Pat* (1935) document Montgomery's own longing for a stable, unchanging home and world through her heroine's fear of change and love of home.[52] References to Hitler and to her fear of another war are sporadically scattered throughout her journals, just as First World War veterans increasingly invade her fiction.[53]

Montgomery returned to her first and most successful heroine, Anne Shirley, in the mid-1930s, filling in the gap between Anne's university graduation and her marriage to Gilbert Blythe in *Anne of Windy Poplars* (1936). *Anne of Ingleside* (1939), the last novel she published in her lifetime, focuses on Anne's growing children and Anne and Gilbert in mid-life crises. Jane Stuart was her last new heroine, in *Jane of Lantern Hill* (1937), a novel in which Jane finds freedom and joy in living with and keeping house for her father in Prince Edward Island, in contrast to the tyranny and darkness of her home with her grandmother and mother in Toronto. War, in this novel, was the means of creating her parents' marriage, but also of forcing them apart. With the prospect of another world war looming, both *Jane of Lantern Hill* and *Anne of Ingleside* recall the emotional and physical impact of the First World War.

L.M. Montgomery died in 1942, at the height of the Second World War. She feared that her adult sons would serve and be killed, giving her a personal emotional connection to war that she had not had since her father fought in the North-West Resistance. The experience of the impact of the First World War fuelled her despair during the Second. Kate Macdonald Butler, Montgomery's granddaughter, believes that she committed suicide through a drug overdose.[54] Mary Rubio, Montgomery's biographer, believes the overdose may have been accidental.[55] Both interpretations acknowledge Montgomery's deep despair at the end of her life. Her final letter to her penfriend G.B. MacMillan admits, frankly, "The war situation kills me along with many other things."[56] Curiously, Montgomery's last manuscript, which remained unpublished in its entirety until Benjamin Lefebvre edited and published it as *The Blythes Are Quoted* in 2009,[57] was delivered to her publisher on the day of her death.[58] *The Blythes Are Quoted* is structured around war, with the first section focused on the First World War and the second part on the postwar era, extending into the Second World War. Montgomery created a new genre with this work, blending short stories with interludes with the Blythe family in which they discuss Anne's and Walter's poetry and their responses to war and to its impact. This work reflects Montgomery's embittered and disillusioned response to war, a sea change from her naive and enthusiastic response to the South African War and her belief in the justness of the cause of the First World War. Yet at the same time, through the character of Rilla, now the mother of adult sons who fight in the Second World War, Montgomery both questions and defends the myths of sacrifice that pervade *Rilla of Ingleside*. Montgomery's ending to *The Blythes* illuminates her ambivalence about war: she recognizes its terrible costs and the myths that cover up its horrors. Yet even while she undermines the myth of sacrifice for sons and mothers, she appears to uphold it. It is as though she believes that self-sacrificial myths are necessary if the world is to fight Hitler's tyranny. At the end of her life, Montgomery was caught in the terrible dilemma of fully realizing the horrors of war as they might affect her personally through her sons while recognizing that Hitler and his allies had to be defeated to end their unjust reign of terror.

L.M. Montgomery: Writing War

Scholarship about *Anne of Green Gables*, Montgomery's most popular work, has been and remains prolific.[59] In comparison, scholarship about Montgomery's war writing is slim, whether on the novels that overtly or subtly invoke war or on her poetry, her short stories, her journals, or her correspondence.[60] Perhaps not surprisingly, Montgomery's *Rilla* and her other war works have not been included in the canon of Canadian war literature.[61] According to Janet S.K. Watson, during the war, men and women were depicted as working together to win the war, much as the community does in *Rilla of Ingleside*.[62] But in the postwar era, as foundational women's war scholar Margaret Higonnet argues, an artificial divide was created between the men who fought and all those who did not: "soldiers' truth" was set against "civilian propaganda."[63] In essence, soldiers' combatant experience was considered privileged and legitimate beyond all others, and women's voices were mostly forgotten or lost. For instance, Vera Brittain's *Testament of Youth*, a best-seller in 1933, went out of print and was not republished until 1978, when its rediscovery kick-started the field of women's war scholarship. In contrast, Montgomery's *Rilla of Ingleside*, which also depicts women's experience of war, remained popular as part of the *Anne* series, one of the few women's war books to remain so through the century since the First World War. Montgomery's position as a female author (in a world of male critics) and her demotion to the children's section of bookstores and libraries excluded her from the recognized war canon despite her influence on Canadian cultural memories of the war.[64] Another complication with *Rilla of Ingleside* occurred because the complete text was mostly unavailable in North America for forty years, until Lefebvre and McKenzie published a restored version of Montgomery's original work in 2010.[65] The cut version left out telling details about characters' attitudes towards war, especially in the first third of the novel.[66] In their introduction to the original text, Lefebvre and McKenzie placed Montgomery's novel in the context of women's war scholarship and literature.[67]

Montgomery's reputation as a war writer has risen in recent decades, coinciding with the publication of her personal journals, edited by Mary Rubio and Elizabeth Waterston, and the burgeoning scholarly field of women's war literature. In 1972, when women were not considered legitimate war writers, Margery Fee and Ruth Cawker summarized *Rilla of Ingleside*'s "attitude to war in one trivializing sentence: 'Rilla degenerates into a chauvinistic tract for Canadian support of Great Britain in World War One.'"[68] In 1992, Sandra Gwyn, though acknowledging the historical accuracy of *Rilla*, described the novel as "jingoistic and sentimental," claiming that Rilla Blythe is not one of Montgomery's "best heroines."[69] This reading was countered by Elizabeth Epperly's book-length study of Montgomery, *The Fragrance of Sweet-Grass*, also first published in 1992, in which Epperly demonstrates the complexity of wartime attitudes in *Rilla of Ingleside* and analyzes the influence of the First World War on Montgomery's other wartime and postwar works.[70] Other scholars who accorded *Rilla* attention include Mary Rubio, Owen Dudley Edwards, Alan Young, and Donna Coates.[71] In the first decade of this century, McKenzie studied the feminist and Canadian twists Montgomery gave to British war myths in *Rilla* and Montgomery's influence on Canadian cultural memories of the First World War, while Paul Tiessen analyzed Montgomery's responses to her pacifist penfriend Ephraim Weber.[72] Amy Tector examined Montgomery's use of violence and war to disrupt the "familiar bucolic harmony" of Glen St Mary and the Blythes' world. Tector, however, like Edwards and Gwyn, found Montgomery's "enthusiasm" for war "troubling," an attitude that reflects British cultural memories of the war as massacre and wastage, rather than the more ambivalent and purposeful Canadian attitudes that Jonathan Vance recounts in *Death So Noble*.[73] Erika Rothwell and Cecily Devereux have each explored Montgomery's "maternal feminism" in relation to the war.[74]

More recently, the centenary of the outbreak of the First World War has drawn new attention to Montgomery's war writing. Mary Beth Cavert, for instance, provided a detailed exploration of the three soldiers Montgomery memorialized in *Rainbow Valley*, illuminating both Montgomery's wartime work in the parish where she lived and the extent of her anguish at the young men's deaths.[75] William Thompson examined the intersection of public events with Montgomery's private life in her war fiction,[76] while Melanie Fishbane analyzed the impact of Montgomery's use of diary writing to alleviate pain in her war fiction and her actual life.[77] To date, Lefebvre and Fishbane are the only authors to have published analyses of Montgomery's final complex work, *The Blythes Are Quoted*.[78] Yet this previous scholarship, for the most part, does not place Montgomery in the larger context of Canadian or international war literature and art.

In the larger realm of Canadian war scholarship – especially literary scholarship – Montgomery is rarely considered.[79] Donna Coates's 1996 groundbreaking article, "The Best Soldiers of All," is one of the few to reclaim English-Canadian women's war writing, including Montgomery's *Rilla*. At the time, Coates declared that "women's wartime writing has been completely ignored."[80] But Coates's feminist reading of first-generation Canadian women war writers is all too rare.[81] In the *Cambridge History of Canadian Literature*, Susan Fisher observes, "We have come to view the First World War as a pointless bloodbath ... Yet during the war years, and indeed for decades after, many Canadians thought otherwise."[82] Neta Gordon's study of literary criticism about Canadian war literature perhaps inadvertently reveals the prevailing attitude towards Montgomery when she uses her only in passing as an example of "aesthetic conformity" to the myth of the war as justified and nation building,[83] the very perspective that, as Fisher notes and Vance concludes, dominated Canada in the inter-war years.[84] Such unquestioning depictions of Montgomery's work overlook the "subversive elements" and "subtle challenges" that per-meate Montgomery's war writing.[85] Then, too, early assessments of Montgomery did not have her posthumously published writings avail-able. Her journals, revealing, as Gammel observes, the performance of a modernist writer,[86] complicate any reading of Montgomery as a "war writer." And *The Blythes Are Quoted*, with its disillusioned end-ing to the story of the Blythes and the First World War while in the midst of the Second, "does not applaud war; its poetry and interludes – the very shape of the book – call war and its rhetoric into ques-tion."[87] As Epperly concludes, there are "no easy answers" to Mont-gomery's intentions.[88]

In Canadian war literature, Timothy Findley's reconstruction of Canada's war in *The Wars* is considered canonical, from Eric Thomp-son's 1981 "Canadian Fiction of the First World War" to Neta Gordon's analysis of recent war novels.[89] (Findley's protagonist is a combatant soldier, and his novel indicts war as brutal and futile.) Thompson, like many others, was influenced by Paul Fussell's *The Great War and Modern Memory* and the British myth of the war as futile – a view still seemingly prevalent in Canadian views of the war.[90] Fussell privileged anti-war male combatant writers such as Siegfried Sassoon and Wil-fred Owen as the "best" British war writers, deeming that "irony" about the war (in service of highlighting its futility) was an essential quality of such work.[91] He also condemned the "high diction" that he claimed perpetuated false idealism about the war. Coates challenges Thompson's work as "patriarchal criticism" and argues that the hero-ines created by Canadian women writers develop their own unique war roles – unlike men, whose role is determined for them by the army and its regulations. Moreover, Coates perceives Canadian women war writers as "forcefully reiterat[ing] that women deserve a place in so-ciety alongside men, not as their subalterns."[92] International women's war scholars such as Margaret Higonnet, Susan Grayzel, Janet S.K. Watson, and a myriad of others have also reclaimed women's war writing, showing that, in Higonnet's words, women's war writing erases the "oppositions between battlefront and home front, public and private, war and peace, men and women."[93] International cultural studies, too, have long challenged the premise that modernism and anti-war soldier-writers are the only legitimate voices of the First World War. Jay Winter's foundational work in *Sites of Memory, Sites of Mourning* argues that "the cutting edge of 'modern memory,' its multi-faceted sense of dislocation, paradox, and the ironic, could express anger and despair, and did so in enduring ways; it was melancholic, but it could not heal. Traditional modes of seeing the war … provided a way of remembering which enabled the bereaved to live with their losses, and perhaps leave them behind."[94] Winter and Blaine Baggett, too, reinforce women's war scholars in *The Great War and the Shaping of the Twentieth Century*, arguing that the First World War impacted all who were involved: "all were mobilized," they claim, and so all voices of wartime experience become equal.[95] In recent years, scholars have widened the scope of war studies further to include the voices of those previously unheard or underheard, looking beyond the earlier emphasis on the Western Front and Europe to other regions and other populations affected by the war, such as children, medical personnel, and populations on the Eastern Front, on the Mediterranean Front and in Africa.[96] Social and cultural studies of war have become diverse and multicultural.

The 2014 centenary of the beginning of the First World War marked a corresponding rise in public interest in Canadian war writing. Ironically, although Montgomery's *Rilla of Ingleside* is the only novel about the First World War by a Canadian author who experienced it to still be in print in a trade edition,[97] her book did not appear on any of the lists of war novels recommended by mainstream cultural institutions. The CBC and *Chatelaine* both recommended Findley's *The Wars* (1977), Jane Urquhart's *The Stone Carvers* (2001), Joseph Boyden's *Three Day Road* (2005), and Frances Itani's *Deafening* (2003).[98] Katherine Ashenburg, writing for the *Globe and Mail*, claimed that the First World War "gave birth to a bitterly disillusioned modern world," and so predictably included all the classic anti-war writers in a list slanted towards European male combatant authors.[99] The Canadian War Museum's current list of nine books for young adult readers includes only one by a woman (Urquhart), with the remainder written by men about or from soldiers' perspectives.[100] The CBC and *Chatelaine* at least recognize the new generation of war novelists, those that represent diverse perspectives and voices – women at home, their soldier lovers, pacifists, and First Nations soldiers, for instance.

Montgomery's war novels, poetry, and life writing do not represent all of these perspectives, but she does present diverse voices and views about war within her works and across her lifetime. Indeed, given Montgomery's influence across the century, she can be considered as a forerunner of later Canadian authors who challenge the male, battle-centred vision of Canada's war or who question the myth of a unified Canada. She represents the continuity of the progressive, nation-building myth, but she also challenges it – and she ended her war writing, in *The Blythes Are Quoted*, by indicting war.[101] Thus, Montgomery's war writing encapsulates the contradiction that causes "anxiety" in current First World War literary criticism:[102] war as "bloodbath" *and* as justified by Canada's progress.

This collection of essays, then, addresses a major gap in Canadian and international studies of war literature by restoring L.M. Montgomery to her rightful place as a major war writer. From the North-West Resistance of 1885 to the closing days of Montgomery's life, war and conflict marked her personal life and her writing life. Given the influence of Montgomery's war writing on Canadian cultural memories, the continuing popularity of her works, and the reassessments necessary due to the posthumous publication of her journals and *The Blythes Are Quoted*, a collection of essays about her war writings, attitudes, and influence is long overdue. It seems fitting that such a collection should be published during the centenary of the First World War, which Montgomery mistakenly hoped would be the "war to end all wars."

Part 1 of this volume, "The Canons of War," contributes assessments and analyses of Montgomery's war writing in the context of the Canadian novelists, artists, and poets of her time, thus better illuminating the first generation of war writers and artists as well as providing new insights about Montgomery as a war writer. Part 2, "Gendering War," raises important questions about Montgomery's subversion of wartime conceptions of masculinity and femininity, sheds new light on Canadian women's actual war work and Montgomery's distinctive use of it in her writing, and extends studies of wartime nationalism and gender. Part 3, "Healing or Hurt?" expands theories of grief and trauma through exploring Montgomery's postwar novels, deepens the theme of art by analyzing the meaning of a century of women's war images in relation to Montgomery's text, and finishes with an ecopoetic critical exploration of Montgomery's postwar attempt to heal the hurt caused by war. *L.M. Montgomery and War* reassesses Montgomery's place in the war canon and the Canadian literary canon, drawing on new scholarship and perspectives from the still-burgeoning interdisciplinary fields of war studies. From literary studies to historical studies, gender studies to visual art, this volume explores a multitude of perspectives and questions about Montgomery's writing and war. How did war influence Montgomery's writing? How did her attitude towards war shift across her lifetime and throughout multiple conflicts? What impact did war have on postwar culture, nationhood, and imperialistic attitudes in her characters and their communities? Do Montgomery's texts perceive war as liberating women or confining them? Why does her war novel, *Rilla of Ingleside*, continue to fascinate readers, while writings by other first-generation war writers have fallen out of favour? These are only a few of the questions that renowned historians, literary scholars, and Montgomery scholars explore in this collection.

Part One: The Canons of War

This section decisively restores Montgomery to the historical, literary, and artistic canons of Canadian and international war history, literature, and art. Historians such as Jonathan Vance and Sandra Gwyn have considered *Rilla of Ingleside* to be a social history of the First World War, but Montgomery has been overlooked or only briefly mentioned in literary studies that favour the new generation of late-twentieth- and early-twenty-first-century war novelists. Yet these novelists write about war as it is remembered, whereas Montgomery wrote about war as she experienced it; her work both "reflected and shaped" Canadian cultural memories of the war during the interwar

years. This section, then, reassesses Montgomery's novels and poetry
in the context of her time. The authors in this section contextualize
Montgomery's fiction within local, national, and international trends,
from the historical experiences of her community to the canonical literature and art of war.

Historian Jonathan Vance, in his chapter "'Some Great Crisis of
Storm and Stress': L.M. Montgomery, Canadian Literature, and the
Great War," explores the very different public and private personae
that Montgomery performed during the years of the First World War.
His essay uncovers the tensions between Montgomery's local war –
the war as she experienced it in her community and township – and
the war as she publicly wrote about it. Blending archival and historical research with literary criticism, Vance astutely reminds readers
that Montgomery's international appeal as a writer is based not only
on her intense engagement with locality, but also with global and cos-
mopolitan agendas that reached into her life and the communities
where she resided. Vance examines Montgomery's war novel, *Rilla of
Ingleside*, in the context of the actual historical experiences of her
community during the war, then in the context of first-generation
Canadian war literature. He argues that Montgomery's "immersion"
in the local was the very reason that she succeeded in creating a
"national" representation of war that is still read and remembered
when so many of her contemporaries – authors such as Katherine
Hale, Charles G.D. Roberts, and Robert J.C. Stead – failed. He thus
firmly establishes Montgomery as a successful and canonical Canadian war writer, with *Rilla of Ingleside* becoming truly representative
of "Canada's war."

While Vance focuses on historical experience, Canadian war literature, and Montgomery's contribution to it, Irene Gammel brings
Montgomery's life and writing into conversation with the life and art
of war artist Mary Riter Hamilton. Following the end of the Great
War, Hamilton travelled to Europe to witness and document the scars
of European cities and landscapes. In "Mapping Patriotic Memory:
L.M. Montgomery, Mary Riter Hamilton, and the Great War," Gammel interrogates forms and meanings of war commemoration and
where *Rilla of Ingleside*, written in the immediate postwar era, fits
within that canon. Gammel is also preoccupied with what consola-

tions can be found in women artists' active and aesthetic engagement with literal and figurative war landscapes. Gammel argues that Montgomery and Hamilton "narrate and visualize complementary stories as they confront trauma and memory" and that their aesthetic actions and decisions problematize the opposition of a (masculinized) battlefield with a (femininized) home front through the "complexity of [their] intertwining empathy and patriotism in fiction and art."

As an interpretation of cataclysm and consolation, Montgomery's *Rilla* has remained more available to the public than Hamilton's paintings, highlighting that *how* we remember war is affected by what art and whose work is privileged. E. Holly Pike offers an insightful reading of the representations of war canonized in the textbooks of Montgomery's childhood and the web of allusion these texts provide for Montgomery's fictional characters. "Education for War: *Anne of Green Gables* and *Rilla of Ingleside*" allows contemporary readers a glimpse into the Royal Readers, which Pike says on the whole created a "literary vision of war as a romantic adventure – a glorious sacrifice for homeland and love" and carried a romantic vocabulary for war forward from the nineteenth century into a horror-strewn twentieth century earlier writers could never have imagined. The poems Anne Shirley and Rilla Blythe memorize – take into their very bodies – in *Anne of Green Gables* and *Rilla of Ingleside* are poems of imperial patriotism. The imagery and values of the poems become all the more important, given that Pike describes *Rilla of Ingleside*'s suggestive echoes of and deliberate recursions to key moments from the entire *Anne* series, drawing attention to the "the continuity of values." But continuity is challenged by war. Rilla's recitation of poems goes beyond the emotional transport her mother Anne might have described and becomes a means of troop recruitment. And, Pike argues, the discontinuity with earlier values embedded in the Royal Readers through the cataclysm of the war is what creates conditions for Rilla to take her place in nation building and Montgomery to take her place in building a new Canadian national literature.

How did the martial poems so prominent in Montgomery's education inflect her own verse? *The Watchman and Other Poems*, published in 1916 in the midst of the Great War, was the only volume of Montgomery's poetry published in her lifetime. And yet, as Susan

Fisher's "'Watchman, What of the Night?': L.M. Montgomery's Poems of War" points out, the volume lacks topical war poems or distinct images of the war Montgomery and Canada were experiencing. Dismissing attempts to redeem the quality of Montgomery's early poems, Fisher agrees with Montgomery's self-assessment of her poems as "commonplace" – but it is worth noting, as Paul Keen has, that the etymology of "commonplace" is contradictory, and that this word invokes "intimacy rather than a gulf between that which is striking or notable, and therefore worthy of being remembered, and that which is trivial, ordinary, or mundane."[103] Fisher questions the adequacy of the vocabulary of the "commonplace" to contend with war, characterizing the poetry as unfulfillingly wrestling with conventional morality in the moral quagmire of war. In this context, poems from *The Watchman* contrast in telling ways with poems from Montgomery's last book, *The Blythes Are Quoted*. Montgomery's war poems in this final manuscript are attributed to a character, the soldier-poet Walter Blythe, and, instead of returning to the poetic models of Montgomery's education, contend with the most famous Canadian war poem of the Great War, John McCrae's "In Flanders Fields." Fisher argues that in the closing poem of *The Blythes Are Quoted*, "The Aftermath," Montgomery perhaps finally refutes the assertion that moral certainties can be found with a bayonet in hand.

Part Two: Gendering War

Following from the observation that "war must be understood as a *gendering* activity"[104] and that wartime work was both gendered and gendering, this section explores work and war with a gender lens in *Rilla of Ingleside*. Montgomery's classic chronicle of women's active war work, *Rilla* explores women's varied roles beyond sweetheart, soldier mother, or sister. *Rilla* places the girl-maturing-into-womanhood at the centre of a nation-building project that war is ostensibly meant to serve. The novel details the value of gendered work on the home front. But to what extent does this germinal text challenge gender stereotypes and problematize the gender binaries that came to prominence during the First World War, and then to dominance in many literary and historical narratives that followed? To what extent does fiction follow purported historical fact? And to what degree does Rilla's story contribute to or undercut nationalistic agendas?

Laura Robinson challenges the critique of *Rilla of Ingleside* as too patriotically cheerful a response to the horrors of war and undermines the superficial assumption that the novel "entrenches" gender categories with its conventional, happily ending narrative structure. In "L.M. Montgomery's Great War: The Home as Battleground in *Rilla of Ingleside*," Robinson traces gender weirdness, perverse pronouncements, and profound ambivalence about gender roles from the Blythes' gender-switching cat to their maid, Susan Baker, and even to the soldier Walter Blythe. Robinson argues that through subtle touches throughout the novel, Montgomery "valorizes feminine values," while "offer[ing] a critique of the masculine heroic ideal that destroys the boys and men." It is women whose labour builds the nation, Montgomery insists. But what experience builds up women in war's destructive wake? Two contradictory marriage plots in the book offer contrasting models for women to build new lives after the war. The wartime setting of *Rilla* permits a fresh questioning of what adequately defines a woman or defines a man, and whether gender categories are adequate at all to deal with the harshness or humour of human experience.

Montgomery's deliberate choices as an author come through clearly when compared with historical accounts of real-life Canadian women. In her chapter, "'I Must Do Something to Help at Home': *Rilla of Ingleside* in the Context of Real Women's War Work," Sarah Glassford examines Montgomery's purposeful narrative decisions in the light of historically documented war work in Prince Edward Island and throughout Canada. Glassford's effort is not to establish accuracy and inaccuracy; rather, she argues that "considering where the historical and fictional records agree and disagree, speak or are silent, offers insights into those aspects Montgomery particularly wished to emphasize as an author." By examining women's actual war work, Glassford demonstrates that in Montgomery's *Rilla*, the knitting, sewing, and other war work do serve practical and emotional purposes by offering the moral succour of *usefulness*; however, the activities being *organized* also bring characters together to allow a multiplicity of points of view on war. Compellingly, Glassford makes the case that to serve the dramatic interests of her story and of character development, the novel in fact "underplays [the role of women's war work] in bringing the community together." Character, rather than documentary evidence, is what ultimately creates the affecting and representative themes Glassford sums up as the heart of *Rilla of Ingleside*: a "young but maturing Canada; capable Canadian womanhood; [and] the purifying spirit of service and sacrifice."

Rilla of Ingleside represents Canadian girlhood and womanhood at war, but in the chapter "Across Enemy Lines: Gender and Nationalism in Else Ury's and L.M. Montgomery's Great War Novels," Maureen Gallagher brings to light extraordinary parallels between L.M. Montgomery's Canadian girl, Rilla Blythe, and German author Else Ury's German girl, Annemarie Braun. This essay is especially significant because Montgomery, writing in the immediate postwar era, incorporates the myth of a nation born through war, wherein the sacrifice of men and women will help to build a progressive nation. Ury, writing during the war years, also sees the war as a unifying force, in this case for Germany, a myth that, as Gallagher points out, was prevalent in Germany at the war's beginning – and yet Ury's novel remained popular even in the postwar years, when Germany underwent hardship as the result of losing the war. Gallagher thus illuminates the workings of war on nationalism, but through the important lens of gender. Both heroines mature from girlhood to young womanhood during the Great War, but, as Gallagher argues, the similarities of narrative incident, plot structure, and character are less notable than the ways in which both Montgomery and Ury, from "across enemy lines," use gender to "simultaneously bolster and undercut wartime nationalist narratives." Both books were parts of popular series, and both books' reception was affected by events in the years that followed the First World War. As Gallagher reveals, *Rilla*'s complex depiction of war, nationalism, and gender meant that it remained the most prominent and important fictional treatment of Canadian women's homefront experience, and it was never out of print. Else Ury's book, the most popular book in its series when it was first published, was "excised from the series following the Second World War, when the nationalism and patriotism it expressed became politically unpalatable," despite its undermining of deterministic nationalism. Neither Montgomery nor Ury would survive to see the end of the Second World War. Else Ury, of Jewish heritage, was barred from publishing when the Nazis began their murderous program to strip Jews of their rights and lives, and she died at Auschwitz in 1943.

Part Three: Healing or Hurt? The Aftermath

This section focuses on the aftermath of war as requiring a new and urgent engagement with meaning-making in the face of destruction, grief, suffering, futility, and death. Montgomery was one of the first Canadian authors to write openly about the grief that war caused for women and the community, a theme that is prevalent in today's field of war studies. How did grief and the trauma of war impact women during the war and afterwards? How did they justify the war to give their suffering meaning? And how did women attempt to heal their worlds in the postwar era? Was healing even possible? How were women's roles in wartime perceived across the century? The themes in this section engage with aftermath; and it should be noted that Montgomery reifies the idea of "aftermath" in *The Blythes Are Quoted*, figuratively through the poem "The Aftermath," attributed to the soldier-poet Walter Blythe, and formally through Walter's family's struggle to interpret the poem, to *come to terms with it*, in the wake of its fictional author's wartime death.

Caroline Jones explores "The Aftermath" and the "war-shadowed" fictions Montgomery created in the 1930s and into the 1940s in her essay, "The Shadows of War: Interstitial Grief in L.M. Montgomery's Final Novels." Through Sarah Cole's definitions of "enchantment and disenchantment," Jones traces how "these later novels foreground conflict, offering happy endings that do not always overcome ... notes of futility." In the aftermath of the First World War, conflicted characters who are war veterans emerge and bring with them broken or unfulfilled family bonds and fractured connections with community. Written during the Great Depression and Montgomery's own losses and depression, these novels feature out-of-proportion arguments, dark secrets, hypocrisy, *schadenfreude*, cruelty, and violence. Many of these themes are superficially familiar from Montgomery's earlier work, but in the war-shadowed work Jones describes as "defined more by its undertones than its surface," new shadows of cynicism and horror infuse the text. As Janice Fiamengo concluded in her study of Montgomery's life-writing and the writer's relationship with depression, "Montgomery crafted an autobiographical 'I' whose record of private pain had the power to shatter and rebuild her public identity"; however, these personal and fictional guises strain under the pressures of war.[105] What Jones refers to as "the smaller theatre of Montgomery's grief" is profoundly entwined with the aftermath of war and the unaccounted injuries to the imaginative spirit; Montgomery seeks meaning for herself and for the characters and communities of her life, her art, and her heart.

Montgomery's *Rilla of Ingleside* is extraordinary partly because it is one of the few depictions of women's experience of the First World War that remains in print and widely read over the century since the war. Andrea McKenzie explores a century of women's war images in "Women at War? One Hundred Years of Visualizing *Rilla*," examining Montgomery's textual representations of women in light of the illustrations of women and war that appear on its covers. These illustrations provide a cultural history of how women's wartime roles and Montgomery's text are visually imagined across time and place. While McKenzie argues that *Rilla* "has influenced successive generations of readers with its complex perceptions about war and women's active and influential part in it," she demonstrates the troubling erasure of this legacy in the cover illustrations. Throughout a century marked by international conflict and upheaval, and despite shifting cultural and national attitudes about warfare, war and its aftermath are rarely part of the visual representation of *Rilla* on book covers. Thus, McKenzie argues, images of Rilla undercut the very active wartime roles that women play in Montgomery's text. Problematically, most of the images deny women's empowered wartime roles, leading McKenzie to conclude, "To de-contextualize Rilla from Montgomery's war is to limit all women caught up in similar conflicts – to downplay the depth of emotion that they experienced and the very real work they undertook."

If women's war images erase the shadows of war from the covers of *Rilla of Ingleside*, the same was not true of Montgomery's life. Before the war, Montgomery expressed her intention to "keep the shadows of my life out of my work."[106] As her life and the twentieth century progressed, the deeper and sharper the shadows, the more complex the avowed task. Much of the critical response to Montgomery's fiction and life-writing explores the darkness that invades the lightness of her writing. In contrast, Elizabeth Epperly explores the healing and beauty that Montgomery offers, through an extraordinarily attentive reading of *Emily's Quest*, the third of the trilogy to feature emergent writer Emily Byrd Starr. The *Emily* series' implicit chronology would historically encompass the First World War, but the novel's narrative does not, in fact, include it.[107] With subtle dexterity, Epperly's "*Emily's Quest*: L.M. Montgomery's Green Alternative to Despair and War?" examines Emily's "consuming human struggle with meaning and despair" through images and metaphors of proximal life in the natural world and the constructed dwelling, rather than distant and distal wars. Epperly employs insights from ecopoetic readings of Romantic literature, contemporary learnings of synaesthetic perception from cognitive neuroscience, and a profound understanding of Montgomery's multi-modal metaphor. Montgomery's Emily experiences the rapture of beauty through nature, but, to be truly rapturous, the experience of beauty must be mediated by the quotidian experience of suffering and loss. In Epperly's terms, "the lesson Montgomery ... wanted to embrace freshly after war, grief, and madness assault her house of life" is that "she must engage with the dailiness of living, trusting to a larger, inclusive pattern where 'Nature never did betray the heart that loved her.'" Image and illusion, and, centrally, the "Disappointed House," which Emily "claimed ... as her own when she was eleven," become her dwelling, where she may dwell on what meaning and beauty can be derived from embodied experience in a war-ravaged century.

Conclusion

Jay Winter and Blaine Baggett write, "At some time between 1914 and 1918, virtually the whole world put on the clothes of war. In terms of outlook, of pessimism, of fear, few have completely shed them since."[108] Yet though L.M. Montgomery struggled to cope with the immediate aftermath of the First World War, in her novels she sought optimism in the midst of horror, shaping her postwar fictional world to show the beauty of imagination and the loveliness of the natural world as forces greater than the darkness and cruelty that were the legacy of global warfare. The war may have become "a permanent feature" of her "mental landscape,"[109] but to a large extent, the delights of her fictional world were her escape – and her readers' escape – from the personal catastrophes and global threats of the interwar years. It seems somehow fitting that the last of Montgomery's novels published during her lifetime, *Anne of Ingleside*, was published in 1939, the same year that saw the beginning of the Second World War.

The 2009 publication of Montgomery's complete Second World War book, *The Blythes Are Quoted*, complicates any reading of her lifetime legacy of war writing. Dark themes of insanity, adultery, and tyranny are juxtaposed with romance, love, humour, and optimism.[110] In one of the final stories, "The Road to Yesterday," the heroine falls in love with a man whom she remembers from childhood as vindictively cruel towards people and animals – a boy seemingly beyond redemption. In a twist of plot, she discovers that she has mistaken her lover's identity; that although on the surface he looks like that cruel boy, he is, in fact, a look-alike cousin with a kind, generous nature, a worthy suitor and lifetime mate, though she may lose him, since he is a soldier on leave. Montgomery thus acknowledges that although cruelty, violence, and brutality do exist, they exist alongside romance, beauty, and a love of the natural world. Yet such redeeming qualities seem fragile and subject to potential loss if not nurtured – and the violence of war threatens them, always. This final reckoning with war illuminates the distance that Montgomery's attitudes have travelled since the North-West Resistance, when she experienced the suspense of her father's fate, and the Boer War, when her attitude succumbed to its "meretricious glory."[111] Her attitudes in *The Blythes* are still embedded in the local, just as Vance argues they were in *Rilla of Ingle-side*, her First World War novel; and just as *Rilla* still resonates with audiences today because Montgomery encapsulated the emotions and experiences of a community at war, so *The Blythes* echoes the more harshly delineated cruelty and beauty that emanated in the aftermath of the First World War and the approach to the Second World War.

This volume of essays establishes the complexity of Montgomery's war writing, examining her novels and poetry in the context of war literature and art, exploring her questions and attitudes about gender roles and work during wartime, and illuminating how she treated the themes of grief, loss, sacrifice, and healing in the aftermath of global conflict. Today, the world is still at war; themes of nationalism, grief, loss, suspense, gender, and heroism are just as relevant now as they were during Montgomery's lifetime. Because she persevered through grief and loss towards hope and perception, Montgomery's war writings illuminate how the enormity of war both shaped and transformed her era and our century, giving us a better understanding of war's impact on women, on communities, and on nations.

NOTES

1 Abrams, *Prince Albert*, 77.
2 Montgomery, *SJ* 2: 160. Hugh John Montgomery, L.M. Montgomery's father, joined the Prince Albert Volunteers to fight against Riel and the Métis people in the North-West Resistance. In August 1890, L.M. Montgomery travelled west and lived in Prince Albert for a year with her father and stepmother. She returned to Cavendish in August 1891. See Bolger's *The Years before "Anne"* for an account of Montgomery's time in Prince Albert and the letters she wrote home; and see Montgomery, *Selected Journals* (hereafter *SJ*), vol. 1 and *Complete Journals* (hereafter *CJ*), vol. 1, for her personal account of her doings and thoughts about Prince Albert. *CJ* 1 provides a more complete set of Montgomery's journal entries from this time.
3 See McKenzie, "Women at War."
4 Montgomery had "never even seen" her half-brother Carl before the First World War, but when he returned missing a leg, she did meet him and liked him very much. See *SJ* 2: 159–60 and 229–31. Stuart

Macdonald served as a doctor with the Canadian Navy, having joined in March 1943 (Rubio, *Lucy Maud Montgomery*, 591).

5 For instance, see Montgomery's horror about Hitler and the prospect of another war during the Munich crisis of 1938. *SJ* 5: 276–82. The Munich agreement, which promised peace in Europe, was signed on 29 September 1938, and the abrupt change in Montgomery's journal shows its impact. On 5 October 1938, she wrote that she had had "the best sleep in months" and awoke feeling "perfectly *rested* and *well*" (*SJ* 5: 283; italics in original).

6 See Edwards and Litster, "End of Canadian Innocence"; Edwards, "L.M. Montgomery's *Rilla*"; Epperly, *Fragrance of Sweet-Grass*; and McKenzie, "Women at War."

7 Montgomery, *CJ* 1: 449–50.

8 Montgomery, *CJ* 2: 3; *CJ* 1: 464.

9 Ibid., 56.

10 Nicholson, *Canada's Nursing Sisters*, 34–47; Dewar, *Those Splendid Girls*, 4.

11 Montgomery, *SJ* 2: 150.

12 Brittain, *Chronicle of Youth*, 88.

13 Brittain, *Testament of Youth*, 291–2.

14 Sandra Gwyn claims in *Tapestry of War* that "Canada … did not produce a wartime diarist with the intensity and perception of Vera Brittain," though she does use Montgomery's journals as revelatory of Canadian life during the war (164–5). It is possible that Brittain's 1933 *Testament of Youth*, written with hindsight to condemn a war that killed the young men to whom she was closest, influenced Gwyn's perspective. Brittain questioned the war in her diary, but her letters show that she continued to support the war and the concept of duty within it. See McKenzie, "Witnesses to War."

15 *SJ* 2: 249 and 265 respectively. Montgomery worked at the *Halifax Echo* from September 1901 to June 1902. See *SJ* 2: 264–83.

16 See, for instance, Montgomery's journal entry about comforting the parents of Goldwin Lapp after he was killed in the war, *SJ* 2: 207.

17 Montgomery mentions this "khaki row" in her journal entry of 3 February 1917 (*SJ* 2: 207–8). For information about the men who enlisted and whom Montgomery knew, see Cavert, "If Our Women," 2.

18 Montgomery, *After Green Gables*, quoted in Collins, "An Occasional Story," 13.

19 Figures in this paragraph about Montgomery's war writing are from Collins, "An Occasional Story," 15. Her article lists Montgomery's wartime writing and publishing.

20 Epperly, *Fragrance of Sweet-Grass*, 75.

21 Ibid., 95.

22 Ibid., 111.

23 See Epperly, "Chivalry and Romance," for an extended exploration of *Rainbow Valley*, Montgomery's use of chivalry in it, and her revealed "ambivalence about war."

24 Montgomery borrows from the poem of Thomas Babington, Lord Macaulay, "Horatius at the Bridge." Macaulay's lines read "And how can man die better / Than facing fearful odds / For the ashes of his fathers / And the temples of his gods."

25 Montgomery, *SJ* 2: 274.

26 See Montgomery, *SJ* 2: 286–307.

27 Rubio, *Lucy Maud Montgomery*, 217–18.

28 Montgomery, *SJ* 2: 309. Helen M. Buss observes that at the time of Ewan's illness, Montgomery's "personal situation would leave little time for the mature writing career that she might have wanted." We agree with Buss's assessment of Montgomery's journals as an "art" that should be "prize[d]," but question the term "mature writing career." Buss, *Mapping Our Selves*, 170.

29 Coates argues that Montgomery "re-writes the term 'total war' by arguing that war is a catastrophic event which affects every living creature." "The Best Soldiers," 76.

30 See Edwards, "L.M. Montgomery's *Rilla*," 170–1; McKenzie, "Women at War," 338–43.

31 For more about humour in *Rilla*, see Lefebvre and McKenzie, Introduction to *Rilla of Ingleside*, xiii–xiv.

32 Ibid., xiv–xv.

33 Acton, *Grief in Wartime*, 18.

34 Ibid.

35 Joel Baetz, "Anna's Monuments," 96, argues that Canadian women poets such as Anna Durie subvert gender expectations of mourning

because "they become valuable custodians of the past, responsible for
its preservation (at least) and revivification (at most)," Kindle locations 3695–6. McKenzie, in contrast, argues that British wartime
poetry creates the expectation that women mourners will become
"discursive agents" who glorify the memories of their lost men; see
"Witnesses to War," chap. 2.

36 A number of Montgomery scholars have explored the impact of Presbyterianism on Montgomery or examined her religious beliefs. See,
for instance, Gavin White, "The Religious Thought of L.M. Montgomery"; Elizabeth Waterston, *Magic Island*; Mary Henley Rubio,
"L.M. Montgomery: Scottish Presbyterian Agency"; Margaret Steffler,
"'Being a Christian' and a Presbyterian"; and Jean Mitchell, "Civilizing *Anne*." Barbara Carman Garner examines religious thinking on
Montgomery's "auto-discourses" in "A Century of Critical Dissec-
tion."

37 For fuller explorations of the notion of sacrifice in Montgomery's
wartime journals and *Rilla*, see Young, "L.M. Montgomery's *Rilla*,"
and McKenzie, "Women at War."

38 Montgomery, *Rilla*, 67.

39 See McKenzie, "Women at War," for an exploration of this specific
myth in Montgomery's work, and how she used, yet subverted, other
British myths in *Rilla*.

40 Vance, *Death So Noble*, 39–40. Vance also observes that writers such
as Marjorie Pickthall and John Oxenham expressed the same concep-
tion of death. See also Young, "We Throw the Torch," for his comments on Montgomery's attitude and how it conformed to other
writers' attitudes.

41 Kazantzis, foreword, xix.

42 See Vance, *Death So Noble*, 175–6, for more critical responses to
Rilla.

43 The *New York Times Book Review and Magazine*, for instance, mentions the young men enlisting and one of them being killed, but focuses much more on the "captivating, sunny story" of "a very human
young girl." Lefebvre, *L.M. Montgomery Reader* 3: 226.

44 Ibid., 3: 229.

45 Ibid., 3: 234.

46 Ibid., 3: 236.

47 Montgomery, "How I Became a Writer," 3.

48 Vance, *Death So Noble*, 175–6; Gwyn, *Tapestry of War*, 164–5.

49 Urquhart, afterword; Munro, afterword.

50 Epperly, *Fragrance of Sweet-Grass*, 147–8.

51 See Montgomery, *SJ* 4: 237–49, for Chester's marriage and its impact; for Ewan's breakdown in 1934, *SJ* 4: 261–85.

52 Epperly, *Fragrance of Sweet-Grass*, 212–20.

53 See *SJ* 5: 276–82, for examples of Montgomery's response to Hitler. See also Caroline E. Jones's chapter in this volume for an analysis of Montgomery's use of war veterans in her 1930s novels.

54 Butler, "Heartbreaking Truth," F1.

55 Rubio, *Lucy Maud Montgomery*, 575, 578.

56 Montgomery, *My Dear Mr. M*, 204.

57 Montgomery, *Blythes*. An incomplete version of this manuscript was edited by Stuart Macdonald and published as *The Road to Yesterday* (1974). This version omits the wartime structuring, the interludes with the Blythes, and two short stories.

58 Lefebvre, afterword, 513.

59 International scholars have explored *Anne of Green Gables*'s influence on various countries in times of war and its aftermath, even though this novel is not a "war novel." See Samigorganroodi, "Reading and Teaching," on *Anne*'s reception in Iran after the Iran-Iraq war (1980–88); Gammel et al., "An Enchanting Girl," particularly Banwait's analysis of the ideology of the text's introduction into postwar Japan; Akamatsu, "Continuous Popularity," on *Anne*'s continuing influence in Japan after the Second World War; and Wachowicz's "At Home in Poland" for an assessment of Montgomery's writing on Polish readers during times of strife.

60 The volume *Storm and Dissonance: L.M. Montgomery and Conflict* takes a broad definition of conflict, encompassing dissonances and "cultural, gender, generational, and class differences" (Mitchell, Introduction, 1). Chapters that specifically address war are limited to McKenzie, "Women at War"; Tiessen, "Opposing Pacifism"; and Lefebvre, "That Abominable War."

61 See Coates, "The Best Soldiers," 66; Webb, "A Righteous Cause," 31; Gerson, "*Anne of Green Gables* Goes to University."

62 Watson, *Fighting Different Wars*, 9–10.

63   Higonnet, "All Quiet," 220–1.
64   See Gerson, "*Anne of Green Gables* Goes to University"; Rubio, introduction to *Harvesting Thistles*; and McKenzie, "Women at War."
65   Montgomery, *Rilla*.
66   Lefebvre and McKenzie, "A Note on the Text," in *Rilla of Ingleside*, by L.M. Montgomery, xx.
67   Lefebvre and McKenzie, "Introduction," ibid., ix–xix.
68   Tector, "A Righteous War," 76.
69   Gwyn, *Tapestry of War*, 165–6.
70   Epperly, *Fragrance of Sweet-Grass*.
71   Rubio, Introduction to *Harvesting Thistles*; Edwards, "L.M. Montgomery's *Rilla*"; Edwards and Litster, "End of Canadian Innocence"; Young, "L.M. Montgomery's *Rilla*"; and Coates, "The Best Soldiers."
72   McKenzie, "Women at War"; Tiessen, "Opposing Pacifism."
73   Tector, "A Righteous War."
74   Rothwell, "Knitting Up the World"; Devereux, "Writing with a 'Definite Purpose'."
75   Cavert, "To the Memory."
76   Thompson, "The Shadow."
77   Fishbane, "My Pen."
78   Lefebvre, "That Abominable War." See also Lefebvre's Afterword to *Blythes*.
79   For a detailed picture of Montgomery's overall stature in critical assessments of Canadian literature through the twentieth century, see Gerson's "*Anne of Green Gables* Goes to University." In the realm of war literature, Donna Coates noted Montgomery's omission from Great War writers in such critical assessments as Carl F. Klinck's *Literary History of Canada*. Peter Webb, writing in 2011, observes that although authors such as Findley and Boyden receive critical attention in Canada, "little is known about many earlier novels, novellas and short story collections published during and shortly after the First World War." He adds, "Even war-related works by better-known authors of the period ... [such as] L.M. Montgomery's *Rilla of Ingleside* (1921) receive scant critical attention" ("A Righteous Cause," 31). Joel Baetz, writing in 2014, claims that "an important and vibrant constellation of [Canadian] women's war writing ... has almost com-

pletely disappeared from view," echoing Coates's 1996 assessment (Baetz, "Anna's Monuments," Kindle locations 3719–20.)

80 Coates, "The Best Soldiers," 66.

81 See Baetz, "Anna's Monuments," Kindle locations 3719–20.

82 Fisher, "Canada and the Great War," 224. Fisher includes a section on Canadian women war writers, including Montgomery, in her essay, and she also includes Montgomery in *Boys and Girls in No Man's Land*.

83 Gordon, *Catching the Torch*, 40.

84 Fisher, "Canada and the Great War," 224; Vance, *Death So Noble*, 266. Glassford and Shaw rightly question "how … women fit into this narrative of war-leading-to-national-maturity" (Introduction, 3).

85 Tector, "A Righteous War," 73; Fisher, "Canada and the Great War," 230. Colin Hill analyzes *Rilla* as part of a study on the transition from romance to realism in Canadian literature. He explicitly connects the development of literary realism in Canada to the First World War. His analysis of Montgomery finds *Rilla* to be "among the most ambitious and intelligent [accounts] of the period," claiming that it "convincingly presents the war subject and its representation as challenges to lingering Victorian conventions in both literary and societal realms." However, Hill unwittingly demotes her earlier work, noting that "Montgomery, of course, built her reputation primarily as a writer of regional romances." He concludes that Montgomery "resists making a clean break with literary tradition" in *Rilla*, and that she, like others of the time, was "unwilling or unable to abandon tried and true romantic conventions." Hill, "Generic Experiment," 59–60, 65–7.

86 Gammel, "Staging Personalities," 262–5.

87 Epperly, Foreword, x.

88 Ibid., xii.

89 Thompson, "Canadian Fiction," 81; Gordon, "*Catching the Torch*," 29. Thompson omits Montgomery because he considers legitimate war novels to be written by combatants, while Gordon mentions her only once, to illustrate how Montgomery conforms to the progressive, nation-building myth. In 2000, Dagmar Novak devoted the penultimate chapter of her analysis of Canadian war novels to *The Wars*.

Novak, *Dubious Glory*. Sherrill Grace also considers Findley's novel to be canonical, beginning her study, *Landscapes of War and Memory*, with this work, and calling it "magisterial" in a shorter piece. She does not consider war writing from before 1977. Grace, *Landscapes of War*, 11; Grace, "The Great War," 3.

90 Thompson, "Canadian Fiction," 83. See Fisher, "Canada and the Great War," 224, and Gordon, *Catching the Torch*, 39–41.

91 Fussell, *Great War*, 8.

92 Coates, "The Best Soldiers," 66, 68.

93 Higonnet, "All Quiet," 220–1. Scholars of women's war writing are too numerous to mention all. Some of the most influential include Higonnet, Angela K. Smith, Gail Braybon, Penny Summerfield, Susan Grayzel, Sharon Ouditt, Jane Potter, Christine Hallett, Carol Acton, and, in Canada, Donna Coates.

94 Winter, *Sites of Memory*, 115.

95 Winter and Baggett, *The Great War*, 12.

96 The range and volume of war scholarship is now so diverse and prolific that we can list only a few examples. For recent trends in research about children, see Paul, Johnston, and Short, eds., *Children's Literature and Culture of the First World War*. For the war told by a wide range of voices – people from thirteen nationalities and disparate areas – see Palmer and Wallis, *Intimate Voices from the First World War*. Higonnet's 1999 anthology of women's war writing, *Lines of Fire*, still provides an excellent, multi-genre range of women's writing; she includes authors from places such as India, Armenia, and Hungary as well as from Britain and America. For examples of African narratives, see Lunn, *Memoirs of the Maelstrom*. See Das, ed., *Race, Empire, and First World War Writing* for studies of the war's impact on diverse cultures. For an analysis of medical personnel's narratives, including those from the First World War, see Jane Potter and Carol Acton's *Working in a World of Hurt*. For an excellent example of trends in nurses' war narratives and literature, see Fell and Hallett, eds., *First World War Nursing*.

97 Fisher, "Canada and the Great War," 230.

98 CBC, "The Great Canadian War Novels," and Grassi, "5 Must-Read Canadian Novels."

99 Katherine Ashenburg, "Why Literature Written Out of the First World War."

100 Canadian War Museum, "Young Adults."

101 Montgomery, *Blythes*, 510.

102 Gordon, *Catching the Torch*, 40.

103 Keen, "So –, So – Commonplace," 94.

104 Higonnet et al., *Behind the Lines*, 4.

105 Fiamengo, "The Refuge," 184.

106 Montgomery, *SJ* 1: 339.

107 Gabrielle Ceraldi examines the "anxieties of modernity" in Montgomery and the aftermath of war as a healing space where "the pre-war past can truly be remembered forward and become a source of strength for the present." See Ceraldi, "Utopia Awry."

108 Winter and Baggett, *The Great War*, 361.

109 Ibid.

110 Lefebvre, Afterword to *The Blythes*, 512.

111 Brittain, *Testament of Youth*, 291.

Trench on
Vimy Ridge
1914 – 1918

Mary Riter Hamilton

2.2

Mary Riter Hamilton
1919

2.4

2.5

2.6

2.7

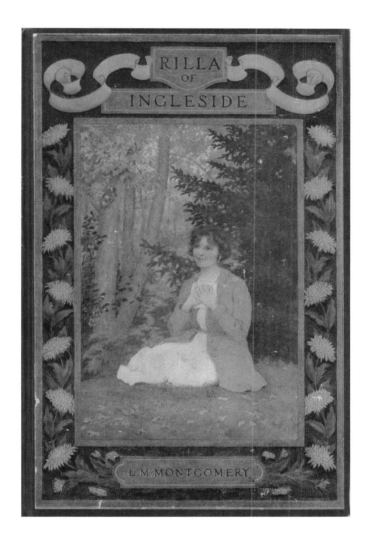

RILLA
OF
INGLESIDE

L. M. MONTGOMERY

9.1

tember 1918 she went to see D.W. Griffith's film *Hearts of the World*, a big-budget epic about a French village ripped apart by the German invasion.⁵ But, according to her journal, her interest was not in the film's blatantly propagandistic tone, nor in the German atrocities that it described. She did not comment on the grand moral issues that it tackled, nor on the strategic importance of the military campaign that was its backdrop. Nothing of broad significance detained her. Instead, she and her aunt Annie Campbell "wanted to see it especially because a battle that Carl [Montgomery, her half-brother] took part in was featured in it."⁶ They were watching for a specific hole in the wall of a specific building that Carl had described. Finally, "Near the end came the hole – unmistakably *the* hole, and we both exclaimed aloud, 'There's the hole.'"⁷ The most important moment in the film, for Montgomery, was the one that reduced the war to a personal level.

She was scarcely more involved in the war on a national level. Most of her fellow writers eagerly embraced the war as a subject, from either a recognition of its dramatic potential or a desire to fight the war with their most potent weapon, the pen. It was also, not incidentally, a good source of income in a vocation that was notoriously fickle. Robert W. Service, after writing a series of war articles for the *Toronto Daily Star*, moved effortlessly from *Songs of a Sourdough* to *Rhymes of a Red Cross Man*. Norah Holland, Marjorie Pickthall, and Katherine Hale all published war poetry that elevated their reputations in a way that their earlier poetry had not. Ralph Connor (Charles W. Gordon), a tireless public speaker before he enlisted with the 43rd Battalion, Canadian Expeditionary Force (CEF), as its chaplain, published *The Major*, and eventually took the Sky Pilot, the titular hero of his 1899 novel, to no man's land. Charles G.D. Roberts wrote some highly regarded war poetry but spent most of his time on non-fiction, serving as a war correspondent and contributing a volume to Lord Beaverbrook's *Canada in Flanders* series. Stephen Leacock, a frequent public speaker before the war, continued in that role after August 1914, and also turned his pen to topics such as finance and economics in wartime, the death of poet John McCrae, "The War Mania of Mr Jinks and Mr Blinks," and even the preface to a book of cookery of the Allied nations.

In contrast, L.M. Montgomery the writer was almost entirely silent on the war while it was in progress. She did not fight the literary war; only a few of her short stories and poems published between 1914 and 1918 directly concern the conflict. Nor did she use her fame to serve the nation in time of emergency; she was not travelling great distances to give patriotic lectures about the war to huge crowds or appear at large recruiting rallies. She did not necessarily subscribe to the view of Saskatchewan artist Augustus Kenderdine, who argued that the role of art in war was "to nourish those cultural and spiritual forces for which we are fighting."[8] In fact, she found her own art form quite unsuited to the great national questions that were at stake, and balked at writing "for schoolgirls and their little doings while the nations are locked in a death struggle."[9]

Montgomery's reluctance to engage the war on a national or international level should not be taken as a sign of shallowness or self-absorption. Instead, it reflects what she recognized at the time in herself: an inability to come to terms with the war while it was in progress. We know from her journals that Montgomery was overwhelmed by the coming of war and that it frequently induced in her a sense of emotional paralysis. In this regard, she is unusual only in her candour in reflecting on her mental state. Indeed, many writers during the First World War recognized the enormity of the situation they were in and the impossibility of dealing with it in a broad sense. In 1915 critic J.E. Hoare, writing in *University Magazine*, praised Canadian poets who realized "the futility of attacking the whole vast subject in a few verses."[10] The most successful war poets, in his view, were those who elected to focus on small parts of the experience. In his preface to *Heartbreak House* (1919), George Bernard Shaw made a similar point: "The enormity of it [the war] was quite beyond most of us. Its episodes had to be reduced to the dimensions of a railway accident or a shipwreck before it could produce any effect on our minds at all."[11]

Consequently, it was on the local level that Montgomery most engaged with the war, and where we must seek her connection to it; to look at the war at a local level accords with how people at the time tried to make sense of it. Fortunately, it is relatively easy to sketch the extent of Montgomery's local world. By combing through her letters, journals, scrapbooks, and other accounts, we can record the various places she visited between August 1914 and November 1918 and, at the same time, get a sense of her activities. The methodology is not perfect; Montgomery probably did not record every single trip she made or activity in which she participated. However, one can assume that she noted the most important journeys and activities; any that she opted not to record likely involved nearby communities.

Over those four years, Montgomery made two trips to the United States, one before the United States entered the war and the other after, to visit relatives of her husband, Reverend Ewan Macdonald. As well, she travelled to Toronto, Montreal, and Prince Edward Island, trips that combined business (usually meeting with people in the book trade) and pleasure. The vast majority of her wartime travelling was local. The most frequently visited communities were Uxbridge (the nearest town with a rail connection and newspapers, something that she mentioned frequently in her journal), Zephyr (the church there constituted part of her husband's charge), Sunderland, and Udora. Most of Montgomery's war was spent in three rural townships: Scott, and its more developed neighbours, Brock (which had two local newspapers during the war, the *Beaverton Express* and the *Cannington Gleaner*), and Uxbridge (the most populous of the three townships, and the one with the largest community).

For decades, historians have argued that between 1914 and 1918 rural Canada had a lower enlistment rate than the cities and that, by extension, interest in and support for the war were weaker in rural Canada than in urban centres. "The towns were readier than the countryside," noted Donald Creighton in 1957, an observation that has been repeated by many historians over the past sixty years.[12] Farm families cared about farming, we are told, and not much else. We might be tempted to imagine that Montgomery, isolated in the fastnesses of Leaskdale, was content to let the war bypass her. Disconnected from the national recruitment and propaganda efforts, declining to write much of substance about the war, travelling only for purposes unconnected to it, surrounded by farmers whose horizons rarely stretched beyond their own fields – surely it would have been easy for her to live her life without significant interruption from the conflict overseas.

There are two reasons why this assumption is unsustainable. First, because Montgomery was married to a Presbyterian minister, she had little choice but to be deeply involved in the war. Canada's established churches were solidly pro-war, and, even had Ewan been soft on the cause, he would have been expected to be an active recruiter and propagandist in the area. As the lady of the manse, it fell to Maud to manage the patriotic effort, organizing and hosting patriotic teas and socials, raising funds for charitable causes, assuming (albeit reluctantly) the presidency of the local Red Cross group, planning craft bees to make comforts for soldiers, and calling on bereaved families who suffered the loss of a loved one in uniform. Almost the only mentions of her personal involvement with the war relate to these kinds of local charitable activities.

Second, the notion of rural Canada being unenthusiastic about the war is based on very shaky evidence; documents have been misinterpreted, broad conclusions have been drawn on dubious grounds, and little effort has been made to test assumptions. Historians rarely take into account the fact that the census definition of an urban resident was someone living in an incorporated village, town, or city, regardless of size.[13] The threshold for incorporation in the late nineteenth century was a population of 750, hardly what we consider "urban." Nor do they allow for the practical obstacles to enlistment in rural areas; for much of the war, it was actually quite difficult to enlist in rural Canada, for the enlistment apparatus was confined to the cities and larger towns. Finally, the peculiar accounting method employed by the Department of Militia and Defence meant that soldiers were classified by their place of enlistment, not their place of residence; we simply do not know whether soldiers came from urban or rural areas.

Measuring support for the war is a tricky proposition at best, but a careful examination of local records from Scott, Montgomery's home township, is essential if we are to understand the response to the war in her milieu. According to the 1911 census, the population of Scott Township and its four villages, Leaskdale, Zephyr, Sandford, and Udora, was 1,109 men and 1,010 women.[14] Granted, that was three years before the war began, but those are the best available statistics, and other local sources make it possible to gauge movement in and out of the township between the census and the outbreak of the war. Furthermore, because 1911 was the year that the Macdonalds moved to Leaskdale, there is a certain logic in using that census as a baseline for analysis.

The census reveals that in 1911 Scott Township had 571 men of military age; that is, they were between the ages of eighteen and forty-five sometime between 1914 and 1918. Obviously, this is an imperfect means of measuring the pool of available manpower. We know that younger teenagers and older men did enlist, yet they would have been outside the pool of potential soldiers. We must also admit that there are likely errors in the census data – birthdates not remembered or recorded incorrectly or illegibly. Two other groups that might have further reduced the eligible male population, First Nations peoples and members of historic peace churches, did not live in Scott Township in numbers that are statistically significant.[15] Any figure can only be approximate, but for lack of a better place to start, let's assume that 571 male residents of Scott Township were eligible for military service.

But that is not quite true. Technically, enlistment was open only to British subjects; men of foreign birth were supposed to be rejected (although they were often enlisted, especially when a unit was having trouble reaching full strength). Roughly 8 per cent of men in Ontario were of foreign birth; Scott Township was overwhelmingly British, but the census reveals that 2 per cent of the male population were foreign born.[16] They were most likely itinerant labourers of military age, a group that normally had a high enlistment rate, but they would have been ineligible for service.

Furthermore, physical fitness was a requirement for enlistment in the Canadian Expeditionary Force, although the expectations were relaxed as the war dragged on and the torrent of volunteers coming forward slowed. The only scholar to have looked at rejected volunteers during the First World War has calculated that roughly 25 per cent of volunteers to the First Contingent in August and September 1914 were rejected on the basis of physical unfitness.[17] Attestation papers reveal that volunteers were also rejected for other reasons. Recruiting officials used a variety of terms to describe such men – "dissolute" and "incorrigible" were popular, but more often they resorted to a single damning verdict: "Unlikely to become an efficient soldier." On the basis of an analysis of later enlistments, this group could constitute as much as 10 per cent of any unit. Finally, there were a number of men of military age who, for other physical reasons, would not have attempted to enlist. The 1911 census lists such men in four categories: "Blind," "Deaf and Dumb," "Insane," and "Idiotic."[18] Their numbers were small, but they nevertheless further reduce the pool by roughly 5 per cent.

With these disqualifications (which, again, can only be estimates), we might conclude that fully 42 per cent of the pool of Scott Township's men of military age were in fact ineligible for service on various grounds, primarily lack of physical fitness. This accords with contemporaries' judgments of the generally poor levels of health in rural Canada at the time.[19] We are left with 331 men from Scott Township who were actually eligible for service and would likely have been accepted had they volunteered.

Cataloguing the men from the township who enlisted is more difficult. The database of attestation papers at Library and Archives Canada cannot yet be searched by place and, in any case, for part of the war, volunteers were not asked to state their place of residence.[20] The records of the Post Office Department pertaining to rural mail delivery routes in the early twentieth century would allow us to determine if an address such as RR#3 Uxbridge was in Uxbridge Township or Scott Township, but those records no longer exist. The only option is to compile a list of township residents, from church records, cemetery registers, the manuscript census returns, and other local sources, and cross-reference those names with the CEF database, which can be searched by name or service number (many of which were allotted on a geographic basis). It is even more difficult to find enlistments outside the Canadian Expeditionary Force, particularly in units from other countries. Tens of thousands of Canadian men enlisted in the Royal Flying Corps or Royal Air Force, British Army units (reservists who left to return to their units at the beginning of the war, as well as later volunteers), the Royal Navy and Royal Canadian Navy, militia and ad hoc formations like the Railway Service Guard, American units, and even those of other nations. But identifying them, not to mention determining their place of residence, can be a challenge. And what about the thousands who enlisted in local Home Guard units? The Cannington Home Guard in neighbouring Brock

Township began soliciting volunteers in February 1915 and within a month had signed up over a hundred volunteers, many of whom were too old or unfit for other military service.[21] Should they be considered part of the patriotic response as well?

By carefully examining contemporary sources, one finds at least 122 men who left Scott Township to serve in the First World War (82 volunteers and 40 conscripts). This should be regarded as a minimum. At the very least, then, 36.9 per cent of Scott Township's eligible adult male population served in uniform during the First World War. The most comprehensive analysis of national and provincial enlistment rates, Chris Sharpe's article in the *Journal of Canadian Studies*, calculated that 39.6 per cent of Canada's eligible male population, and 45 per cent of Ontario's eligible male population, enlisted.[22] Scott Township was thus a little under the national average, but not dramatically so.

It is abundantly clear that Montgomery was surrounded by people going off to war. She mentioned a few of the local men by name in her writings, most notably Goldwin Lapp (killed in January 1917 while serving with the 20th Battalion), Robert Brooks (killed in action at Amiens on 8 August 1918), and Morley Shier (a Royal Air Force pilot lost over the North Sea in September 1918), three young men to whom she dedicated *Rainbow Valley*. But it was a small enough community, and she had a significant enough position, that she would have known *of* all of them, even if she did not personally *know* them. In January 1916, she wrote to Ephraim Weber, "On Xmas eve I gave a dinner party for the boys who have enlisted from our church and I wondered how many of them would ever sit at my table again."[23] In the same letter, she noted that "about 17 of our finest boys have enlisted."[24] Of significance here is her implicit value judgment. It was seventeen of the "finest" who enlisted, a group that, in her mind, stood head and shoulders above men who had declined to enlist, such as her neighbour Mrs Leask's "strapping slackers," to whom she referred in another letter.[25]

And other men in Montgomery's life were in uniform: her half-brother Carl Montgomery, who enlisted in October 1914 and lost a leg at the Battle of Vimy Ridge; Cameron McFarlane, an officer with Princess Patricia's Canadian Light Infantry and the husband of her dear friend and cousin Frederica Campbell; her English fan and pen-pal Ken Cruit. The conclusion is inescapable: Montgomery's world was deeply involved in the war, as she herself was. But she was not in-volved by writing bracing war poetry to encourage recruitment or do-nations. When she spoke at recruiting meetings in Scott Township, she preferred John McCrae's "In Flanders Fields" to anything she had written herself.[26] There is little indication that she was keen to use her fame for the benefit of the war effort, as so many of her fellow authors did. She was involved in the war not as a celebrity but as a commu-nity leader and resident of a deeply committed rural township. It was the mothers of soldiers in *her* church that moved her, the boys from *her* township that she worried about (aside from the 122 Scott Town-ship men in uniform, a further 30 listed their next of kin as living in the township). She was involved in the war in precisely the same way as tens of thousands of other Canadians were.

Montgomery recognized the degree of her immersion only when she left the country. As she wrote to Ephraim Weber in January 1916, "Unless you have been in Canada since your last letter was written I do not think you can even partially realize how earnestly we are 'at war.'"[27] She repeated this notion in her journal in September 1916, on a trip to visit Ewan's family in Indiana: "I did not realize until I came here how deeply Canada *is* at war – how *normal* a condition war has come to be with us. It seems strange to go out – on the street or to some public place – and see no Khaki uniforms, no posters of appeal for recruits, no bulletin boards of war despatches."[28] This feeling only deepened as the war dragged on. In November 1917, at almost the lowest point of the conflict as far as the Allies were concerned, she confided to Weber, "When you live and breathe and eat and drink and sleep and *pray* war, you can't ignore it even in a letter."[29]

Local matters consumed so much of Montgomery's mental and emotional energy that she had little left to devote to the national and the international. But that was also a conscious decision on her part, a conclusion that emerges from her earlier reflection on Canadian lit-erature. The fusing of the various elements into a harmonious whole, as she put it, had to come first; only later could something bigger emerge. "I think the war will give birth to a great literature," she wrote to Ephraim Weber, "but it will be thirty years or more before it comes. This generation will not give it. It will come from the generation that is being born now and suckled on the new ideas that must come from such a world upheaval."[30]

Not only did she find it very difficult to deal with the war while it was in progress, but she also saw the wisdom in waiting for a conclusion, or better, a resolution, before she attempted to make sense of it. In this regard, it is instructive to contrast her novels with the work of some writers who did publish extensively through the war and postwar period. Robert J.C. Stead was an Ontario native who started a newspaper in Cartwright, Manitoba, when he was still a teenager. By 1914, he had a solid reputation as a novelist (based on his 1914 novel *The Bail Jumper*) and a poet (thanks to his 1908 collection *The Empire Builders and Other Poems*). He traded on his literary fame to become active in national patriotic causes during the war, acting as chief fund-raiser for Alberta during the 1918 Victory Loan campaign, and also continued to write. Stead's verse collection *Kitchener and Other Poems* (1917) is very conventional, just like his novel *The Cow Puncher* (1918), which follows its hero Dave Elden from his ranch to his death at the Battle of Courcelette. But in 1920, Stead published *Dennison Grant*, a very different novel reflecting a new social baseline. Its hero, profoundly dissatisfied with the merciless character of prairie capitalism, finds in the war the opportunity to build a better world. But the world he hopes to build is just as complicated as the one he wants to replace. The war has not been the panacea he imagined; it solved some problems, only to create new ones. Stead's 1926 novel, *Grain*, the story of a young western farmer wrestling with notions of duty in wartime, is more sophisticated and challenging still. The hero, Gander Stake, is not entirely likeable, and his response to the war bears little resemblance to Dave Elden's. Gander is not impressed by soldiers; his heroes are the men who run the steam-powered threshing machine that comes to his farm. He feels an obligation to enlist but has no desire to; quite apart from his very reasonable belief that he can best serve his country by using his skills as a farmer, the patriotic rhetoric of military service rings hollow in him. When he finally does enlist, his decision is not a positive affirmation of values he treasures, but a kind of penance; the uniform becomes a hair shirt that he feels he must wear. *Grain* is a nuanced portrait of a deeply conflicted young man, made possible by a period of contemplation and reflection on the part of the author.[31]

Montgomery, in declining to write a lot of conventional wartime material and allowing herself that period of contemplation, did herself a great favour. She has no wartime potboiler to her name that she might have rued once the "death grapple" had ended. Granted, she did use parts of her journal in *Rilla*, but she was able to temper those elements with postwar reflection. This is not to suggest that she necessarily regretted anything she wrote during the war. On the contrary, her use of wartime rhetoric in the novel indicates that her views on the rightness of the cause remained conventional. For example, on the frontispiece to *Rilla*, she used a line from Virna Sheard's poem "The Young Knights," published in her collection *Carry On!*: "Now they remain to us forever young / Who with such splendour gave their youth away."[32] In the novel, Montgomery writes, "More than one recruit joined up because Rilla's eyes seemed to look right at *him* when she passionately demanded how could men die better than fighting for the ashes of their fathers and the temples of their gods."[33] The last phrase is taken from Macaulay's *Lays of Ancient Rome,* but, more significantly, it was used by Sir Clifford Sifton in a speech at the Canadian Club of Montreal in January 1915.[34] The speech was widely reported in national media, and it is quite possible that Montgomery read of it. Even if she did not, the sentiment meant enough to her that she was willing to use the line after the war with no sense of irony.

Even so, with the wisdom of hindsight, Montgomery was able to contextualize the war in *Rilla*, adding nuance without compromising the novel's verisimilitude. To balance the characters and scenes that beautifully capture the emotions and thoughts of the war years, Montgomery drew other characters who seem to be experiencing those four years with the knowledge of one who has already lived through them. Gertrude Oliver's dream, in which a blood-tinged wave breaks over her feet and stains her dress, hints at the tragedy that Montgomery knows is coming, but that she must keep from her characters. And then there is Walter Blythe's agonized warning to Mary Vance:

> Before this war is over ... every man and woman and child in
> Canada will feel it – you, Mary, will feel it – feel it to your

heart's core. You will weep tears of blood over it. The Piper has
come – and he will pipe until every corner of the world has
heard his awful and irresistible music. It will be years before
the dance of death is over – years, Mary. And in those years
millions of hearts will break.[35]

Few Canadians in August 1914 felt that sense of foreboding but, by
highlighting the prescience of Walter and Miss Oliver, Montgomery
is able to reflect with the full benefit of hindsight on what the war
did to her world. This gives *Rilla* the edge over many novels published
around the same time, which a century later seem too one dimensional.

The other great strength of *Rilla* is its authenticity. Critics at the
time praised it for capturing so accurately the essence of small-town
life in wartime. Glen St Mary, observed one reviewer, "could be a
thousand other small towns in Canada."[36] The *Regina Post* lauded
the book for possessing "in a very high degree that natural, life-like
semblance of being a chronicle of actual happenings,"[37] while a Vancouver librarian thanked Montgomery for having "given a true picture of what we went through during five long years of agony."[38] In
Rilla, in the view of many reviewers, fictionalization was merely a device that allowed Montgomery to write what was essentially a work
of local history.

There is no question that Montgomery was helped by the fact that
she was working with existing characters who already had lives in
the minds of readers. This allowed her to imagine how they would
have reacted to the war within a very specific local context. In contrast, Henry Beckles Willson, in his novel *Redemption*, seems to have
started with the great national ideals that interested him and then
hung characters on them.[39] Gregory Vant and Gustave Lanctot are
not so much people as national archetypes that have been given flesh.
Willson was typical of novelists who had to, or felt they had to,
interpret the war in its broadest sense right away; all too often, that
meant falling back on clichéd characters and boilerplate episodes, as
in *Redemption*.

But more important is the fact that Montgomery lived the war on
the local level in a way that many writers, by choice or by chance, did
not. Montgomery not only accepted but embraced the need to look at

the war in microcosm. She related those years as she lived them in Leaskdale; her novel became autobiography. She wrote the war as countless Canadians lived it, so that readers could recognize their own past in the story. In British Columbia or Saskatchewan, Ontario or New Brunswick, or even Quebec, they could find in *Rilla* truths about their own experience. As a novelist, Montgomery succeeded where so many of her contemporaries failed. Despite her prediction that a national literature was another generation away, she succeeded in writing that *national* literature precisely because her focus was *local*. In writing Glen St Mary at war, she wrote Canada at war.

NOTES

1 Entry of 27 August 1919, in Montgomery, *SJ* 2: 339–40.
2 The original article, published in the *Globe*, has been reprinted in Lefebvre, ed., *L.M. Montgomery Reader* 1: 48–9.
3 Morrow, *The Great War*, xi.
4 Entry of 7 December 1914, in Montgomery, *SJ* 2: 157.
5 *Hearts of the World*, dir. D.W. Griffith, 1918. The film starred Lillian Gish, Robert Harron, and Dorothy Gish.
6 Entry of 5 September 1918, in Montgomery, *SJ* 2: 267–8.
7 Ibid.
8 University of Saskatchewan Archives, MG 87, A.F.L. Kenderdine Papers, vol. 3, f. 10, untitled talk.
9 Letter of 16 October 1914, in Montgomery, *My Dear Mr. M*, 70–3.
10 Hoare, "The Muse in Khaki," 201.
11 Shaw, *Heartbreak House*, xxvii.
12 Creighton, *Dominion of the North*, 448; see, for example, Bothwell, Drummond, and English, *Canada, 1900–1945*, 144.
13 Basavarajappa and Ram, "Section A: Population and Migration."
14 Canada, Census and Statistics Office, Department of Trade and Immigration, *Fifth Census of Canada, 1911*, vol. 1, table 2, 338–9.
15 The census records Rama Township as having the only First Nation population in the county of Ontario North, and counts three Quakers living in Scott Township. Ibid., vol. 2, table 7, 234–5; table 2, 68–9.
16 Ibid., vol. 2, table 7, 234–5.
17 Clarke, "You Will Not Be Going," 161–83.

18 *Fifth Census of Canada*, vol. 2, tables 39, 40, 41, and 42, 514–625.

19 For one study that references rural health at this time, see Martin, "The Right Course," 55–89.

20 Service Files of the First World War, 1914–1918 – CEF, http://www.bac-lac.gc.ca/eng/discover/military-heritage/first-world-war/first-world-war-1914-1918-cef/Pages/search.aspx.

21 *Cannington [ON] Gleaner*, 4 March 1915, 4.

22 Sharpe, "Enlistment in the Canadian Expeditionary Force," table 5.

23 Letter of 12 January 1916, in Montgomery, *After Green Gables*, 60.

24 Ibid.

25 Entry of 20 April 1918, in Montgomery, *SJ* 2: 246.

26 Letter of 7 April 1918, in Montgomery, *My Dear Mr. M*, 81.

27 Letter of 12 January 1916, in Montgomery, *After Green Gables*, 59.

28 Entry of 5 September 1916, in Montgomery, *SJ* 2: 191–2.

29 Letter of 25 November 1917, in Montgomery, *After Green Gables*, 67.

30 Ibid., 70.

31 There is a similar contrast between Douglas Durkin's poetry collection *The Fighting Men of Canada* (1918) and his novel *The Magpie* (1923).

32 Sheard, *Carry On!*, 8. Sheard's son Paul was an officer in the Canadian Army Service Corps.

33 Montgomery, *Rilla*, 122–3.

34 *Montreal Herald and Daily Tribune*, 25 January 1915.

35 Montgomery, *Rilla*, 45.

36 University of Guelph Archives, L.M. Montgomery Collection, scrapbook of book reviews, 1911–36, 183–91.

37 Ibid.

38 Ibid.

39 Willson, *Redemption*.

CHAPTER 2

Mapping Patriotic Memory: L.M. Montgomery, Mary Riter Hamilton, and the Great War

Irene Gammel

On a recent trip to Ypres, on my way to the medieval Cloth Hall, I crossed the cobblestone Grote Markt, past the tour guides. Where once shells fell, annihilating the city over the course of four years, the commemoration industry bustles. On the wall of the lobby of a nearby hotel where I stayed is a large-lettered floor-to-ceiling inscription of "In Flanders Fields." The museum commemorating the Great War in the old Cloth Hall also bears the name of John McCrae's poem: the In Flanders Fields Museum. A few kilometres north of Ypres, in St Julien, is the Brooding Soldier, the St Julien Memorial, high up on a stone plinth, his helmeted head bowed as he quietly faces Ypres. In the twilight of the July day, with drizzle turning into rain, the soldier mourns: "18,000 CANADIANS ON THE BRITISH LEFT WITHSTOOD THE FIRST GERMAN GAS ATTACKS THE 22–24 APRIL 1915. 2,000 FELL AND LIE BURIED NEARBY."

How do we remember events of mass trauma? How do individuals and nations memorialize events as cataclysmic as the Great War? Denise Thomson argues that the First World War spawned a new tradition of commemoration of the war dead in Canada that "gradually came to reflect an increasingly assertive nationalism."[1] Peter Hoffenberg's study of Australia corroborates that war continues to shape collective memory in the major combatant nations. This intersection of patriotism, memory, and mourning is the concern of this essay. L.M. Montgomery experienced two world wars, and the "shadows of war" are evident in her writing, through the darker tone in her wartime *Anne* novels such as *Anne's House of Dreams* and *Rainbow Valley*,[2] the local patriotism of Prince Edward Island as a microcosm for the emergent nation, and Hamilton by recording the scenes where regiments from various parts of the dominion and from Newfoundland had fought, thus mapping the emergent nation through memorializing. They did so in the years immediately following the war, a time that was deeply unstable and troubled by new scourges that kept the mood severely depressed, as the influenza pandemic, unemployment, and quarrels among former allies cut off the brief euphoria of the armistice in November 1918. While the male modernist artists such as Hemingway or Sassoon reacted with anger, Montgomery and Hamilton, whose family members and friends had served in the war, took radically different positions, and their work requires different approaches and perspectives to appreciate the texture of their commemorative aesthetic. As Jay Winter observes: "Irony's cutting edge – the savage wit of Dada or surrealism, for example – could express anger and despair, and did so in enduring ways; but it could not heal"; in fact, it was often more traditional modes of expression that "provided a way of remembering which enabled the bereaved to live with their losses, and perhaps to leave them behind."[22] Just so, Montgomery and Hamilton were hoping to heal, experimenting with the cultural codes of mourning, which are also infused with patriotism. In doing so, they created Canadian landscapes of war memory in which specific locales become sites of both patriotism and mourning, of war memory and nation building. While Winter suggests that these healing narratives were "at times less profound," my concern is precisely with documenting their complexity and depth.[23]

In the following, then, I juxtapose Montgomery and Hamilton's depiction of three prominent war sites – Vimy, the Somme, and Ypres – associated with Canadian military victories and intense commemoration. Fusing personal memories of loss with efforts to comfort, their constructions of Vimy, the Somme, and Ypres proffered opportunities for replicating, and also for subverting, to varying degrees, available rhetorical and cultural moulds of commemoration. As we shall see, Montgomery's and Hamilton's emergent landscapes of memory and mourning are embodied, unsettling, and querying, even as they console with a powerful aesthetic that resonates more than a hundred years later.

Mapping Memories of War

Vimy Ridge

One of the myths of the birth of Canada is related to the victory at the Battle of Vimy Ridge, 9–12 April 1917, the site where the four Canadian divisions fought together for the first time. Vimy looms large in the war memory in the immediate postwar era, claimed as Canadian land; Canada's contributions were enshrined even on the pages of the 1919 Michelin guide to Arras.[24] Interestingly, Montgomery's mapping of Canadian war memory is at once thoroughly *local*, in focusing on the Canadian home front, and ambitiously *global*, in incorporating her military analysis of world events and military maps printed in the newspapers. In the latter, her focus is less distinctively Canadian than it is Allied (and British), following the events on *all* battlefronts, including Verdun, the Marne, the Aisne, as well as the Russian Front, the Southern Front (Italy, Greece), and the Near East. Verdun is referenced over a dozen times in *Rilla*, even though no Canadians fought there, whereas Vimy, so important in the Canadian postwar imagination, appears in only two passages. And yet these two Vimy references are each highly charged, the first appearing midway through the novel:

> The moon sank lower into a black cloud in the west, the Glen went out in an eclipse of sudden shadow – and thousands of miles away the Canadian boys in khaki – the living and the dead – were in possession of Vimy Ridge.
>
> Vimy Ridge is a name written in crimson and gold on the Canadian annals of the Great War. "The British couldn't take it and the French couldn't take it," said a German prisoner to his captors, "but you Canadians are such fools that you don't know when a place can't be taken!"[25]

By filtering the memory of Vimy through the backhanded compliment of German prisoners, Montgomery troubles the formula. This ironic subversion is all the more remarkable given that Vimy Ridge presented an outstanding military achievement. The success of Vimy helped mobilize new recruits and culminated in the completion, in 1936, of the Canadian National Vimy Memorial, inscribed "To the valour of their countrymen in the Great War and in memory of their sixty thousand dead this monument is raised by the people of Canada."

This site of a grand, national gesture of mourning, embraced by the government, was troubling for Montgomery, cathected with personal memories of losses that prompted more textured methods of mourning. Montgomery's half-brother Carl Montgomery suffered severe wounds at Vimy, "his leg blown off above the knee," as she noted with distress in her journal on 2 June 1917: "It seems dreadful that he should be maimed for life like that."[26] A few months later, Montgomery preserved a telling portrait in her journal (fig. 2.1). Dressed in his uniform, Carl sits in the garden, his good leg on the ground. On his lap is her son Stuart, whose dangling leg provides an optical illusion, taking the place of Carl's missing leg like a prosthesis.[27] The photograph, taken by the author, performs a visual restoration of the leg, such that its aesthetic composition works as a metaphor for the process of mourning itself – both proclaiming a loss and performing a gesture of empathy in helping repair that loss. Vimy hit close to home all the more through its connection to the death of Colonel Sam Sharpe, an Uxbridge military man whom Montgomery knew, who had played a tactical role in the success at Vimy Ridge, and whose career had been cut short. In 1918, as Montgomery reports in the tiniest notation in her journal, "insane from shell-shock, [he] jumped from a window in the Royal Victoria at Montreal."[28] Even though he received a burial with full military honours following his suicide (which Montgomery is careful to note) the very brevity of her entry speaks to her discomfort. Such mental afflictions do not belong to the realm of what British war poet Siegfried Sassoon in his sardonic and hostile poem "Glory of Women" called the "mentionable" wound that is a trope of women's discourse on war.[29]

In her second highly charged passage referring to Vimy, Montgomery employs perhaps her most innovative representational strategy, celebrating the Canadian victory sideways, in a deeply gendered way. Montgomery projected her passion for her country, her hostility towards the Germans, and her contempt for Woodrow Wilson into sixty-four-year-old Susan Baker, the Blythe family housekeeper who hoists the flag, knits socks, and never loses confidence in the cause. She

2.1
Vimy veteran Carl Montgomery with Stuart Macdonald, Leaskdale, 1918.
Photograph by L.M. Montgomery.

becomes the spirit of Vimy: "neither a beautiful nor a romantic figure; but the spirit that animated her gaunt arms was the self-same one that captured Vimy Ridge and held the German legions back from Verdun."[30] Montgomery chose as the flag bearer for Vimy an older woman, not teenaged protagonist Rilla Blythe, or her soldier brothers. More subversively, Montgomery associates the spirit of Vimy with the generation of women born before Confederation, forcefully advancing the idea of this generation of women, as well as Montgomery's own, having done "their bit" for decades and coming into their own. By associating the spirit of this Canadian victory with Susan, Montgomery claims for herself and other women of the home front an active, patriotic identity.

Where Montgomery inscribed the memory of Vimy Ridge from the perspective of the female home-front worker-cum-mourner, Hamilton problematized the grieving process from the entrenchments of Vimy. "The first day I went over Vimy ... it was cold and snowing," she later wrote. "I am glad to have seen it under hard conditions."[31] The allusion is clear: it was snowing on 9 April 1917 – Easter Monday – when the Canadians attacked Vimy Ridge in a dramatic blizzard that swept the ridge, impeding visibility and wrapping the soldiers in snow and cold. Exposing herself to the elements was Hamilton's way of getting close to the soldiers whose spaces she was aiming to record with her brush. Her perspective was deeply immersive and empathic, as illustrated in paintings such as *Trench on Vimy Ridge* (fig. 2.2), which takes the viewer inside a communication trench. The artwork depicts the trench's red clay with chalk subsoil on top, showing the earth still in turmoil, even as wildflowers grow out of the wreckage to proclaim new growth. Her composition draws attention to the landscape as a witness of war, revealing the remains of weapons and spaces and tactics. The camouflage in the background consists of wire with rushes attached, "the movement in the breeze rendering long distance observation impossible," as *The Gold Stripe*[32] explained when it reproduced the picture in 1919.[33] The wooden cross in the background signals the presence of a body buried where the soldier had fallen, waiting to be exhumed and reburied in one of the large concentrated war cemeteries nearby. With the flowers blooming red and yellow in the foreground, we are reminded of Samantha Vice's concept

2.2
Mary Riter Hamilton, *Trench on Vimy Ridge, 1914–1918*. 1919.
Oil painting.

of mourning through "practices of beauty." Vice argues that the
beauty of art, memorial, or requiem can be experienced as consoling,
and "these practices can be carried out by the victims themselves or
by those more indirectly affected – relatives, friends, [or] local and
national communities."[34]

   In order for such beauty to console, there needs to be some organizing form or composition – an aesthetic to which Hamilton draws attention through her use of shape and colour. A case in point is her oil
painting *Gun Emplacements, Farbus Wood, Vimy Ridge* (fig. 2.3),[35] an
extraordinary Canadian war memory captured on the eastern slope of
the ridge, painted in vibrant hues – green, blue, brown, yellow, teal,
black, and white – that highlight the artistic construction. The title ref-

erences a significant military story, for Canadians won these German gun emplacements in 1917, as part of the Vimy offensive. A screen of stumped trees reveals the remains of the forest that once helped to hide the formidable gun emplacements that allowed the enemy to maintain their position on the ridge; dark openings of the thick-walled concrete structures suggest the subterranean world inside the ridge. This remarkable scene includes two isolated graves, and Hamilton's trademark trench figures as a violent gash in the foreground. As Hamilton put it in an interview in 1922: "If ... there is something of the suffering and heroism of the war in my pictures it is because at that moment the spirit of those who fought and died seemed to linger in the air. Every splintered tree and scarred clod spoke of their sacrifice. Since then nature has been busy covering up the wounds, and in a few years the last sign of war will have disappeared."[36]

2.3
Mary Riter Hamilton, *Gun Emplacements, Farbus Wood, Vimy Ridge.* 1919. Oil on wove paper. 43.5 cm × 33.4 cm.

Hamilton's project consisted of witnessing and recording, in capturing the savage yet ephemeral traces of war, visually rendering a story of violence and annihilation, as well as of endurance and regeneration. Tracking Vimy Ridge and its district in more than a hundred paintings, Hamilton memorialized the places where Canadians lived and fought: Villers-au-Bois, where they had their billets; Zouave Valley, Ablain-Saint-Nazaire, and Thélus, where many fell. During battle, the dead received burial where they fell before these isolated graves and smaller graveyards were moved to concentrated cemeteries. Because Canada's 67,000 war dead could not be repatriated, Hamilton's Vimy paintings had special meaning for the families at home. When these pictures were first exhibited in Vancouver in the fall of 1919, they were vehicles of mourning for Canadian families who could visually connect with the sites where their loved ones died and lay buried in France and Belgium. In this way, Hamilton's art was meant to help console by conceptualizing the remains in the major theatres of war. At the same time, these paintings were powerful reminders of the destruction of war.

Courcelette (The Somme)

Both Montgomery and Hamilton tracked the battlefield scenes at the Somme, where over 3,000,000 soldiers died, including 8,000 Canadians. In *Rilla of Ingleside*, the Somme, notorious for its bloodbaths, is the site that arouses Anne's anxiety most profoundly. Even before the news of Walter's death there arrives, she is the grieving yet resilient mother who is strong for her son and the cause but is also dwarfed by the pressure. When she hears that the Canadian forces have been moved to the Somme, "for the first time Mrs. Blythe's spirit fail[s] her a little, and as the days of suspense w[ear] on the doctor beg[ins] to look gravely at her."[37] A key location in the Somme for *Rilla of Ingleside* is Courcelette. Canadians stormed and took this town from German hands in a major battle on 15 September 1916, during which they also deployed tanks for the first time. The fighting took place at the sugar refinery close to Courcelette, which the Germans had occupied and turned into a formidable stronghold reinforced with iron and concrete. In her novel, Montgomery records this victory but contains Susan's celebratory impulse: "One day the glorious news came that the Canadians had taken Courcelette ..., with many prisoners and guns. Susan ran up the flag and said it was plain to be seen that Haig knew what soldiers to pick for a hard job. The others dared not feel exultant. Who knew what price had been paid?"[38]

As readers learn after much foreshadowing, Courcelette is the location where Anne and Gilbert's son Walter dies in combat. The family receives his final letter, written to Rilla, posthumously. He writes, "We're going over the top tomorrow, Rilla-my-Rilla ... I shall never be afraid of anything again – not of death – nor of life, if after all, I am to go on living."[39] Implicit in this death is the idea that the others must keep faith – continue the fight – not make peace. "It isn't only the *living* who are fighting – the *dead* are fighting too," Walter writes, echoing the dead from "In Flanders Fields." "Such an army *cannot* be defeated," he insists.[40] Courcelette is thus a location that signals intense commemoration, with Montgomery launching into nationalist rhetoric and echoing McCrae's battle cry to continue the fight no matter what.

In contrast, Hamilton represents Courcelette without heroics. Her painting *Interior of the Sugar Refinery, Courcelette* (fig. 2.4) depicts a large unsightly hole in the brick wall, which provides the aperture into a pastoral scene outside. (Hamilton's orifice also reminds us of the "big round hole in a brick wall" that Montgomery remembers from her brother Carl's accounts of "the battle of Courcelette," a hole Montgomery keenly tracked in the documentary footage of D.W. Griffith's popular 1918 war movie *Hearts of the World* to connect with her brother's battlefield experience.)[41] Hamilton's odd perspective takes the viewer inside the former German stronghold, enabling a response similar to what Roland Barthes in his discussion of photography describes as a *punctum* – a detail that rises from the scene, "shoots out like an arrow, and pierces me."[42] In the work of commemoration, as Palmer and Minogue propose in their study of memorializing poetry, the *punctum* can produce a powerful moment of identification, defying the official closure brought about by grand monuments such as cenotaphs. Just so Hamilton's unusual view from inside the site – standing in the place of the enemy during battle – can be seen to act as the *punctum* that pierces the viewer with the realization of identification. The viewer takes the place of Canadian soldiers who had stood here after the battle, after dislodging the enemy from their long-term stronghold. Through this immediacy and immersion, Hamilton ruptures the distancing involved in abstract historical accounts of Canada's success at Courcelette, the very emptiness inviting mourning for the loss of life associated with this site. Hamilton's almost haptic identification with the soldiers' experience complicates an abstract or romantic understanding of Glory, rendering the site in terms of the Pyrrhic victory it was.

Ypres

In a third example of Montgomery writing the scene from the home front, and Hamilton painting it overseas, the two artists return to Ypres, the most dangerous place on the Western Front. The Ypres Salient was a principal site of resistance in Belgium, where the Germans had entrenched, and Canadians fought several critical battles there to dislodge them. Among these was the Second Battle of Ypres, the first major battle in which Canadians fought, during which the first chlorine gas attack of the war took place, at St Julien, eight kilometres northeast of Ypres, on 22 April 1915. In the first forty-eight hours, 2,000 Canadians died (15,000 Canadians died in Ypres Salient battles in total), but despite their faulty Ross rifles and the gas attack, they were successful in holding St Julien – the site of the Brooding Soldier monument today. Hamilton commemorates this event in a painting with the elaborate title *St Julien, First Gas Attack Launched Here* (fig. 2.5), which features a bunker, one of the strongholds used by the Allies to defend the Ypres Salient. However, this memorial to the valour of Canadian soldiers ultimately testifies to the overpowering nature of the war itself: the objects of war depicted are monumental while the people in the picture are tiny and dwarfed in comparison.

Hamilton's picture *Canadian Monument, Passchendaele Ridge* (fig. 2.6) captures the monument for the 85th Canadian Infantry Battalion (Nova Scotia Highlanders), who lost 148 soldiers during the Battle of Passchendaele, or the Third Battle of Ypres, in 1917. This unit was called "Neverfails" because of their perseverance,[43] and the monument was built by the surviving soldiers of the battalion in April 1919 on the site of their old headquarters, the cement mixed with water

2.4
Mary Riter Hamilton, *Interior of the Sugar Refinery, Courcelette*. N.d.
Oil on wove paper. 23.9 cm × 19.4 cm.

and sand from no man's land. The monument is unique, as it is among
the few non-government-funded memorials on the Western Front, representing the personal experience of a small group of soldiers. Hamilton frequently focuses on such non-official forms of memorializing.
Hamilton's entire project is infused with empathy, recalling Palmer
and Minogue's paraphrase of Jay Winter's concept of "memorials as
an act of compassion,"[44] which gives her work its strong appeal. The
absences inscribed in her text rhetorically compel the viewer's engagement: as Helmers notes, "Due to the absence of human figures,
the viewer is able to be the protagonist, ordering his or her own
story."[45] Viewers enter the space of Hamilton's painting to fill the absences with their impulse to connect with the traces of war. In this
process, different timelines blend, the past fusing with the present;

today, this painting, and the collection of which it is a part, is a vehicle for viewers to connect with century-old individual family history and Canada's collective history.

In *Rilla of Ingleside*, Ypres and the gas attacks appear as objects of both repression and return through Rilla's diary: "I've forgotten Ypres and the poison gas and the casualty lists. Now it rushes back."[46] Rilla's journal also reports the news on Passchendaele, two years after St Julien, in November 1917. She writes: "Our Canadian troops have won another great victory – they have stormed the Passchendaele Ridge and held it in the face of all counter attacks. None of our boys were in the battle – but oh, the casualty list of other people's boys!"[47] Passchendaele Ridge, some kilometres northeast of Ypres, is the site where Canadians had triumphed but also suffered many casualties between late October and early November 1917. The Third Battle of Ypres is a place of intense emotion for Canadians and also intense controversy. Strategically, Passchendaele Ridge was important, as the Germans held the high ground; they could observe the enemy lines from high up. However, during the two weeks it took to conquer Passchendaele, more than 4,000 Canadians lost their lives – the "other people's boys" of Rilla's diary.

Interestingly, the town of Ypres, which gave its name to a number of major battles that involved Canadians, features most memorably in *Rilla of Ingleside* as the unpronounceable place that Susan calls *Yiprez*.[48] The name itself becomes background, its horror recalled by its absence. In contrast, for Hamilton, Ypres is in the foreground. She painted a total of 120 paintings of the Ypres Salient. She was fascinated by the Cloth Hall of Ypres (fig. 2.7), which was left in ruins by the war and today houses the In Flanders Field Museum. Despite the

2.5 *Opposite top*
Mary Riter Hamilton, *St Julien, First Gas Attack Launched Here*. 1920. Oil on wove paper. 34.5 cm × 26.8 cm.

2.6 *Opposite bottom*
Mary Riter Hamilton, *Canadian Monument, Passchendaele Ridge*. 1920. Oil on cardboard. 34.7 cm × 25.9 cm.

shelling, there is a solidity about its body in Hamilton's painting. The famous Cloth Hall is in ruins but is still standing after years of bombardment. It is a robust icon of endurance, and thus a symbol for Ypres itself.

❦

The works of both Montgomery and Hamilton are a product of their active and passionate involvement in the war and immediate postwar eras, at the home front and overseas. The two women, like hundreds of thousands of ordinary Canadian women, became engaged in the war effort. Lord Beaverbrook and his advisers in Canada were commissioning artists to paint female workers in munitions factories, in shipyards, in the fields, including iconic representations of munitionettes. Even so, the actual statistics about women in these new roles were much more modest, as historian Joan Sangster has noted,[49] and most women continued to work in traditionally domestic roles. With Susan Baker and Rilla Blythe, Montgomery's work gave the female domestic war worker her due and made her part of the nation (albeit a version of the nation that, like the 1917 Wartime Elections Act, excluded French, Aboriginal, and other non-anglophone women). Montgomery's *Rilla of Ingleside* sold a remarkable 27,000 copies during the interwar years,[50] showing the widespread appeal of her love of country, domestic feminism, and motivational message.

Like Montgomery, Hamilton approached her tributes to the war with determination, persistence, and conviction. When she was rejected from Beaverbrook's war scheme and learned that she could not go to the battlefields, she did not take no for an answer. Undaunted, she went to work in Europe on her terms, producing more than 320 war landscapes, her life's work. Refusing to benefit from her war work, Hamilton donated her collection as a gift to Canada – to the Dominion Archive for the benefit of the wounded veterans and the families of those who had died. Sadly, today, the name of Mary Riter Hamilton is still a well-kept secret, even though selections of her oeuvre are available digitally on the Library and Archives Canada website. In sacrificing her health and career, Hamilton was deeply invested in her work, just as her war art collection made viewers

2.7
Mary Riter Hamilton, *Ruins at Ypres, Cloth Hall*. 1919.
Oil on plywood. 58.2 cm × 45.6 cm.

connect with the soldiers' experience in immersive ways. Ultimately, Hamilton's overseas war work and Montgomery's work at the home front stand for women's agency and engagement during the war, and their efforts to create a consoling aesthetic after the cataclysmic trauma that was the First World War. Deeply intertwined and complementary, theirs are powerful Canadian stories of remembrance.

NOTES

1   Thomson, "National Sorrow," 5.
2   Edwards and Litster, "The End of Canadian Innocence." ·
3   Lefebvre, "That Abominable War."
4   See for instance, Epperly, *Fragrance of Sweet-Grass*, 112–30; Rothwell, "Knitting Up the World."
5   McKenzie, "Women at War," 326.
6   The majority of Mary Riter Hamilton's works are held at Library and Archives Canada (LAC).
7   Helmers, "Visual Rhetoric," 79.
8   See Rubio, "Subverting the Trite," for an argument for Montgomery's use of a double discourse: an overt discourse affirms the convention, whereas a second discourse critically subverts it.
9   Dyer, *Missing of the Somme*, 32.
10 See for example, Harrison, *Generals Die in Bed*, whose graphic anti-war depictions anticipate Findley's *The Wars*.
11 Vance, *Death So Noble*, 5.
12 Quoted in Fisher, "Canada and the Great War," 227.
13 Shaw, *Crisis of Conscience*, 11.
14 Fussell, *Great War*, 248–50.
15 McCrae, "In Flanders Fields," line 10.
16 Aitken, *Canada in Flanders*, xiv.
17 Ibid., xiv.
18 Ibid., 5.
19 Ibid., 6.
20 Ibid., 13.
21 Ibid., 26–7.
22 Winter, *Sites of Memory*, 115.
23 Ibid.
24 *Arras*, 17. The guide reads: "The Canadians of the 1st Army dashed to the assault of Vimy Ridge, which had so far proved impregnable ... In a single rush they carried La Folie Farm and the hamlet of Les Tilleuls; further south, they captured Hill 132 ... and the village of Thélus, between Neuville and Farbus."
25 Montgomery, *Rilla*, 265–6.
26 Entry of 2 June 1917 in Montgomery, *SJ* 2: 219.
27 Reproduced in ibid., 230.

28 Entry of 29 May 1918, in ibid., 247.

29 Sassoon, "Glory of Women," line 2.

30 Montgomery, *Rilla*, 276.

31 Quoted in "Mary Riter Hamilton," 11.

32 A periodical dedicated to the Amputation Club of British Columbia, which sponsored Hamilton's journey to Europe.

33 "Trench, Vimy Ridge," 17.

34 Vice, "Beauty, Mourning," 144.

35 Two paintings are featured in the LAC's digital collection under this name, including a painting with two white crosses and wreaths in the foreground, which is clearly not the painting described by the title. This is a digital cataloguing error.

36 Quoted in Falla, "Dauntless Canadian Woman."

37 Montgomery, *Rilla*, 239.

38 Ibid., 240.

39 Ibid., 244–5.

40 Ibid., 246. Italics in original.

41 Entry for 5 September 1918, in Montgomery, *SJ* 2: 267.

42 Quoted in Palmer and Minogue, "Memorial Poems," 168.

43 Roy MacGregor, "Halifax Keeps Memory of Passchendaele Alive," *Globe and Mail*, 6 November 2002.

44 Paraphrased in Palmer and Minogue, "Memorial Poems," 162.

45 Helmers, "Visual Rhetoric," 91.

46 Montgomery, *Rilla*, 134.

47 Ibid., 285.

48 Ibid., 124.

49 See Sangster, "Mobilizing Women."

50 Vance, *Death So Noble*, 176.

CHAPTER 3

Education for War: *Anne of Green Gables* and *Rilla of Ingleside*

E. Holly Pike

In *Anne of Green Gables*, war takes place long ago, far away, or both, and this distance creates romance and glamour, reinforced by the way war is depicted in the poetry referenced in the novel. When Anne describes her previous education to Marilla, she lists "The Battle of Hohenlinden," "Edinburgh after Flodden," and "Bingen on the Rhine" as poems she has already memorized, and refers to the "thrills" of reading "The Downfall of Poland."[1] She later recites "Mary, Queen of Scots" in school and "The Maiden's Vow" at a concert and learns the battle canto from "Marmion" for recitation.[2] In *Rilla of Ingleside*, on the other hand, war takes place in the here and now, as Rilla's siblings and schoolmates enlist or do war work at home. However, the rhetoric of war and the themes developed in the poems about war that Anne learned remain: Jem's eagerness to support the mother country, Walter's battlefield longing for the scenes of his childhood, Una's lost chance at love, and Rilla's projected marriage to a returned soldier all pick up on themes from the poems referenced in *Anne of Green Gables*. This resonance suggests that despite her fidelity to actual events and reporting of the Great War, L.M. Montgomery develops some aspects of *Rilla of Ingleside* to fit a literary vision of war as a romantic adventure – a glorious sacrifice for homeland and love.

Scholars have identified elements in *Rilla* that suggest Montgomery did not wholeheartedly accept the view that war is a glorious adventure,[3] but *Rilla of Ingleside* fits a pattern identified by historian Jonathan Vance, who argues that immediately after the war, Canadians favoured "positive" recollections of the war "that retained essentially nineteenth-century images to describe a twentieth-century war."[4] Just as Vance refers specifically to Wordsworth's "Character of the Happy Warrior," written after the battle of Trafalgar, as prefiguring the persistently cheerful accounts of life at the front written after the First World War, the poems about and attitudes towards war mentioned in *Anne of Green Gables* prefigure the connection between war, home, love, and nationhood in Montgomery's depiction of the war in *Rilla of Ingleside*. Montgomery also develops parallels between Anne's and Rilla's experiences to recall to readers the initial novel of the series and the world it depicted. By emphasizing continuity in this way, Montgomery both enacts the intention expressed in her journal to "end Anne – and properly" with *Rilla of Ingleside* and supports the view expressed in her journals that the war will mark a dividing line in Canadian history and literature[5] and therefore in the country's national identity.

Rilla's girlhood experiences replicate Anne's in a number of ways. Anne's vanity in dyeing her hair and decorating her hat with buttercups and wild roses is echoed in Rilla's purchase of the expensive and showy hat that she then stubbornly wears for the duration of the war, a choice that also parallels Anne's stubbornness over Gilbert Blythe. Anne's pre–Green Gables childcare experiences are replicated in Rilla's care for the "war baby," Jims Anderson, and Anne's treatment of Minnie May Barry's croup is echoed in Jims's croup, when another clever and mistreated orphan, Mary Vance, saves the child's life. The Hopetown orphanage, from which Anne (and Mary Vance) came, is mentioned as a place Jims could be sent. Anne's preparation for her first hotel concert, with its focus on her concern with her appearance and on Diana's help, is paralleled by Rilla's preparation for her first dance, assisted by Miss Oliver. Just as Anne is concerned that her recitation will not be a success, Rilla is worried that no one will ask her to dance. Anne must choose between her "fashionable" and "pretty" blue dress and her white organdy, and Rilla must choose between her white dress and her new green one, which is "by far the prettier."[6] Like her mother, Rilla receives pretty slippers as a Christmas gift, though while Anne is able to use hers right away for the school concert, Rilla must wait several months for the lighthouse dance to wear hers. Anne loses Matthew, the person she feels closest to; Rilla loses Walter, her adored brother. By creating these parallels, Montgomery revives in the minds of readers the Anne of *Anne of Green Gables*, who in *Rilla of Ingleside* is a middle-aged woman hardly recognizable as the original Anne.

The social contexts in which Anne and Rilla grow up are also quite similar. Like Avonlea, Glen St Mary is a fishing and farming community with long-standing traditions and assumptions regarding religion, education, and social standing. In Avonlea, Marilla and Mrs Lynde ascribe certain characteristics to local families: Mrs Lynde states that "the Sloanes are all honest people," and Marilla claims that "Josie is a Pye, so she can't help being disagreeable."[7] In Glen St Mary, Miss Cornelia refers to "those terrible Dillons from the Harbour Head," and Susan notes that "the Deans were always high-spirited."[8] In *Anne's House of Dreams* the community definition of family characteristics is made more explicit when Miss Cornelia recites the "prayer" of the Four Winds people: "From the conceit of the Elliotts, the pride of the MacAllisters and the vain-glory of the Crawfords, good Lord deliver us."[9] While all of Anne and Gilbert's children except Rilla take it for granted that they will attend university, they also put in stints as schoolteachers, as their parents did – presumably, like their parents, to finance university education. The forms of entertainment also seem to have changed little. While there are no references to dances in *Anne of Green Gables* as there are in *Rilla of Ingleside*,[10] the concerts for various charitable causes (the library, the Charlottetown hospital, and a school flag) in *Anne of Green Gables* are replaced by patriotic society recruiting meetings and Red Cross concerts in *Rilla*,[11] and the nature of the entertainment is unchanged: choruses, solos, dialogues, and recitations, with a flag drill being added in wartime.[12]

To emphasize these echoes, Montgomery also has Rilla record in her diary a reference to the slate incident of *Anne of Green Gables* and her impression that her mother was "a limb when she was a little girl"; Anne herself refers to the ankle she broke "when Josie Pye dared me to walk the Barry ridge-pole in Green Gables days" and the time "years ago at Green Gables, when I dyed my hair."[13] The explicit references to Green Gables in these reminiscences further remind readers of the original novel. Montgomery also includes references to incidents and characters from other books in the *Anne* series, emphasizing the continuity of the world depicted in the novels up to this point. Gilbert recalls "a buggy ride … the first fall [Anne] taught in Avonlea," which would be the period covered in *Anne of Avonlea*. Anne lists all of her friends from Avonlea, Queens, and Redmond whose sons are enlisting, recalling episodes of those novels to readers.[14] When Jem enlists, Anne and Gilbert are described as remembering "the day years ago in the House of Dreams when little Joyce had died."[15] Rilla recalls Mary Vance chasing her with a codfish and Walter's fight with Dan Reese in "Rainbow Valley days," and before he leaves, Walter recalls how the children spent time in Rainbow Valley.[16] In these ways, the whole series is recalled, as is appropriate if Montgomery is consciously planning this installment as a finale. These reminiscences do not deny the existence of difficulty and grief in the agrarian world depicted in the earlier novels, but they do emphasize the continuity of values such as close friendship, small communities, and connection with the natural world. The references to Anne's ongoing relationships with friends of her past further emphasize continuity and point sharply to the new experience of uncertainty, loss, and fear that readers know these characters are about to share.

As noted above, recitation is a regular feature of community entertainment in Avonlea, and George Peabody's account of Empire Day celebrations and the visits of school inspectors in *School Days: The One-Room Schools of Maritime Canada* suggests that such performances were in fact a regular aspect of Maritime school life.[17] For Anne and Diana, being invited to recite is clearly a mark of prestige. As Diana tells Anne after the first public concert they attend together, "They're always wanting the big scholars to recite," and Anne says, "It must be splendid to get up and recite there."[18] When Anne prepares to recite for the first time at her own school concert, she tells Marilla, "I just tremble when I think of it."[19] She further emphasizes the importance and stress of the event in her comments to Diana after it is over: "I felt as if a million eyes were looking at me and through me, and for one dreadful moment I was sure I couldn't begin at all."[20] The source of these recitations seems to be the Royal Readers, the series Anne refers to as the source of the poetry she has memorized.[21] Peabody notes that "even in 1925, the number of books in rural libraries averaged only twenty-four per school," so school books may have been the only source for recitation material in many communities.[22] The Royal Readers were widely used in Britain and its dominions and colonies from the 1870s through the early twentieth century, though the contents were revised from time to time. Some items in the readers were specifically identified as appropriate for recitation, which both trained students in memorization and prepared them with pieces for school concerts and examinations, which at the time generally included an element of public display. The preface to the 1882 edition of *Royal Reader V* includes a note indicating that the outlines of British history have been removed in order to create room for "additional POETRY for READING and RECITATION ... at the urgent solicitation of many Teachers," demonstrating the importance attached to recitation at the time.[23] Felicity Ferguson argues, in "Making the Muscular Briton," that the Royal Readers were used to "transmit the ideology of imperialism" to the colonial readers of the texts, focusing on "heroic military and naval exploits in the history of the nation" and "the affective qualities of the leaders," precisely the themes raised in the poems associated with Anne and recitation.[24] Amy Tector claims that "the boys go to fight, not only for ideas of Canada and Empire, but also for the physical space of home," based on Jem's and Jerry's references to the disrupted European landscape in their letters home; this supports Ferguson's interpretation of the Royal Readers and is also consonant with the poems Montgomery references in *Anne* and *Rilla*, though Ferguson argues that it is the "values" of imperialism, which extend British attitudes, rather than the idea of home that lead young men to enlist.[25]

The poems that Anne claims to know well depict a romanticized and adventurous version of war. For instance, the glorification of sacrifice and veneration of leaders are seen in "The Downfall of Poland," found in *Royal Reader V*, which Anne had described to Marilla as "just full of thrills."[26] The poem as presented in the reader is an excerpt from "The Pleasures of Hope," published in 1799 by Thomas Campbell (1777–1844), depicting the unsuccessful Polish uprising against Russia led by Tadeusz Kosciusko in 1794. The poem links Poland's cause to the general cause of freedom by invoking other patriotic leaders: "Oh! Once again to Freedom's cause return / The patriot Tell – the BRUCE OF BANNOCKBURN!"[27] Kosciusko, "Warsaw's last champion," calls on his countrymen to live for their country or die with it. His few "trusty warriors" are "dreadful as the storm," and the passage that may well contain the "thrills" Anne refers to describes the carnage: "fires of ruin," "blood-dy'd waters," "the smouldering piles with thunder fall," "red meteors flash'd across the sky."[28] While in its original context in "The Pleasures of Hope," the example of the fall of Poland illustrates a time when hope was lost, the extract selected for the Royal Reader serves simply as a description of battle, approval of nationalism, and glorification of sacrifice.

"Edinburgh after Flodden," by William Edmonstoune Aytoun, which Anne memorized from *Royal Reader VI*, where the first eight of the original fifteen stanzas appear, similarly celebrates sacrifice and defeat in a nationalist cause. The events in "The Fall of Poland" are contemporary to the writer, though not to Anne's generation as readers, but "Edinburgh after Flodden" describes an event of the distant past (1513), though the poem itself was published in *Lays of the Scottish Cavaliers* in 1849. Nevertheless, the values it espouses in its description of war are similar to those in Campbell's poem. Like the "trusty warriors, few but undismay'd" of Poland, the Scots who fought at Flodden are characterized as "the valiant and the strong / ... Grimly dying, still unconquered," and the "blood-dy'd waters" of Prague are matched by the Scottish banner stained with the king's blood.[29] "The Battle of Hohenlinden," from *Royal Reader IV* and also by Thomas Campbell (1803), which recounts a battle of the Napoleonic wars, likewise has images of blood, staining both the Iser River and the snow, and the soldiers are "ye brave, / Who rush to glory, or the grave."[30] In Caroline Norton's "Bingen on the Rhine" (1847), in *Reader VI*, the focus is on the individual rather than the force. As a "soldier of the legion," the central character is not fighting for his homeland, but the other aspects remain the same: they "fought the battle bravely," and "the red sand of the battle-field" was "with bloody corpses strown."[31] Because the battles in these poems are European or British, they are remote in both time and place from the Canadian children who read them. The most contemporary of the poems mentioned in *Anne of Green Gables* – "Mars La Tour, Or the Maiden's Vow," published in 1883 by Stafford MacGregor and set in 1870–71 – develops themes consistent with the earlier poems. In the young woman's vision of the defeat of France,

"The Seine shall run red," and she vows to remain faithful to her lover, who dies "to love and country true" in a hopeless cause.[32]

These poems, with their vivid if somewhat stereotypical imagery, clear narrative lines, and strong rhythms, are eminently suited for recitation. Anne justifies participation in her first concert on the grounds of its objective – it will "cultivate a spirit of patriotism" by raising money to purchase a flag for the schoolhouse.[33] Having noticed "old Mrs. Sloane wiping away tears" after her recitation, Anne says, "it was splendid to think I had touched somebody's heart."[34] In Anne's time, patriotism is merely a community value to be referenced, and the recitation of poems about war and heroism is entertainment for the sake of the "thrills" Anne experiences and the catharsis presumably felt by the Mrs Sloanes of the community. When Rilla recites, the purpose is much more practically patriotic – to encourage recruitment.[35] Unlike Anne, who thinks "it must be splendid to get up and recite there," Rilla has avoided reciting, being embarrassed about her tendency to lisp.[36] However, feeling that she must live up to Jem's standards, she overcomes her reluctance in order to support the war effort in one of the few ways open to her. The specific poems that Rilla recites seem to be T.B. MacCauley's "The Story of Horatius" (in *Reader VI*) and Thomas Mordaunt's "The Call" (in *Lyra Heroica*),[37] both of which, like the poems in *Anne of Green Gables*, celebrate sacrifice for the homeland and refer to earlier, distant battles. "The Call" was written during the Seven Years' War (1756–63) and "Horatius" recounts an episode of ancient Rome, though written in the mid-nineteenth century. Montgomery's description of Rilla's recitations obliquely quotes from the two poems and emphasizes the effectiveness of her appearance as well as the content: "More than one recruit joined up because Rilla's eyes seemed to look right at *him* when she passionately demanded how could men die better than fighting for the ashes of their fathers and the temples of their gods, or assured her audience with thrilling intensity that one crowded hour of glorious life was worth an age without a name."[38] The passion and intensity ascribed to Rilla's performance also recall the effectiveness of Anne's recitations, which leave her audience either in tears or captivated.[39]

The poems that Anne memorized from the Royal Readers are not specifically mentioned in *Rilla of Ingleside* as among the works used at patriotic concerts, yet the values and even the incidents in them inform the depiction of war in the later novel. In "Edinburgh after Flodden," the lines "Widows, maidens, mothers, children / Shrieking sobbing in despair"[40] emphasize the effect of war on the people left at home in Edinburgh, who are at risk from invasion. The citizens of Edinburgh, who are to "man the walls like burghers stout, / And fight while fight you may" if the Scottish army is defeated, are recalled in *Rilla of Ingleside* by Susan, who says, "The Huns shall never set foot in Prince Edward Island as long as I can handle a pitchfork."[41] Susan also echoes the implicit faith in leaders evidenced in the poems in her adherence to Lord Kitchener and British prime minister Lloyd George. Walter's statement in his final letter to Rilla that "the *dead* are fighting too – such an army *cannot* be defeated"[42] also recalls "On the Downfall of Poland," which calls on "Departed spirits of the mighty dead! / Ye that at Marathon and Leuctra bled!" to "restore your swords to man, / Fight in his sacred cause, and lead the van!"[43]

Caroline Norton's "Bingen on the Rhine," in which a dying soldier sends a message to his home, specifically sets up themes and incidents of *Rilla of Ingleside*, particularly Walter's letter to Rilla the night before he dies, when he has had a premonition that he will follow the piper "west" the next day.[44] In the opening stanzas, the speaker emphasizes the bravery of his companions in the recent battle and reveals that he had always wanted to be a soldier, a sentiment also implied in Jem's excitement at the possibility of war, of which he speaks "gaily" and "cheerfully" and which he regards as an adventure,[45] an attitude that Jonathan Vance also found in postwar recollections.[46] The fourth stanza, in which the speaker sends a message to his sister telling her not to weep for him, as he was "not afraid to die," prefigures Walter's telling Rilla, "I'm not afraid" after recounting his new vision of the piper.[47] In the same stanza, the speaker also asks his sister to listen favourably to any soldier who seeks her affections, much like Walter's "premonition" that Ken Ford will return, and he and Rilla will have "long years of happiness."[48] The next stanza, referring to the other girl at home as "not a sister," as well as recalling Gilbert's recitation of the poem in *Anne of Green Gables*, alludes to Walter's wish for Rilla to share his final letter with Una. The young woman in the poem, like Una, has blue eyes and is clearly

associated with the speaker's childhood, as indicated by his recollection of their strolls "down many a path beloved of yore and well-
remembered walk."[49] Her characteristics, however, are split between
Rilla and Una: the soldier recalls the "merriment" and "light heart"
of the young woman,[50] invoking Rilla's attributes ("Wherever Rilla
Blythe was, there was laughter"; "Is there laughter in your face yet,
Rilla?"), and also recalls a heart "too innocent for coquetry," invoking Una's characteristics ("Una was as sweet and shy as she had been
in the Rainbow Valley days").[51] The soldier's focus on the young
woman's eyes ("the merriment that sparkled in her eye," "her glad
blue eyes were on me"[52]) is echoed in Walter's statement "somehow I
see [Una's] eyes very plainly tonight, too."[53] The soldier's detailed recollection of the river and hills of home in the sunshine parallels Walter's recollection of the harbour, hills, and haze of the glen.[54] Because
this poem was explicitly referred to in *Anne of Green Gables*, and in
particular was regarded as significant by Gilbert in relation to Anne,
it seems possible that Montgomery's reworking of it in *Rilla* is conscious and deliberate.

Rilla is susceptible to the romance and glamour of war and thinks
in terms of the literary version of war in pursuing her activities in support of the conflict. She says, "I think a war would be so exciting,"
and she "reacted to the romance of it all," feeling that she would, like
the young men enlisting, respond to "the call of their country." She
quotes *The Lady of the Lake* in her journal, again something learned
from excerpts in the Royal Readers, to express her wish that she could
take part in the adventure.[55] This wish echoes Anne's early desire to
"train as a nurse and go with the Red Crosses to the field of battle,"
which she classes with being a foreign missionary as "romantic."[56]
While Rilla feels that her war work "lacks the romance" of Nan and
Di's, she is alive to the romantic possibilities of Miranda Pryor's wedding, and though disappointed in the wedding itself, "found nothing
lacking" when she saw "that ever-burning, sacred fire of devotion and
loyalty and fine courage that [Miranda] was mutely promising Joe she
and thousands of other women would keep alive at home."[57] Like
Jem, however, Rilla learns that war is less about romance than about
disagreeable realities. Just as Jem writes in a letter home that "one
soon gets used to horrors here"[58] and acknowledges, "I thought it was

fun. Well, it isn't,"[59] Rilla adjusts to doing tasks she dislikes as she comes to understand what fighting a war is really like, even at home and far from battle: "I have done so many things I hate since the fourth of August that one more or less doesn't matter."[60] The change from a romantic to a realistic attitude towards the war is further illustrated in the description of Shirley's attitude towards enlistment: he went "not radiantly, as to a high adventure, like Jem, not in a white flame of sacrifice, like Walter, but in a cool, business-like mood, as of one doing something, rather dirty and disagreeable, that had just got to be done."[61] The title of chapter 16, "Realism and Romance," places Rilla's last evening with Ken Ford in the same context of changed expectations and learning to deal with real conditions.

Early in her work on *Rilla of Ingleside*, Montgomery, rereading her journals, found a comment she had made on Canadian literature in 1910 arguing that "some great crisis of storm and stress" would be needed to create a true national literature. She recognized that the war was likely to be that crisis, echoing her comment on starting *Rilla* that the *Anne* series belonged to "the green untroubled pastures and still waters" before the war[62] – a use of biblical imagery that calls up the economic structure and the peace of the communities she depicts in the *Anne* books. Montgomery places her beliefs about how the war has changed the world as predictions in the mouths of her characters in *Rilla of Ingleside*.[63] A week after war is declared, Walter tells Rilla, "I'm afraid our old world has come to an end," and, shortly afterwards, Mr Meredith voices the belief that the war has a purpose, that it is "the price humanity must pay for some blessing," a development of Montgomery's journal prediction about the crisis that will "purge away all our petty superficialities and lay bare the primal passions of humanity."[64] Similarly, Faith Meredith's statement that "I remember telling old Mrs. Taylor long ago that the world was a world of laughter. But it isn't so any longer" is followed by Walter's belief that "Nobody whom this war has touched will ever be happy in quite the same way. But it will be a better happiness, I think, little sister – a happiness we've *earned*."[65] Mr Meredith's description of the war as "the birth-pangs of a new era" expresses as a confident prediction the questions about the outcome and possible futility of the war that Montgomery raised in her journal and put in Gertrude Oliver's mouth.[66]

Although Montgomery has Mr Meredith speak with confidence that the war will benefit humanity, even at the signing of the armistice, Montgomery herself was not sure what had been achieved: "*What has been born?* The next generation may be able to answer that. *We* can never fully know."[67] Signs of this new era created by the war that are mentioned in the novel include the advent of automobiles and aeroplanes, the upheaval in political affiliation among the Crawfords, Elliotts, and MacAllisters, and Miss Cornelia's more liberal attitude towards Methodists, though it is not clear what the long-term effects of those changes will be.[68]

Further developing the idea of the war as a dividing line in history, in the middle of the war Montgomery has Anne say, "it seems hundreds of years since those Green Gable days"[69] and suggest that the world will have changed beyond recognition when the war ends – "it can't be a bit like the past. I wonder if those of us who have lived half our lives in the old world will ever feel wholly at home in the new?"[70] Miss Oliver responds that "everything written before the war seems so far away now, too. One feels as if one was reading something as ancient as the Iliad,"[71] placing Anne's past in the same remote past as the battles depicted in the poems she found so thrilling as a child. The poetry that Rilla recites, which also belongs to that era "before the war," must seem just as remote, and perhaps it works as a recruiting tool because it recalls values the young men learned in childhood. Montgomery thus creates an explicitly literary past to which both romantic views of war and the *Anne* novels belong. While, as Amy Tector argues, Walter is both Montgomery's representative of the Canadian literature coming out of the "crisis" and a hero, he significantly is not attracted by the literary version of war and heroism that initially motivates Jem and Jerry.[72] Instead, Walter thinks of "everything I've read in old histories … the blood and filth and misery of it all."[73] Yet Walter has been unable to write poetry since war was declared, and only after he enlists can he say to Rilla, "I could write poetry … I've never been able to write a line since last August. Tonight I'm full of it,"[74] suggesting that the crisis that is to give Canada a national literature is also to give Walter his mature voice as a poet. This reading of Walter's role is strengthened in *The Blythes Are Quoted*, in which the introduction to Part 2 states that "he destroyed most of his poems before going overseas but left a few with his mother,"[75] showing a clear break between the poetry he wrote at home and "The Piper," the poem that became famous. Walter's significance as a Canadian poet of the war is highlighted by the absence of references to Canadian writers in *Anne of Green Gables* and *Rilla of Ingleside* and in the Royal Readers, in which the authors studied are overwhelmingly British, as would be inevitable in the late nineteenth century. Walter's death, preventing him from fulfilling Gertrude Oliver's prophecy that he will be "perhaps the first really great poet that Canada has ever had,"[76] is also in keeping with Montgomery's belief that "the great Canadian literature will come from the generation born of this conflict not from the generation that fought through it" and that "surely some new Homer will arise to sing [Verdun]."[77]

Montgomery also specifically alludes to Canada's development of nationhood during the war. Although initially the young men who join up are doing so to save Britain, over the course of the novel their service becomes defined as defence of Canada. Jem expresses his first intention to fight if England enters the war as supporting "the 'old grey mother of the northern sea,'" a paraphrase of a line from Lachlan MacLean Watts's "The Grey Mother," a poem of the Boer War, and he continues the reference to the natural relationship between Britain and Canada by saying, "We're the cubs – we've got to pitch in tooth and claw if it comes to a family row."[78] Kenneth Ford reiterates that version of the relationship when he tells Rilla, "We are part of the British Empire. It's a family affair. We've got to stand by each other."[79] If it is a family affair, Canada is clearly the child and will earn maturity through the struggle. However, Gilbert says that Rilla is "saving a little life for Canada," not for the empire, and when Walter enlists, he tells Rilla, "I owe life and Canada *that*, and I've got to pay it."[80] In Walter's last letter, he expresses his sense of how the war has changed him, knowing that after what he has seen, life would be "ugly and painful always for me," but he recognizes that he has "helped to make Canada safe for the poets of the future," that the war affects "the future, not of Canada only but of the world," and that he expects a "golden harvest – not in a year or two, as some foolishly think, but a generation later."[81] He thus states Montgomery's belief in a changed world and matured Canada to come out of the war, not in his generation, but in the following one.

By 1920, Montgomery was tired of writing *Anne* books and wanted to develop "a new heroine," already "christened" Emily, and write "a book dealing with grown-up creatures."[82] Since, however, it would not be possible to just stop the *Anne* series, Montgomery needed to create a natural closure. To "end Anne – and properly," Montgomery needed to make the world of the final novel consonant with the earlier ones while acknowledging that the world she depicts will disappear. Amy Tector asserts that "*Rilla* reflects Montgomery's struggle to chronicle the impact of the First World War within the expected parameters of the Anne series,"[83] which in effect means doing what Jonathan Vance argues was done frequently during and after the war – depicting a twentieth-century war in nineteenth-century terms, the terms expressed in the poetry taught through the Royal Readers. Mr Meredith's notion that the war is the birth of a new era identifies a clean break with the past, just as Walter's assertion that the fight is not just national, as were the wars in the poems referenced in *Anne of Green Gables*, indicates a basic change in the causes of war that separates his experience from that of previous generations. Gertrude Oliver's reference to Wordsworth as if he were a contemporary of Homer, as if "everything written before the war" is equally remote and belonging to a world where "classic calm and repose"[84] were still possible, suggests that the war has disturbed previous conceptions of all aspects of culture. The "green, untroubled pastures"[85] that Montgomery refers to as an image of the prewar world and the close ties to the natural world she attributes to her characters support her view that the world will be changed because of this crisis; she thus justifies her attempt to assign the *Anne* series to that past, closing the series (or so she thought) by identifying Rilla's experiences with Anne's and having them both learn the reality of war, which may be "full of thrills," but disrupts forever the secure and unchanging world in which the generations depicted in the series have been raised and educated.

NOTES

1 Montgomery, *Anne of Green Gables*, 91.
2 Ibid., 227, 298, 262.
3 See Edwards, "L.M. Montgomery's *Rilla*"; Edwards and Litster, "End of Canadian Innocence"; Tector, "A Righteous War"; McKenzie, "Women at War."
4 Vance, *Death So Noble*, 74.
5 Montgomery, *SJ* 2: 309, 339–40.
6 Montgomery, *Anne of Green Gables*, 295; Montgomery, *Rilla*, 25.
7 Montgomery, *Anne of Green Gables*, 276, 324.
8 Montgomery, *Rilla*, 13, 198.
9 Montgomery, *Anne's House of Dreams*, 212.
10 There is a dance associated with convocation in *Anne of the Island*, 220.
11 Montgomery, *Anne of Green Gables*, 191, 294, 228; Montgomery, *Rilla*, 122, 132.
12 In her journal Montgomery lists the entertainment she is preparing for a Sunday school concert for Christmas 1919 as "recitations and dialogues and drills" (*SJ* 2: 352), further attesting to the unchanged nature of these events.
13 Montgomery, *Rilla*, 111, 11, 198.
14 Ibid., 272, 99–100.
15 Ibid., 56.
16 Ibid., 33 (cf. Montgomery, *Rainbow Valley*, chap. 7); 37 (cf. *Rainbow Valley*, chap. 17); 162.
17 Peabody, *School Days*, 93–6.
18 Montgomery, *Anne of Green Gables*, 194.
19 Ibid., 229.
20 Ibid., 238.
21 Ibid., 91, 129.
22 Peabody, *School Days*, 64. Miller, in *Rural Schools in Canada*, notes that in Prince Edward Island, annual grants of up to twenty dollars were available to match local funds in support of school libraries (42), but he is unable to confirm whether any such libraries exist (98).
23 *Royal Reader V*, iv. Emphasis and capitalization in original.
24 Ferguson, "Making the Muscular Briton," 253, 255, 264.
25 Tector, "A Righteous War," 72–86.

26 Montgomery, *Anne of Green Gables*, 91.

27 Campbell, "On the Downfall of Poland," 472. This poem, as excerpted for the Royal Reader series, is reprinted in Barry, Doody, and Doody, *The Annotated Anne of Green Gables*, so that work will be used as the source for this and other poems referenced in *Anne of Green Gables*.

28 Campbell, "On the Downfall of Poland," 471, 472.

29 Aytoun, "Edinburgh after Flodden," 469.

30 Campbell, "The Battle of Hohenlinden," 467.

31 Norton, "Bingen on the Rhine," 470, 471.

32 MacGregor, "Mars La Tour," 482.

33 Montgomery, *Anne of Green Gables*, 229.

34 Ibid., 239.

35 Montgomery, *Rilla*, 122–3.

36 Montgomery, *Anne of Green Gables*, 194; Montgomery, *Rilla*, 122.

37 "The Story of Horatius" is excerpted in *Royal Reader VI*. "The Call" does not appear in any of the Royal Readers I was able to consult, but it was anthologized in *Lyra Heroica: A Book of Verse for Boys*, edited by William Ernest Henley and first published in 1892, which remained in print until at least 1921, including school editions.

38 Montgomery, *Rilla*, 122–3.

39 Montgomery, *Anne of Green Gables*, 301.

40 Aytoun, "Edinburgh after Flodden," 469.

41 Aytoun, "Edinburgh after Flodden," 468; Montgomery, *Rilla*, 305.

42 Montgomery, *Rilla*, 246.

43 Campbell, "On the Downfall of Poland," 472.

44 Montgomery, *Rilla*, 244–6.

45 Ibid., 28, 29.

46 Vance, *Death So Noble*, 96.

47 Montgomery, *Rilla*, 245.

48 Ibid., 246.

49 Norton, "Bingen on the Rhine," 471.

50 Ibid., 470–1.

51 Montgomery, *Rilla*, 6, 246, 34.

52 Norton, "Bingen on the Rhine," 470, 471.

53 Montgomery, *Rilla*, 246.

54 Ibid., 244.

55 Ibid., 25, 57.
56 Montgomery, *Anne of Green Gables*, 228.
57 Montgomery, *Rilla*, 218, 195, 207–8.
58 Ibid., 128.
59 Ibid.
60 Ibid., 117.
61 Ibid., 264.
62 Montgomery, *SJ* 2: 339, 309.
63 Discussions of the connections between Montgomery's journals during the war and *Rilla of Ingleside* include Epperly, *Fragrance of Sweet-Grass*, 112–30, and Young, "L.M. Montgomery's *Rilla*."
64 Montgomery, *Rilla*, 60, 67; *SJ* 2: 340.
65 Montgomery, *Rilla*, 136, 161.
66 Ibid., 213; Montgomery, *SJ* 2: 160.
67 Montgomery, *SJ* 2: 274.
68 Montgomery, *Rilla*, 284–7.
69 Ibid., 199.
70 Ibid.
71 Ibid.
72 Tector, "A Righteous War," 83.
73 Montgomery, *Rilla*, 62.
74 Ibid., 154.
75 Montgomery, *Blythes*, 363.
76 Montgomery, *Rilla*, 21.
77 Montgomery, *SJ* 2: 340, 198.
78 Montgomery, *Rilla*, 28, 29.
79 Ibid., 47.
80 Ibid., 100, 154.
81 Ibid., 245, 246.
82 Montgomery, *SJ* 2: 390. See also Gerson, "Dragged at Anne's Chariot Wheels."
83 Tector, "A Righteous War," 72.
84 Montgomery, *Rilla*, 199.
85 Montgomery, *SJ* 2: 309.

CHAPTER 4

"Watchman, What of the Night?": L.M. Montgomery's Poems of War

Susan Fisher

Throughout 1916, the Great War was much on L.M. Montgomery's mind. Anguished references in her journals and letters indicate that the war was as urgent and present a concern to Montgomery as her family's health or the machinations of her unscrupulous publisher Lewis Page. It was to her "a black year."[1] In a June 1916 journal entry she declares, "This war is slowly killing me. I am bleeding to death as France is being bled in the shambles of Verdun."[2] Many similar statements appear throughout the entries for 1916. After the war, when she came to write *Rilla of Ingleside*, Montgomery was at pains to show how the war had permeated life on the home front. Day after day, the household at Ingleside waits anxiously for the newspapers and the mail. The news from the battlefields – from the Marne, the Balkans, the Eastern Front, Gallipoli, and Mesopotamia – so dominates thought and conversation that Gertrude Oliver laments, "How *everything* comes back to this war ... We can't get away from it – not even when we talk of the weather."[3] Yet *The Watchman and Other Poems*, the only book that Montgomery published in 1916, is not a collection of war poetry. After the dedication – "To the memory of the gallant Canadian Soldiers who have laid down their lives for their country and their empire" – there is no further reference to the war. It contains no words such as *trench, gas, helmet, flare*, or *bayonet* that would instantly signal the battlefields of the Western Front. The word *poppies* appears, but it is definitely used in a pre–"In Flanders Fields" sense: "The poppies aflame with gold and red / were the kisses of lovers in days that are fled."[4]

How could it be that in 1916, when Montgomery was following the war news with such intensity, the only book she published that year was silent on the conflict? Virtually every other Canadian writer of note rushed into print about the war.[5] Why not Montgomery?

One obvious reason has to do with Montgomery's attempt to manage her reputation. *The Watchman* was never intended as a topical book. Rather, it was an opportunity to present another side of her literary talent: her achievements as a poet. Rea Wilmshurst has established that at least twenty-four of the ninety-four poems in the collection were originally published elsewhere.[6] The acknowledgments page for *The Watchman* lists nineteen periodicals that held copyright to poems included in the collection, so a significant number of the poems were written before Montgomery was plunged into despair about "this awful war ... hideous – unbelievable – unthinkable!"[7]

The only reference in her journal to the collection is very restrained: "Today my volume of poems *The Watchman* came from my Canadian publishers. It is very nicely gotten up. I expect no great things of it."[8] Yet, according to Mary Rubio, Montgomery was "deeply involved with this book on an emotional level."[9] It certainly included poems of which she was especially proud, poems that would remain favourites all her life: in 1938 she mentions that she has given recitations of "To My Enemy" and "The Call."[10] Moreover, *The Watchman* had special significance in Montgomery's ongoing struggles with Page. Rubio notes that Montgomery was "furious" when Page rejected the manuscript on the grounds that poetry would not sell.[11] Given all the money that Page had made from her novels, Montgomery felt that he should have published her poetry. She turned to the firm of McClelland, Goodchild & Stewart, which readily accepted her manuscript and became her Canadian publishers, thus initiating Montgomery's long and harrowing legal battle to break free of Page.[12]

Montgomery's apparent indifference to the fate of *The Watchman* may reflect her assessment of her own talent. Back in 1903 when she introduced herself to the Scottish writer G.B. MacMillan, with whom she would correspond for the next forty years, Montgomery described her aspirations and abilities:

I don't know whether I call verse my specialty or not. I know
that I touch a far higher note in my verse than in prose. But I
write much more prose than verse because there is a wider market for it, especially among the juvenile publications. In 1903
I have made $500 by writing of which less than $100 came
from verse ...

But I am frankly in literature to make my living out of it. My
prose sells and so I write it although I prefer writing verse. I
know that I can never be a really great writer. My aspiration
is limited to this – I want to be a *good workman* in my chosen
profession.[13]

Unfortunately, the "far higher note" of Montgomery's poetry has little charm for the modern reader. Kevin McCabe, in his introduction to
The Poetry of L.M. Montgomery, praises the "relative simplicity of
style and lack of ornate poetic diction" in her verse.[14] But "relative" is
the key word here. Rather than addressing outright the limitations of
Montgomery's poetry, he softens his criticism by discussing her among
other "Late Romantic" poets: "The long-term effect of producing large
quantities of verse on a limited number of subjects was often a vague
and general style which took refuge in 'poetical' phrasing and literary
platitudes. Poets such as Tennyson and Masefield who attempted to
write verses every day showed a progressive decline in poetic verve and
expressiveness. Montgomery is no exception to the rule that the demand for quantity rather than quality eventually showed itself in repet-
itiveness and undistinguished work."[15] It is kind of McCabe to suggest
that Montgomery was no less a poet than Masefield or Tennyson on a
bad day, but Montgomery herself knew better.

In her final book, *The Blythes Are Quoted*, Montgomery offers her
own view. This unusual work, which (not entirely successfully) weaves
together poetry and short fiction, contains forty-one poems by Montgomery, some attributed to Anne, others to her son Walter.[16] Gilbert
Blythe finds Walter's poetry "commonplace," even though he recognizes that, despite Walter's youth and inexperience, his poetry has
emotional intensity: "the boy had something in him."[17] The poems
attributed to Walter share themes, diction, settings, and even titles

with those in *The Watchman.* Of course, they are by the same hand, but Montgomery did little to differentiate those supposedly written by Walter from those published under her own name; perhaps she felt that the "higher note" of her own youthful verse was well-suited to an idealistic and talented young poet like Walter. Compare, for example, Walter's "A June Day" with "A Day in the Open" from *The Watchman.*[18] Both offer the time-honoured pastoral prescription for low spirits. "A June Day" begins with an invitation: "Come, 'tis a day that was born for dreaming / ... we will have done with worry and scheming." In "A Day Off" each stanza begins "Ho, a day / Whereon we may up and away." Both poems favour the poetic diction of the Late Romantic mode: "tryst," "gypsy," and "empearled" appear in "A June Day"; "A Day in the Open" refers to "gypsying breezes," "orient distances," and "a lyric of flowers." In "A June Day," the speaker and his companion will "march with the windy firs"; in "A Day in the Open," they will "roam / where the pines in green gloom of wide vales make their murmuring home." Given that Walter's lyrics are hardly distinguishable from those in *The Watchman,* it seems reasonable to take Gilbert's judgment of Walter's poetry as Montgomery's assessment of her own: for all its passion, her verse was no more than "commonplace."

Another perspective on Montgomery's poetry can be derived from *Emily of New Moon,* which Montgomery described as "more autobiographical than any of my other books."[19] In her father's books, Emily marks "every beautiful word" with "a tiny pencil dot" so that she will remember it: "dingles, pearled, musk, dappled, intervales, glen, bosky, piping, shimmer, crisp, beechen, ivory: I think those are all lovely words."[20] Elizabeth Epperly has pointed out that in Emily's list "we hear the Romantic and Victorian preferences that characterize Montgomery's own volume of verse, *The Watchman and Other Poems.*"[21] Emily, like Montgomery, has precocious talent and a deep feeling for poetry, but she will find distinction and success as a writer of fiction. Her teacher Mr Carpenter recognizes this when Emily accidentally hands him her notebook of stories and sketches instead of the one containing her poems. Although he himself is the object of some of the mocking "word-painting" in Emily's stories, Mr Carpenter declares,

"Why, I wouldn't have missed this for all the poetry you've ever written or ever will write."[22] In *Emily's Quest*, the response of another mentor, Miss Royal, to Emily's novel could also be read as self-assessment: "Your story is like a wild rose, dear, all sweetness and unexpectedness with sly little thorns of wit and satire."[23] Those "sly little thorns" served very nicely to offset the sentimental romance plots of her fiction, but they would not have accorded with the "far higher note" Montgomery wanted to strike in her poetry. Kevin McCabe claims that, "for Montgomery writing poetry was more than a literary activity: it was almost a form of Holy Communion."[24] This may seem an extravagant claim, but in "A Day in the Open" Montgomery describes the "cup of wild wine" that makes the speaker "elate with a laughter divine."[25] It is not just being in nature but writing poetry about it that is sacred. In Montgomery's writing life, poetry served two somewhat contradictory functions: on the one hand, it was a readily produced (though not lucrative) commodity, and on the other, an expression of her deepest spiritual impulses.

This combination might help explain why *The Watchman* is the least read of Montgomery's works. The commodity side is evident in the limited range of themes and subjects: the sea, the woods, spring, sunset, storms, love and marriage, the sanctity of home. These topics, and Montgomery's conventional treatment of them, would not have troubled the editor of any church magazine. The spiritual side manifests itself in Montgomery's affinity for an animistic classicism: dryads and nymphs inhabit her forests; even Pan dwells there. For Montgomery and her contemporaries, classical literature was an unquestioned part of the knowledge of any educated person, and such references would not have seemed inappropriate, even in poems about Prince Edward Island.[26] But to modern readers and to those of Montgomery's own time with modernist tastes, such classicism could seem inauthentic.

The banal spirituality and outmoded classicism of her poetry may also explain why Montgomery could not readily find the resources to write war poems. As she would later demonstrate in *Rilla in Ingleside*, she had indeed thought deeply about the cruel contradictions of the war – the high idealism of the soldiers and the utter squalor of their dying, the lofty patriotic rhetoric and the moral bankruptcy of the politicians and the generals. Moreover, she was able to weave all of this complexity into what was, at least superficially, just "a story for girls."[27] But to write poetry about the conflict was a different sort of challenge; it would have required her to overturn the poetic and spiritual verities of her literary apprenticeship. The kind of verse she had written depended on belief in the natural world as a beautiful, healing, holy place, a world in which real battlefields (as opposed to some distant "darkling plain") could not exist. In 1916, the work of soldier-poets such as Wilfred Owen, Siegfried Sassoon, and Isaac Rosenberg, with its conversational plainness and subtle inversions of the pastoral mode, was still to come.[28] Montgomery would have seen plenty of war poetry by her Canadian contemporaries; it appeared regularly in magazines and newspapers. But almost all of it was patriotic doggerel or spiritualized effusions. The most popular Canadian poem of the war – that is, before "In Flanders Fields" appeared – was Katherine Hale's "Grey Knitting." It glorifies death on the battlefields, not with military language or battlefield narrative, but by drawing on the feminine domains of needlework and fairyland:

> I like to think that soldiers, gayly dying
> For the white Christ on fields with shame sown deep,
> May hear the fairy click of women's needles,
> As they fall fast asleep.[29]

If this was the kind of war poetry expected from women poets, then it is not surprising that for the most part Montgomery avoided writing about the war. When *The Watchman and Other Poems* appeared in 1916, it was promoted as a collection of "dainty poems."[30] The publisher's advertising copy offered assurance that nothing in the book would disturb established notions of Montgomery's work: "The author of *Anne of Green Gables* with her joyous outlook on life, vivid imagination, instinct for words and facility in expression could not help being a poet. This beautiful volume of verse will be widely welcomed. The poems are of rare quality, delicate, lilting, and full of music."[31] A writer of "dainty" and "delicate" poems with a "joyous outlook on life" could hardly be expected to tackle the subject of war. And yet, in certain oblique, tentative, and contradictory ways, Montgomery did in *The Watchman*.

The title poem, "The Watchman," provides one such instance.[32] A dramatic monologue narrated by Maximus, a member of the Roman guard set to watch Christ's tomb, it has obvious formal and thematic affinities with "My Last Duchess," which, in a letter to Ephraim Weber, Montgomery had described as her favourite among Browning's poems.[33] Written in blank verse, as is Browning's poem, "The Watchman" allows a man to reveal himself through uninterrupted first-person narrative. But whereas Browning's duke is an unrepentant murderer, Montgomery's narrator Maximus is both forthright and guilt ridden. And his wife, Claudia, is still very much alive, for it is she to whom his confession is addressed.

In contrast to other poems in the collection, "The Watchman" tends towards plain diction; this suits the narrator Maximus, a soldier of the Roman Empire who describes himself as "a man who had no foolish heart / Of softness all unworthy of a man." He is proud that "Red in my veins the warrior passion ran." The poem's epigraph, drawn from Matthew 28:4 – "And for fear of Him the keepers did shake and become as dead men" – foretells the effect the Resurrection will have on Maximus.[34] Gazing upon the resurrected Christ causes Maximus to collapse into a stupor, and when he regains consciousness, he is "no longer Maximus." Gone is the soldier who "gloried in the splendid strife of war, / Lusting for conquest."

Maximus finds his new gentleness shameful; to Claudia he declares his weakness will "surely … pass in time and I shall be / Maximus strong and valiant once again." But the reader can hardly share Maximus's view that the transformation from warrior to comforter is cause for shame. The new Maximus, the man who wants "To help and heal bruised beings, and to give / Some comfort to the weak and suffering" is surely preferable to the old one, who could "[look] upon a tortured slave / As on a beetle crushed beneath my tread."

What might "The Watchman" have to do with the First World War? Maximus has discovered that a soul truly touched by Christ's death and resurrection cannot be a warrior. This makes "The Watchman" seem a simple anti-war poem, a plea for Christian kindness as an antidote to war. But Christianity and the war were not considered antithetical. Montgomery, according to Epperly, believed that "the war against Germany was sacred, a holy cause."[35] So did most Canadians, including the hierarchy of her own church: in 1917 the Presbyterian Church endorsed the war, declaring that "the Cross of Christian sacrifice spreads its arms over the field of war."[36] The motif of sacrifice – Christ's sacrifice and the type that prefigured it, Abraham's willingness to sacrifice Isaac – was repeatedly invoked to apotheosize the fallen soldier and give a Christian meaning to death on the battlefield.[37] Does the story of Maximus's transformation implicitly challenge this analogy and its endorsement of the war? Perhaps. Montgomery certainly did something similar in *Rilla of Ingleside,* when Bruce Meredith drowns his cat Stripey as a propitiatory sacrifice to protect Jem Blythe.[38] This unpleasant episode in the novel suggests that Montgomery did question the Christian rationale for war.

Mary Rubio has suggested that the title "The Watchman" refers to a landmark on Prince Edward Island, the Watch-tower, which was the "largest and highest dune of the sand-hills."[39] In a letter to George MacMillan, Montgomery describes the view from it as "the most beautiful and satisfying I have ever beheld."[40] Given how important Island landscapes are to this collection, it would not be surprising if Montgomery had chosen a title with local associations. (The author of a short review note of *The Watchman* described it as "inspired by her native province."[41])

But this is not an entirely satisfying explanation. "Watchman" has biblical associations that would certainly have been known to Montgomery, and these associations strengthen the case that, albeit obliquely and indirectly, the collection does address the war. In Isaiah 21, a man who has been set to guard the city in time of war is asked, "Watchman, what of the night?" He replies, "The morning cometh and also the night." Perhaps Montgomery saw the watchman as a herald of hope – one who sees the darkness, but also the dawn. From this perspective, the lyrics that make up the bulk of *The Watchman* may be related to the war inasmuch as they depict not only an untroubled prewar pastoral but also a future world to which peace will ultimately return after the dark night of war. Maximus, a member of the watch, has seen the darkness fall over the sepulchre, but then he witnesses the bright dawn that accompanies the resurrection. The combination in the poem of the imperial and the biblical, the Christian and the pagan, perhaps reflects Montgomery's view of the incompatibility of the British Empire's military aims with its Christian principles, never so painfully evident as when it went to war with other Christian nations. As Wilfred Owen put it, "pure Christianity will not fit in with pure patriotism."[42]

Another poem in *The Watchman*, "At the Long Sault," may represent a similarly indirect approach to the topic of war. But here Montgomery takes a patriotic stance; this poem invokes a Canadian precedent for the idea that some lives must be sacrificed for the salvation of the many. "At the Long Sault" recounts the familiar story of Adam Daulac (Dollard des Ormeaux) and his small group of men, whose resistance to the Iroquois (by whom they were greatly outnumbered) in 1660 was regarded as an act of heroic self-sacrifice that saved the colony at Montreal. Wilmshurst identifies "At the Long Sault" as having been previously published elsewhere; in other words, it predated the war. But in wartime, its celebration of a Canadian hero took on new meaning. Hailed as "Canada's Thermopylae," Daulac's heroic stand was used as proof that the martial spirit was deeply rooted in the Canadian character.[43] Montgomery imagines Daulac's final address to his doomed comrades:

Ever thus since the world was begun,
When a man hath given up his life,
Safety and freedom have been won
By the holy power of self-sacrifice;
For the memory of your mother's kiss
Valiantly stand to the breach again.
Comrades, blench not now from the strife,
Quit you like men![44]

With its echoes of *Henry V* and the Bible, "At the Long Sault" retells a Canadian story in the mode of British martial verse. It turns Canadian heroes into heroes of the British Empire (despite the fact that the men who held off the Iroquois at the Long Sault were French and Huron).

"At the Long Sault" could be seen as indirect war propaganda but of a fairly muffled, muted type. To see Montgomery in full patriotic mode, one has to look elsewhere, not in *The Watchman*. "Our Women," Montgomery's only poem explicitly about the war published during her lifetime, appeared in the 1918 collection *Canadian Poems of the Great War*, edited by John Garvin, husband of Katherine Hale, the author of "Grey Knitting."[45] Hale's poem was included in the anthology, and one can see how someone who was enthusiastic about "Grey Knitting" might consider Montgomery's "Our Women" a splendid poem. Each stanza of "Our Women" celebrates women's sacrifice. The first depicts a new bride who smiles because her husband has just "died with a smile on a field of France"; the second, a mother who is happy because her only child "gave himself with a gallant pride"; and the third, a woman who is "shamed and sad" because she has "none of love or kin to go." Montgomery appeared at recruiting rallies, but she nonetheless felt relief that her own sons were too young to join up:[46] "I thank God that Chester is not old enough to go – and as I thank Him I shrink back in shame, the words dying on my lips. For is it not the same thing as thanking Him that some other woman's son must go in my son's place?"[47] One is reminded of Rilla's anguished protest when her brother Walter enlists: "*Our* sacrifice is greater than *his* ... Our boys give only *themselves. We* give them."[48] Clearly Montgomery was much more conflicted about the war than the pat vignettes of "Our Women" or the heroic portrait of Dollard des Ormeaux would suggest.

Long after *The Watchman*, Montgomery wrote two other poems specifically about the First World War: "The Piper," Walter Blythe's poem alluded to but not included in *Rilla of Ingleside*, and "The Aftermath." Both appear in her final book, *The Blythes Are Quoted*. Montgomery introduces "The Piper" with this note about its origins: "Although the poem had no real existence many people have written me asking me where they could get it. It has been written recently but seems even more appropriate than then."[49] The passive "has been written" preserves the illusion that it is Walter's poem. But this might not have been her original intention: Benjamin Lefebvre has noted that the poem "is signed 'L. M. Montgomery' in the first two type-scripts of *The Blythes Are Quoted* and unsigned in the third."[50]

The poem was anticipated at the end of *Rainbow Valley*, when Walter, who has been reading "his beloved book of myths," has his first vision of the Piper: "He pipes – he pipes – and we must follow ... round and round the world."[51] Montgomery's use of this motif probably owes something to Robert Browning's poem, "The Pied Piper of Hamelin." Browning's poem was specifically invoked during the war as an image of how men could be swept away by the stirring music of the bagpipes; somehow the middle European vagabond of the folktale mutated into a heroic Highlander, piping men into battle.[52] Walter's final letter home, which Rilla receives after his death, describes the vision that inspired his poem:

> One evening long ago when [we] were together in Rainbow Valley I had a queer vision or presentiment ... Rilla, I saw the Piper coming down the Valley with a shadowy host behind him ... Last night I saw him again. I was doing sentry-go and I saw him marching across no-man's-land from our trenches to the German trenches – the same tall shadowy form, piping weirdly – and behind him followed boys in khaki ... It was no fancy – no illusion. I *heard* his music, and then – he was *gone*. But I *had* seen him – and I knew what it meant – I knew that I was among those who followed him.
>
> Rilla, the Piper will pipe me "west" tomorrow.[53]

Did Walter's Piper lead him on a right and noble path, or did the beguiling piping lead only to death? By the time Montgomery actually writes Walter's poem, it seems to be the latter.

In addition to Browning's "Pied Piper," another famous poem lies behind Walter's "The Piper": John McCrae's "In Flanders Fields." Montgomery thought McCrae's poem "very fine" and used it as an encore piece when she gave recitations at recruiting rallies.[54] In *Rilla of Ingleside*, the success of Walter's poem – "In a month it had carried Walter's name to every corner of the globe" – is clearly modelled on that of McCrae's poem. But the poem Montgomery produced years later for inclusion in *The Blythes Are Quoted* is not a plausible candidate for "the one great poem of the war."[55] In contrast to McCrae's rondeau, "The Piper" is, as Epperly puts it, a "lackluster lyric," hardly "an epitome of all the pain and hope and pity and purpose of the mighty conflict, crystallized in three brief immortal verses," which is the way it is described in *Rilla*.[56] (As it happens, Walter's poem has only two verses.)

But it is in its treatment of the necessity of war that "The Piper" departs most significantly from "In Flanders Fields." The final stanza of McCrae's poem turns from lament to exhortation, from sentimental pastoral to what Paul Fussell has described as "recruiting-poster rhetoric":[57] "Take up our quarrel with the foe: / To you with failing hands we throw / The torch; be yours to hold it high."[58] In contrast, "The Piper" offers, in Epperly's words, a "tepid endorsement of war":[59]

> Some day the Piper will come again
> To pipe to the sons of the maple tree!
> You and I will follow from door to door
> Many of us will come back no more ...
> What matter that if Freedom still
> Be the crown of each native hill?

The insipid quality of "The Piper" could be attributed to a mimetic intention on Montgomery's part to make it seem the work of an apprentice poet. But its lack of fervour might also reflect Montgomery's disillusion with the rhetoric of patriotic sacrifice.

This disillusion, muted and masked in "The Piper" (which had to sound as if written by a soldier who still believed in the virtue of his nation's cause), is undisguised in "The Aftermath," the final poem in *The Blythes Are Quoted*.[60] If "The Piper" is an imitation of McCrae's poem, then "The Aftermath" is its bleak reversal. While McCrae's speakers are "the Dead," still full of patriotic ardour, the speaker of "The Aftermath" is alive in a hell of tormenting memories:

> The dead are happier than we who live,
> For dying, they have purged their memory thus
> And won forgetfulness; but what to us
> Can such oblivion give?

Epperly likens "The Aftermath" to the war poetry of Wilfred Owen and Siegfried Sassoon.[61] Its repeated image of the bayonetting of "a stripling boy" who "might have been my brother slim and fair" is reminiscent of Owen's "Strange Meeting" – "I am the enemy you killed" – or Sassoon's "The Rank Stench of Those Bodies" – "He was a Prussian with a decent face / Young fresh and pleasant, I dare to say."[62] As Fussell has observed about so many canonical English texts of the Great War, "The Aftermath" operates as an ironic pastoral, an "exploitation of [the] conventions of English pastoral poetry, especially pastoral elegy," to depict the cruelty of war.[63] Metrically, "The Aftermath" fits this mode: its eight-line stanzas in iambic pentameter, with third and eighth lines in iambic tetrameter, fuse the quatrains of the pastoral elegy with Tennyson's *In Memoriam* stanza. In imagery too, it reverses the pastoral, thus repudiating not only the spiritualized patriotism of "The Piper" (and "In Flanders Fields") but also the joyous, nature-loving dreaminess of Montgomery's own verse. The woodland pools so frequent in Montgomery's nature lyrics have become "pits of hell." On the ground are scattered not seeds but "dead men." Spring, a season celebrated in so many of her poems, has become "hateful"; the wind, which features in her lyrics as a divine agent stirring the sea and the trees, brings only the terrible voices of the war dead. Even the title reverses the conventions of pastoral. The aftermath is the new grass that comes back after the mowing. But what has grown after the harvest of those "dead men scattered on the reeking ground"? Only an indelible, terrible memory of the killing. And in the final four lines, Montgomery introduces a rhyme that completely undercuts the pastoral world of Ingleside:

> The wind has voices that may not be stilled ...
> The wind that yester morning was so blithe ...
> And everywhere I look I see him writhe,
> That pretty boy I killed!

To rhyme "writhe" with "blithe," that supremely important adjective in Montgomery's fictional world, seems an unmistakable admission of despair.[64] "The Aftermath" is the final poem in Montgomery's final book. Is it therefore to be taken as her last word, her ultimate assessment of the Great War? If so, we must assume that, by the end of her life, Montgomery had come to the bitter conclusion that the war had been neither noble nor necessary.

NOTES

1 Montgomery, *SJ* 2: 200.
2 Ibid., 185.
3 Montgomery, *Rilla*, 125.
4 Montgomery, *Watchman*, 109.
5 See Fisher, "Canada and the Great War," 225.
6 Russell, Russell, and Wilmshurst, *Lucy Maud Montgomery*, 119–20.
7 Montgomery, *My Dear Mr. M*, 71.
8 Montgomery, *SJ* 2: 194.
9 Rubio, *Lucy Maud Montgomery*, 194.
10 Montgomery, *SJ* 5: 233–4, 291.
11 Rubio, *Lucy Maud Montgomery*, 197.
12 Rubio points out that John McClelland's decision to publish *The Watchman* and thus become Montgomery's publisher "was undoubtedly the best business decision he ever made," for her best-selling novels would subsidize his firm for decades to come. Ibid.
13 Montgomery, *My Dear Mr. M*, 2–3.
14 McCabe, introduction, 2.
15 Ibid., 3.
16 For a discussion of the book's structure, see Lefebvre, "That Abominable War," 112.
17 Montgomery, *Blythes*, 370.
18 "A June Day," *Blythes*, 369; "A Day Off," *Watchman*, 51.
19 Montgomery, *After Green Gables*, 88.
20 Montgomery, *Emily of New Moon*, 190.
21 Epperly, *Fragrance of Sweet-Grass*, 150.
22 Montgomery, *Emily of New Moon*, 349.
23 Montgomery, *Emily's Quest*, 242.
24 McCabe, introduction, 5.
25 "Elate" is used here in the archaic adjectival sense.

26 Doody, "L.M. Montgomery and the Significance of 'Classics,'" 84–5.

27 Montgomery, *After Green Gables*, 88.

28 Fussell, *Great War*, 231–69.

29 Hale, "Grey Knitting," lines 17–20.

30 *Toronto Globe*, 22 November 1916, 2.

31 Ibid., 11 November 1916, 2.

32 Montgomery, *Watchman*, 3–7.

33 Montgomery, *After Green Gables*, 217.

34 The source is incorrectly given in *The Watchman* as "Matthew 23 and 4."

35 Epperly, *Fragrance of Sweet-Grass*, 118.

36 Kilpatrick, "The War and the Christian Church," 17.

37 See Vance, *Death So Noble*, 35–56.

38 Montgomery, *Rilla*, 331. For a discussion of Montgomery's treatment of the theme of sacrifice, see Fisher, *Boys and Girls*, 214–16; Epperly, *Fragrance of Sweet-Grass*, 112–30; Edwards, "L.M. Montgomery's *Rilla*."

39 Rubio, *Lucy Maud Montgomery*, 194.

40 Montgomery, *My Dear Mr. M*, 88.

41 "The Season's Best Books in Review," *Toronto Globe*, 2 December 1916, 15.

42 Quoted in Silkin, introduction to *Penguin Book of First World War Poetry*, 21.

43 "Canadiens," Comité de recrutement canadien-francais poster, 1915–18, available on the Canadian War Museum website at http://www.warmuseum.ca/cwm/exhibitions/propaganda/poster3_e.shtml, accessed 15 August 2014. See also Kennedy, "Lampman."

44 Montgomery, *Watchman*, 116–19.

45 Garvin, *Canadian Poems of the Great War*, 158.

46 Montgomery, *My Dear Mr. M*, 81.

47 Montgomery, *SJ* 2: 160.

48 Montgomery, *Rilla*, 156.

49 Montgomery, *Blythes*, 3.

50 Lefebvre, "That Abominable War," 120.

51 Montgomery, *Rainbow Valley*, 340.

52 See Parrott, *The Children's Story of the War* 4, no. 16 (1915): 2.

53 Montgomery, *Rilla*, 245.

54 Montgomery, *My Dear Mr. M*, 81.

55 Montgomery, *Rilla*, 215.

56 Epperly, foreword, xi.

57 Fussell, *Great War*, 249.

58 McCrae, "In Flanders Fields," lines 10–12.

59 Epperly, foreword, xi.

60 Montgomery, *Blythes*, 509–10.

61 Epperly, foreword, xi; for the description of Walter's poem, see *Rilla*, 215.

62 Owen, "Strange Meeting"; Sassoon, "The Rank Stench," lines 31–2.

63 Fussell, *Great War*, 250.

64 See Lefebvre, "That Abominable War," 122, for a discussion of this rhyme.

PART TWO

Gendering War

CHAPTER 5

L.M. Montgomery's Great War: The Home as Battleground in *Rilla of Ingleside*

Laura M. Robinson

In his book *War Is a Force That Gives Us Meaning*, Chris Hedges argues that, alongside horror and anguish, war "can give us purpose, meaning, a reason for living."[1] Hedges cites several survivors of the Bosnian War who admitted to feeling strangely deflated after the war: "Peace had again exposed the void that the rush of war, of battle, had filled."[2] L.M. Montgomery expressed this very sentiment in her journals on 12 November 1918, the day after the end of what she knew as the Great War: "I am sure no one could feel more profoundly thankful that the war is over than I ... And yet the truth is that everything seems flat and *insipid* now, after being fed for four years on horrors and fears, terrible reverses, amazing victories, all news now seems tame and uninteresting ... one is thankful – and bored!"[3] She adds, "Somehow, there is a blank in life. I suppose it will gradually fill up."[4] It is hardly a wonder, then, that in 1919 she picked up her pen to craft a novel describing life on the Canadian home front. Intriguingly, she places into a minor character's mouth those very words from her journal: "I wonder ... if things won't seem rather flat and *insipid* when peace really comes. After being fed for four years on fears and horrors, terrible reverses, amazing victories, won't anything less be tame and uninteresting? How strange – and blessed – and *dull* it will be not to dread the coming of the mail every day."[5] Scholars such as Amy Tector have detailed how some early responses to *Rilla of Ingleside* (1921) labelled it a patriotic and uncritical celebration of the Canadian war effort, abroad and at home; Tector and others suggest that this interpretation is too simplistic.[6] Rather, Montgomery returns to the war in order to relive an energy missing with the newfound peace;

more specifically, this novel recreates the world of energetic girls and women that the end of war disempowered, lauding those who carried on with daily life during wartime. Ultimately, Montgomery suggests that women are always warriors for maintaining the home front, not only during times of war but also, by corollary, those of peace.

Women and Wartime

After the war ended, the stories of women's efforts were quickly subsumed into a national narrative of healing and moving on. Writing in the early 1920s, Julia Drummond notes in the foreword to Iona Carr's *A Story of the Canadian Red Cross Information Bureau during the Great War* that "when the curtain rang down at last on the greatest Drama in the history of the world, and our work – our bit of the work to which we had given our heart and soul – was no longer required, a silence fell on many of us. How could we talk to the busy world of that manifold experience, a world that seemed for a time only anxious to forget?"[7] On 3 September 1921 Montgomery commented, upon receiving her copy of *Rilla*, that people might not be interested in it because "the public are said to be sick of anything connected with the war."[8] Did Montgomery realize quite quickly after the war that women's labours and sacrifices were being overshadowed by the nation's need to get back to a sense of normalcy? In *Rilla*, Montgomery writes what Susan Fisher calls "a documentary novel about Canada during the war years,"[9] and, as Fisher and other scholars have pointed out, she does so to laud that extraordinary activity by women. Montgomery also stated in her journals that this was her first novel "written with a purpose," in order to describe "the life we lived in Canada during those years."[10] But rather than attempting only to record and reflect a particular moment in time, Montgomery arguably exploits the war setting to draw attention to the ongoing and continuous harsh nature of women's labour, regardless of peace or war. Montgomery's novel shows that women's work is often sacrificial, distasteful, and difficult, and frequently downplayed by members of the larger community.

Rilla of Ingleside is concerned with and appears to entrench rigid gender roles. This novel is a conservative story of a young girl's coming of age – Rilla's only ostensible ambition is to be Kenneth Ford's wife, although she also raises a war baby and starts a Junior Red Cross League. Yet, nestled within this deeply traditional narrative, and troubling it, is a startling gender ambiguity. Several characters disrupt clearly defined gender categorizations. Rilla's friend Faith exclaims, "Oh, if I were only a man, to go too!"[11] Her brother Walter expresses the opposite desire: "I should have been a girl," he cries.[12] The school-teacher Gertrude has "the zest and vigour of a man."[13] Even the very traditional maid, Susan, cheers "like a man."[14]

Most intriguingly, the novel begins with a perplexing if humorous focus on the family cats. Jack Frost, the household tomcat, surprises everyone by giving birth. The family remains undaunted in their male references: "The Blythes had been so accustomed to regard Jack Frost as a member of the male sex that they could not get out of the habit. So they continually used the masculine pronoun, although the result was ludicrous."[15] The family says to the kitten, for example, "Go to your mother and get him to wash your fur."[16] Lest the reader get the idea that Montgomery is laying the groundwork to challenge strict gender roles through this bi-gendered cat, the kitten Jack Frost begets is a monster: the appropriately named Dr Jekyll/Mr Hyde. Dr Jekyll, the quiet, loving, and drowsy side of the feline, occupies a feminine framework in Montgomery's text, whereas Mr Hyde, whose "tread was as heavy as a man's," who had a "savage snarl" and would "bite at any restraining or caressing hand,"[17] represents a masculine facet of the animal. By suggesting that gender ambiguity begets a monster, Montgomery's novel is both advocating for clear-cut gender roles and complicating them. Having the monster unify both extreme masculine and feminine traits suggests Montgomery is attempting something quite radical. It is also worth noting that, in this war novel, masculine traits are savage and cruel.

Men and Wartime

So, rather than only entrenching gender roles, *Rilla* also invites a reappraisal of the degree to which gender is a natural manifestation of biological sex. It is able to do this in large part because it is set during wartime. In *From Chivalry to Terrorism: War and the Changing Nature of Masculinity*, Leo Braudy explains that wartime focuses a particular scrutiny on what constitutes a man: "Wartime masculinity is a top-down and bottom-up effort to emphasize a code of masculine behavior more single-minded and more traditional than the wide array of circumstances and personal nature that influences the behavior of men in nonwar situations."[18] Michael Roper focuses on representations of manliness in war memoirs, concluding that war literature revises the "sense of men's place within patriarchal power."[19] Roper argues that, in these memoirs, men are depicted primarily and perhaps surprisingly as victims. While apparently rendering different conclusions, both scholars would agree that stories of war heighten, expose, and critique what a society normally takes for granted, including gender roles. Montgomery not only exploits the wartime setting to interrogate traditional gender roles in this way; she also seems to endorse a masculinity very different than traditional roles associated with combat. Before war is declared in the novel, Rilla's brother Jem enthusiastically relates a story of heroism from the Balkan War:

> The doctor lost both his legs – they were smashed to pulp – and he was left on the field to die. And he crawled about from man to man, to all the wounded men round him, as long as he could, and did everything possible to relieve their sufferings – never thinking of himself – he was tying a bit of bandage round another man's leg when he went under. They found him there, the doctor's dead hands still held the bandage tight, the bleeding was stopped and the other man's life was saved. Some hero, wasn't he, Faith?[20]

Rilla is revolted by this story, while her teacher, Gertrude Oliver, finds it a wonderful tale showing "godlike" sacrifice.[21] Interestingly, the representation of ideal masculinity here – a selfless nurturing of others – does not reflect a traditional understanding of heroism. The man is a doctor, not a soldier; he saves his comrades rather than vanquishing his foes.

As several critics, such as Benjamin Lefebvre, have argued, Rilla's poetic brother, Walter, embodies the heroic spirit of this novel, du-

here I am doing both regular and I find there is something in politics after all."⁴⁵ She makes public speeches, argues with Dr Blythe, and keeps the home front running smoothly. Furthermore, Montgomery aligns Susan closely with Canadian soldiers. For example, Susan helps bring in the harvest in the absence of enough men: "Susan, standing on a load of grain, her grey hair whipping in the breeze and her skirt kilted up to her knees for safety and convenience – no overalls for Susan, if you please – was neither a beautiful nor a romantic figure; but the spirit that animated her gaunt arms was the self-same one that captured Vimy Ridge and held the German legions back from Verdun."⁴⁶ Susan also runs the flag up the flagpole to celebrate an Allied victory. She salutes the flag as a soldier would, and the narrator writes, "The gingham apron that shrouded her from head to foot was cut on lines of economy, not of grace; yet, somehow, just then Susan made an imposing figure. She was one of the women – courageous, unquailing, patient, heroic – who had made victory possible. In her, they all saluted the symbol for which their dearest had fought."⁴⁷

Montgomery thus establishes equivalence between Susan and the Allied soldiers. The lyrical tenor of these two passages suggests an earnestness to Montgomery's depiction of Susan as bearing the same spirit and heroism as the soldiers who conquered Vimy, an earnestness all the more remarkable because Susan is most often figured in a humorous or gently ironic manner. Moreover, because the successful battle at Vimy Ridge has often been regarded as a crucial moment in Canada's birth as a nation,⁴⁸ aligning Susan with soldiers at Vimy places her and her work as central to Canada's nation-building, as other scholars have argued. She may be a symbol, but she is also actively part of the victory, just as much as the men are. Indeed, Susan declares, "'The Huns shall never set foot in Prince Edward Island as long as I can handle a pitchfork,' … looking and feeling quite equal to routing the entire German army single-handed."⁴⁹ The irony here is similar to Walter's irony about Rilla's caring for an infant being harder than Jem's facing Germans. While it makes Susan's determination lighthearted, it also clearly positions her as ready and able to fight in her own way. Moreover, her instrument of violence – the pitchfork – is also decidedly domestic. In *Rilla*, then, war necessarily

empowers the girls and women, as they have no choice but to carry
on in the absence of men, and the novel expands the notions of heroism to validate and valorize the home front and domestic labour.

Critics argue that Susan and young Rilla each represent the new
nation of Canada emerging through the fire and baptism of war. For
example, McKenzie reasons that Susan reflects a maturing Canada and
its role on the international stage and that Rilla represents Canada's future.[50] While I agree wholeheartedly that Montgomery upholds Susan
and Rilla as representatives of an emerging and future Canada, I would
also suggest that Montgomery is offering a subtle challenge to her readers to read past the wartime narrative. Alan Young argues that Montgomery "ultimately sidesteps the implicit challenge" of revealing the
horror of war and overturning the pastoral in her novel by "fall[ing]
back into the conventional solutions of romance"[51] at the end. I would
argue that Montgomery uses the conventional solutions of romance
precisely in order to challenge women's role in early-twentieth-century
Canada. Montgomery enfolds both Rilla and Susan into a traditional
domestic romance narrative at the end of the novel, and each romance
story provides perspective on the other. Susan's romance, if cloaked in
humour, overturns the traditional "happy ending" of heterosexual
marriage to endorse a single, financially independent woman. Susan
receives a proposal of marriage from Mr Pryor, the despised pacifist
whom locals believe to be a closet Hun. She defeats him roundly by
chasing him from her domestic sphere, the kitchen, wielding a pot of
boiling dye. Mr Pryor had proposed to gain a free housekeeper: he
mulls to himself, "If [my son-in-law] Milgrave comes home alive I'll
lose [my daughter] Miranda and hired housekeepers cost more than a
wife and are liable to leave a man in the lurch any time."[52] Susan's rejection of him is an affirmation of her economic independence and perhaps reflects Canada's emergence as a nation more independent from
England after its success at Vimy.

Unlike Susan's romance, Rilla's conforms to convention. Rilla too
receives a proposal, but from soldier Kenneth Ford before he heads
into action. While she is unsure if it is an actual proposal, she responds
with a definitive "yes," with a clear "s" even though she is given to
lisping. Early in the novel, the reader learns of Rilla's impediment

when she lisps a "yeth" in response to Kenneth: "Rilla had lisped in early childhood; but she had grown out of it pretty thoroughly. Only on occasions of stress and strain did the tendency reassert itself."[53] However, over the course of the novel, she manages to conquer the lisp. She gives a series of recitations for the Patriotic Society, for example. During the first one, she lisps several times; later, as she does several more, she "became resigned to an occasional lisp."[54] Not lisping in response to Kenneth's rather vague proposal indicates that she is decisive and sure.

The domestic characters of Susan and Rilla are each ensconced in a marriage plot. The climax of each occurs when armistice is declared, even if that is not immediately obvious in Susan's case. When the war ends, Susan takes herself on a honeymoon. In response to Anne's surprised cry, "A *honeymoon?*" Susan replies, "Yes, Mrs. Dr. dear, a honeymoon ... I shall never be able to get a husband but I am not going to be cheated out of everything and a honeymoon I intend to have."[55] Because Susan is going to Charlottetown to visit family, she, and Montgomery, could very well have represented this trip as a vacation. However, Montgomery ironizes the discourse of domestic romance by sending this empowered single woman off by herself on a trip meant for newlyweds.

On the other hand, when the war ends, Ken Ford returns to Rilla and queries her as to whether she is still his. "Yeth," she replies, lisping this time.[56] The return of Rilla's childish lisp signifies on many levels; indeed, highlighting the deliberation that went into that one small word, Montgomery's manuscript shows that she scrawled the "th" over the "s" of the original "yes."[57] First, this regression might be a way to make Rilla's determined maturity of the preceding chapters lighthearted and more palatable to readers. As Mary Rubio astutely points out, "For male and female readers alike, the only acceptable closure of a story about a young woman was the sound of wedding bells. Thus, Montgomery had to portray marriage as the site of the ultimate female happiness."[58] Rubio notes that Montgomery still manages to find clever ways to create subversive messages alongside the traditional ones. Thus, Montgomery might be both placating her readers and indicating the losses that women incurred with the end of the war. Rubio states that by 1920 Montgomery would not have known how many rights women would lose,[59] but I would argue that she might have already realized that women's stories were not being told.

Susan R. Grayzel points out the immediate effect of war's end on women in the labour force in the United Kingdom: "By March 1918, many thousands of women had been dismissed from munitions factories with one week's notice. On the eve of armistice in November 1918, women munitions workers marched in London and Glasgow to protest their being laid off, but that had little effect. By 1921, the percentage of women in the labour force was 2 per cent lower than in 1911."[60] Grayzel emphasizes that, postwar, "women's roles were quickly relegated to the sidelines."[61] Montgomery was an avid reader of news, so she most likely would have been aware of the larger global response to women after the war, especially as the *Globe*, the newspaper she read religiously, covered the plight of women's munitions workers, among many other issues surrounding women's wartime labour.[62] Montgomery might indeed have seen the future as regressive.

Reading Rilla's acceptance in the light of Susan's violent and righteous rejection of Mr Pryor and taking herself on a honeymoon emphasizes the submission inherent in marriage at the time. Marriage entailed economic dependence on a man. McKenzie regards Rilla as the future "mother and guardian of a new nation," which is representative of Montgomery's "new vision."[63] Indeed, in another book, *Women's Identities at War*, Grayzel demonstrates that the primary identity for women during the First World War was that of motherhood: "motherhood came to represent for women what soldiering did for men, a gender-specific experience meant to provide social unity and stability during a time of unprecedented upheaval."[64] While Rilla's diligent care of Jims and her engagement to Kenneth set her up as a future mother, Montgomery's message is more ambivalent than it may first appear. As her lisp testifies, Rilla's position is regressive, both as the war ends and her possibilities for power diminish, but also because she is poised to become a housewife, chained to the very labour she complained bitterly about through the majority of the novel. Although the battle and the sacrifice of the boys and men is complete, Rilla's will continue.

And yet, the final word is affirmative and spoken by Rilla, whose voice increasingly dominates the novel as her diary takes up more and more space in it. In this way, Montgomery achieves a double aim, as Rubio notes that she often does. Montgomery shows the inevitable disempowerment of her heroine while, at the very same moment, encouraging the reader to see what a sacrifice it will be for Rilla to labour in the domestic sphere. In doing so, Montgomery highlights the daily, ordinary heroism of women that becomes apparent in wartime but in actuality always underwrites daily life. War simply allowed a time for women's ordinary labours to be acknowledged and praised.

Clearly Montgomery valorizes and renders heroic women's wartime work, a move that was consistent with the tenor of the times. For example, on 28 August 1918, a women's parade and demonstration of their war labours took place during the Canadian National Exhibition in Toronto. This demonstration included factory workers, nurses, flax pickers, and mothers of soldiers. What is fascinating is that *Rilla of Ingleside* does not highlight the heroism of women's work centring on a war-specific theme, such as nursing or factory work, but rather focuses on the labour that women always perform: cooking, sewing, knitting, housekeeping, raising children. In this way, Montgomery exploits the wartime setting to exalt women's usually unsung household labours. And the novel ends with a sense that Rilla's sacrifice and heroism will continue, as she is poised to become a housewife. While undeniably about the war, Montgomery's novel, at its deepest level, celebrates not only women's ability to rise to the challenge of war but also their typically unacknowledged and primarily unpaid labour that underpinned Canadian society in the first decades of the twentieth century.

NOTES

1 Hedges, *War Is a Force*, 3.
2 Ibid., 7.
3 Montgomery, *SJ* 2: 276–7.
4 Ibid., 277.
5 Montgomery, *Rilla*, 338.

6 Tector, "A Righteous War," 76. See also Epperly, *Fragrance of Sweet-Grass*, 112–30, and Edwards, "L.M. Montgomery's *Rilla*," 163–5.
7 Drummond, foreword, 5.
8 Montgomery, *SJ* 3: 17.
9 Fisher, *Boys and Girls*, 213.
10 Montgomery, *SJ* 3: 17.
11 Montgomery, *Rilla*, 54.
12 Ibid., 61.
13 Ibid., 44.
14 Ibid., 76.
15 Ibid., 7.
16 Ibid.
17 Ibid., 8.
18 Braudy, *From Chivalry to Terrorism*, xvi.
19 Roper, "Between Manliness and Masculinity," 361.
20 Montgomery, *Rilla*, 35.
21 Ibid., 36.
22 Lefebvre, "Walter's Closet," 15.
23 Montgomery, *Rilla*, 155.
24 Ibid., 345.
25 Ibid., 306, 348.
26 Edwards, "L.M. Montgomery's *Rilla*," 171.
27 Ibid., 172.
28 Montgomery, *Rilla*, 89.
29 Ibid.
30 Ibid., 104.
31 Ibid., 142.
32 Epperly, *Fragrance of Sweet-Grass*, 114.
33 Tector, "A Righteous War," 73.
34 Ibid., 84.
35 McKenzie, "Women at War," 343.
36 Montgomery, *Rilla*, 95.
37 Ibid., 108.
38 Ibid., 88.
39 Ibid., 70.
40 Ibid., 116–17.
41 Ibid., 293, italics in original.

42 Ibid., 260.
43 Ibid., 58, italics in original.
44 Ibid., 98.
45 Ibid., 127.
46 Ibid., 276.
47 Ibid., 314.
48 I need to acknowledge here that there is much debate about the truth to this statement. See, for one example, Grodzinski, "The Use and Abuse of Battle."
49 Montgomery, *Rilla*, 305.
50 McKenzie, "Women at War," 336–8, 338–9.
51 Ibid., 109, 118.
52 Montgomery, *Rilla*, 276.
53 Ibid., 41.
54 Ibid., 122.
55 Ibid., 342, italics in original.
56 Ibid., 350.
57 The manuscript is in the Montgomery Collection of the University of Guelph Archives.
58 Rubio, introduction to *Harvesting Thistles*, 5.
59 Ibid., 11.
60 Grayzel, *Women and the First World War*, 106.
61 Ibid., 118.
62 For some examples of the issue in the *Globe*, Montgomery's daily Toronto newspaper, see "Object to Lose War-Time Wages: Women Munitions Workers Demand Immediate Withdrawal of Discharges," 4 December 1918, 2; "Think No Hard Times Coming: Women Munitions Employees Optimistic as to Future Conditions," 20 November 1918, 4; and a poignant letter from a Canadian woman longing for munitions work in Canada, 13 April 1918, 6.
63 McKenzie, "Women at War," 339.
64 Grayzel, *Women's Identities at War*, 87.

CHAPTER 6

"I Must Do Something to Help at Home": *Rilla of Ingleside* in the Context of Real Women's War Work

Sarah Glassford

"Mother, I want to do something. I'm only a girl – I can't do anything to win the war – but I must do something to help at home."[1] With these breathless words, L.M. Montgomery's fifteen-year-old home-front heroine Rilla Blythe earnestly begins her personal journey into the Great War and, through war, to self-knowledge and maturity. Rilla's speech, or something like it, had real-life counterparts in the minds and conversations of millions of Canadian women. Following Britain's declaration of war on Germany on 4 August 1914, these women's empire, their country, and, perhaps most importantly, their home communities and families were transformed – called to action in a great tidal wave of patriotic propaganda and popular discourse. But they lived in a society that hemmed them in with boundaries of gender and class, boundaries that sharply curtailed the ways in which they could participate in the great national struggle. What was a young woman to do when she grew tired of waiting around for the men to sort out the fighting?

Montgomery's journals and letters to Ephraim Weber explain that she wrote *Rilla* "with a purpose" and strove to depict the Canadian home front of the Great War era as accurately as she could.[2] The novel remains the most popular and oft-cited fictional depiction of Canadian women's home-front experiences nearly a century later, in part because readers – beginning with contemporary reviewers, as Jonathan Vance notes – have "universalized" Montgomery's version of the war, reading Glen St Mary as a substitute for any Canadian town.[3] Yet, the Prince Edward Island setting is integral to the story and Montgomery based her depiction of the war years on her specific personal wartime experiences in Leaskdale, Ontario. Moreover, Maud herself could hardly be considered a model for the average Canadian woman, as her journals will attest.[4] This chapter therefore places the fictional war work of Montgomery's Glen St Mary women in the context of real Canadian (and, when possible, specifically Prince Edward Island) women's voluntary war work to determine whether, from a historical perspective, Montgomery got it right in *Rilla of Ingleside*. This is not just historical nitpicking. As a novelist, Montgomery had every right to ignore the historical record and turn her characters and their actions to her own thematic ends. But considering where the historical and fictional records agree and disagree, speak or are silent, offers insights into those aspects Montgomery particularly wished to emphasize as an author and the degree to which her personal experiences did or did not accurately reflect those of women elsewhere in Canada. The broad outlines of her Ontario experience prove reasonably universal, but her fictional depiction emphasizes and omits certain elements of the historical record, the better to draw out her chosen themes of national rebirth and maturity. As it does to readers today, *Rilla of Ingleside* rang true to its first readers, but its author's goal was to evoke the war years rather than strictly to document them. Assessing the difference between the two approaches helps illuminate more clearly the craftsmanship in Montgomery's writing, as well as her significant influence on post-1918 Canadian cultural understandings of the war – an influence that continues today.

꙳

When Bertha Marilla Blythe, known to everyone as Rilla, approaches her mother, Anne, with her plea for some sort of war-related role, she is beginning to feel left behind: her mother, father, and older sisters are busy with war charities, her oldest brother has enlisted and is about to leave for Valcartier, and her other two brothers are exempt from enlisting because of poor health or youth and are shortly to return to university. Suddenly everyone has a purpose but the baby of the family. Despite the uncertainties the war has already introduced into her family circle, Rilla has decided to be "as *brave* and *heroic* and *unselfish*" as possible – all in italics, of course – and she means it, in her naïve, youthful way. The answer she receives from her mother is

therefore completely deflating: "The cotton has come up for the
sheets," says Anne. "You can help Nan and Di make them up."⁵
Sewing hospital sheets with her sisters – a most unromantic task, to
be sure – is almost certainly not what starry-eyed Rilla had in mind.
Anne's answer, however, is quite in line with historical fact: domestic
work for war charities had to satisfy millions of Canadian women
who felt the urge to actively participate in the national war effort.

Fighting was out of the question for all Canadian women, but some
found non-traditional outlets for their energies. Many single, work-
ing-class women in industrialized cities like Toronto or Montreal made
up for the male labour shortage in wartime industries, joined by a
smaller number of married or middle-class women; other single women
stepped into the breach as bank clerks or business secretaries. A select
group of women translated their professional nursing skills into tick-
ets overseas as military nurses.⁶ But the overwhelming majority of
Canadian women, particularly those who were married, middle class,
or rural, did not have access to these options. Instead, most women
who wished to support the war effort threw themselves into applying
their peacetime organizational and domestic skills – in particular knitting, sewing, and food preparation – to the wartime context. In church
groups, family groups, and on their own, or through large national organizations such as the Women's Institutes, Imperial Order Daughters
of the Empire (IODE), Canadian Red Cross Society, and Canadian
Patriotic Fund, women raised millions of dollars and created tens of
millions of comfort items, supplementary hospital supplies, and pris-
oner of war food parcels.

Erika Rothwell notes that knitting served as a "coping mechanism" in the face of anxiety over loved ones, giving women something
to do while they waited. But it was more than that. As Jeffrey Reznick
argues, the wartime "culture of caregiving" through war charities and
voluntary organizations helped sustain both manpower needs and
civilian morale. Supplementary medical aid meant more soldiers returning to the trenches, comforts helped keep soldiers' spirits up, and
civilians felt good about making a contribution to the war effort.⁷ As
added bonuses, voluntary organizations mobilized pools of labour
(women, children, the elderly, the infirm) that the military and industry could not (or would not) tap into, and the money and supplies

they provided cost the government nothing.[8] It should come as no surprise, then, that contemporaries praised the work of these organizations, and especially the women who did the lion's share of their work. But beyond the many practical benefits of the work, contemporary Canadians saw in women's voluntary war work something less tangible, and very much in line with the period's view of women's special gifts for caring and nurturing. Sir Andrew Macphail, who wrote the official history of the Canadian Army Medical Corps, praised women's work for the Canadian Red Cross by claiming that it "brought into the austere life of the soldier a touch of the larger humanity, an element of the feminine ... The soldiers knew they were not forsaken by their womenkind."[9] Other voluntary organizations received similar praise. Some women used this praise and approbation for their patriotic war work to leverage greater access to public life.[10]

What contemporaries called "war work" – women's unpaid labour for voluntary organizations and war charities – is an integral part of Montgomery's vision of the Canadian home front, as depicted in *Rilla of Ingleside*. Indeed, as Amy Tector writes, "Female work is a central fact of the novel."[11] It is worth pointing out that, over the course of the novel, Rilla Blythe steps well outside of her comfort zone to raise a war baby and temporarily work behind the counter at Carter Flagg's store during the 1917 harvest, while Susan Baker and Mary Vance break the usual gendered divisions of labour to help in the fields at harvest time.[12] All of these labours could be considered "war work," as they were forms of work that took place as a direct result of the war. However, this chapter concerns itself specifically with the kind of organized, sustained, semi-official work that women did through voluntary organizations during the war, because this was, by far, the most common form of war work for Canadian women.[13]

In the later chapters of the novel, we learn that Rilla gives recitations at recruiting meetings, and we hear of the Blythe family's housekeeper, Susan Baker, delivering a stirring address in support of the 1917 Victory Loan campaign.[14] These are both ways by which real Canadian women contributed their labour and skill to the war effort. However, women's voluntary war work in the novel takes place largely under the banner of the Canadian Red Cross Society. During the initial period of mobilization in August 1914, Anne Blythe and

her friend Miss Cornelia organize a local Red Cross Society around
the same time that eager young recruits Jem Blythe and Jerry Meredith enlist in the army, and at exactly the same time that Gilbert Blythe
and Reverend Meredith organize the local men into a Patriotic Society. This swift mobilization, and the gender-based division of labour
between war charities with different aims and approaches, is entirely
accurate. For instance, less than six months after the outbreak of the
war, the Canadian Red Cross Society had expanded from a handful
of branches to hundreds across Canada, including many on Prince
Edward Island. The Red Cross devoted itself to the care of sick,
wounded, and captured soldiers, while the Canadian Patriotic Fund
(Gilbert's "Patriotic Society") cared for soldiers' wives and depen-
dants. These two organizations quickly became Canada's largest and
best-supported war charities of the period. Although both organizations had heavily male-dominated national and provincial executives,
women were crucial to branch-level success.[15]

Soon Anne and her older daughters, Nan and Di, are busy with
the Red Cross, while Rilla mopes about aimlessly. It is at this point
that she asks her mother for something to do and is told to help with
the Red Cross. Rilla launches into sewing with her sisters (something
she does not enjoy) and, at her mother's suggestion, organizes a
"Junior Red Cross" among the girls of her own age. The Junior Red
Cross as an official, organized program of the Canadian Red Cross
Society began as a postwar nation-building project in 1919–20, but
the idea of organizing young people into age-specific groups for Red
Cross work became relatively common in Canada after 1915. No
evidence of such groups has yet surfaced on PEI, but documented examples from rural Saskatchewan and urban Toronto show that, in
certain places, young Canadians were formed into "junior" groups
for war work.[16] These two forms of volunteer work – the senior Red
Cross for the older women and Rilla's junior Red Cross for the
younger women – serve as a running theme through the remainder of
the novel. In a similar way, women's work producing and supplying
comforts and medical supplies for troops and refugees overseas became ubiquitous throughout First World War Canada – so much so
that the term "red cross work" came to signify women's voluntary

war work for *any* organization, not just for the actual Canadian Red Cross Society.[17]

The Ingleside women's Red Cross work serves several purposes in *Rilla*. Not only does Montgomery pepper the story with references to battles and military turning points in the war (making the activities of Canada's fighting men an integral component of the home-front narrative), but she similarly makes regular passing reference to knitting or sewing – references that serve as shorthand for "meanwhile, the women were still working diligently at home." This technique highlights a theme Andrea McKenzie identifies in the novel: "the forging of a new nation based on *shared* sacrifice and *shared* suffering," with women as equal partners in the new Canada.[18]

Several times Montgomery presents knitting as a useful distraction and calming activity for anxious women: minds may be in turmoil, but hands can still work. Or, in Susan's colourful turn of phrase, "knitting is something you can do, even when your heart is going like a trip-hammer and the pit of your stomach feels all gone and your thoughts are catawampus."[19] This draws directly upon Montgomery's own experiences, but was equally true for many women across the country. Bruce Scates calls women's wartime volunteer work "emotional labour" for this very reason, arguing that the act of making comforts for soldiers could be comforting to women themselves, offering them an outlet for their anxiety, grief, frustration, and feelings of powerlessness. Anne Blythe, who stands in for every anxious, suffering mother in the country, voices this very sentiment when a concerned Gilbert attempts to convince her to scale back some of her feverish Red Cross activity for the sake of her health. "Oh, let me work – let me work, Gilbert," she cries. "While I'm working I don't *think* so much. If I'm idle I imagine everything – rest is only torture for me." With Jem and Walter in constant danger at the Somme, Anne's war work helps her get through each day.[20]

Rilla's involvement with what she calls her "Junior Reds" is the most memorable instance of women's war work in the novel: as organizer and chief visionary, Rilla stage manages the group throughout the war – through charm and determination, one assumes, since she serves as secretary, rather than as president. Here, Montgomery drew

upon her own service as president of the Leaskdale Red Cross, be-
stowing on Rilla and the Junior Reds not only the kind of patriotic
concert fund-raising work Maud herself likely helped organize, but
also the frustrations and personality conflicts she experienced in the
process. The difficulties of managing group dynamics would also have
rung true for many Canadian women.[21] Foisting these troubles on a
group of fictional teenage girls allowed Montgomery to highlight the
pettiness of some of these upsets while distancing them sufficiently
from real life to avoid offending the women in her community from
whom these trials drew their inspiration. But Montgomery used Rilla's
Red Cross work for more than sociological purposes. The Junior Reds
constitute a central pillar of Montgomery's attempt to show Rilla's
growing maturity over the course of the war. Through Rilla's frustrations and personality conflicts with fellow members Irene Howard
and Olive Kirk, and her triumph of pulling off the Belgian Relief
concert in the face of devastating personal news, readers see Rilla –
and by extension the young country of Canada she metaphorically
represents – rise to the occasion and demonstrate real ability in the
face of a crisis.[22]

Montgomery also adeptly uses her characters' Red Cross involvement in more practical ways. It often serves as a convenient excuse to
gather a number of characters in the same room, where they can express contrasting opinions on the war or react in a variety of ways to
the same piece of war news, thereby allowing Montgomery to effi-
ciently incorporate varied strands of opinion and a wide range of emotional responses that would otherwise have required several scenes to
convey. One example sees Gertrude Oliver, Anne and Gilbert Blythe,
and Susan Baker gathered in the Ingleside living room on a December
evening, the women all "busy sewing or knitting." The occasion gives
rise to comments on the war having expanded their geographical
knowledge, how to deal with the kaiser if he turned up in person, and
the difficulty of pronouncing Eastern European place names.[23] Montgomery also uses Red Cross work as a tool to advance her plot on at
least three occasions. First, Red Cross errands take Rilla – who might
otherwise be expected to stay close to home – to Mrs Anderson's,
where she discovers and adopts her war baby Jims. This development

is vital because Jims plays such a central role in Rilla's growth over the course of the war. Women's work for recognized war charities did in fact increase women's authority and freedom of movement in the public sphere (whether canvassing door-to-door or organizing community events), a fact Montgomery cleverly draws on to engineer this otherwise somewhat unlikely meeting of girl and baby.[24] Miranda Pryor then comes to Ingleside on the pretext of Red Cross business in order to advance her plans for a secret marriage. This is another example of women's war work serving to open doors otherwise closed, because Miranda's cantankerous pacifist father (who opposes the match) does not feel he can prohibit his daughter from doing Red Cross work without incurring more community censure than he can handle.[25] Finally, Red Cross business again takes Rilla away from home, this time to Charlottetown; on the way there, Jims falls off the train, leading him and Rilla to meet Mrs Matilda Pitman. This misadventure and new friendship ultimately wins Jims an inheritance.[26]

Although Montgomery subtly reminds readers throughout the novel that the Ingleside women unceasingly work for the Red Cross, she sticks very close to her own experience in depicting that work. Maud did not have personal knowledge of the types of Red Cross and Voluntary Aid Detachment (VAD) nursing work she assigns to Nan and Di Blythe and Faith Meredith, which is almost certainly one reason why she does not describe their war work in any detail. Instead, their work takes place offstage in Kingsport, Nova Scotia and, in Faith's case, in England. (One could also argue that Nan and Di do not receive much attention because they are attending Redmond College, while the story centres on Glen St Mary and the Ingleside family still at home.) As Benjamin Lefebvre and Andrea McKenzie point out, neither does Montgomery deal with women's non-traditional wartime work in factories and elsewhere. But whereas readers see glimpses of trench life overseas through snippets from the enlisted Blythe and Meredith men's letters – Jem even writes of a "cootie-hunt" at one point – Montgomery includes no such descriptive detail from Nan, Di, or Faith. Rilla assumes their work must be more romantic than hers because it takes place in and around a military camp in Kingsport, and Faith's journey to England to nurse as a VAD only increases the romance.[27] But Montgomery·provides no further detail. As the example of the Blythe and Meredith soldiers suggests, Montgomery could have found creative ways to incorporate a fuller sense of what the three young women's work looked like, but clearly chose not to do so. This may be a conscious decision to keep the focus on the less glamorous work women did in their own homes, but also likely reflects the fact that Montgomery had less access to what women engaged in these forms of war work experienced than she did to soldiers' experiences. Despite the frequent misperception today that Canadians at home had no idea what their men experienced at the front, the voluminous correspondence flowing across the Atlantic, newspaper accounts, and extensive written, photographic, and artistic renderings produced by the Canadian War Records Office combined to give Canadians at home *some* notion of what the war looked like.[28] Nothing to compare with the actual experience of being there, of course, but a general idea nonetheless. Women's work as military nurses, or as volunteers working with soldiers in Canadian training camps or on leave in England, by contrast, received far less publicity. As Susan Mann writes, "to a wartime nurse, silence was both armour for herself and a tool of her trade," this silence urged by her hospital training, military propriety, and even Matron-in-Chief Margaret Macdonald.[29] Some nurses did write letters or later memoirs about their work and living conditions, but Canadian women as a whole were not raised to consider women's activities historically important. So unless she had access to Mary Macleod Moore's 1919 volume *The Maple Leaf's Red Cross* (which described overseas Red Cross work) or knew a military nurse or VAD personally, Montgomery would have found it more difficult to access these women's experiences.[30]

The absence of any detail about Nan, Di, and Faith's work highlights the fact that although Montgomery wrote what her contemporaries considered to be a very true-to-life story of the war years, it is not the *complete* story. It also indicates that while Montgomery strove to infuse her novel with period details, these details were meant to serve her broader themes rather than simply offer a documentary glimpse into the war years. Several important elements are therefore missing from her portrait of Canadian women's war work.

First, *Rilla* glosses over some of the distinctions among Canadian women produced by socio-economic class, geography, and other variables of identity. Montgomery's narrative revolves around the semi-leisured white, Anglo-Saxon, Protestant Blythe family of Ingleside, who do not live on a farm.[31] The Ingleside women are thereby members of a privileged ethnic and religious majority *and* freed from a number of time-consuming and laborious tasks that rural PEI women would have had to do – and more than 80 per cent of the Island's population was considered rural in this period. For instance, the rural PEI women who did their war work through the Women's Institutes had to fit their knitting, sewing, and fund-raising around not only housework and childrearing, but also outdoor work such as market gardening and poultry keeping, as well as tending livestock and harvesting crops when hired men became increasingly scarce.[32] In this sense, the Ingleside women more closely reflect the comparatively well-off urban women who belonged to the Royal Edward chapter of the IODE in Charlottetown. Members of the Royal Edward chapter engaged in the same type of comfort production as the Ingleside women, although the larger, denser population in the provincial capital meant they could rely more heavily upon sales to raise money for their work (for example, their annual Rose Sale at the provincial agricultural exhibition) than could women in small villages like fictional Glen St Mary.[33] Aboriginal, French-speaking, and Catholic women all called PEI home during the Great War, but their experiences are not reflected in the Glen St Mary story. Nor are those of pacifist women – of whom there must have been at least a few on the Island – unless we consider Whiskers-on-the-Moon a male equivalent, which seems unfair.

Evoking the war years rather than documenting them also allowed Montgomery to keep her characters' war work to a manageable scope. Real PEI women worked for the war effort through not only the Canadian Red Cross, but also the YWCA, the IODE, the Women's Institutes, and the Women's Patriotic Association, as well as through congregationally based church groups. In *Rilla*, the women largely confine their efforts to the Red Cross, although Rilla's Junior Reds also organize a patriotic concert for Belgian relief – both a method and a cause taken up by real Canadian women throughout the war years – and the Ingleside women prepare personal care packages for the Ingleside men overseas. If Montgomery wanted to document real PEI women's war work, the Blythes and their two Red Crosses would "adopt" local boys being held in prisoner-of-war camps overseas, send relief supplies to Haligonians after the 1917 Halifax Explosion, and direct at least some of the comforts they produced to local PEI troops through organizations like the 105th Regiment Comfort Circle. They might also send some money to PEI-related causes such as furnishing the PEI ward at the Canadian Red Cross Hospital in Le Touquet, France, or the Rena McLean Memorial Fund in memory of Nursing Sister Rena McLean from PEI.[34] But these additions, despite having equivalents in other communities, would perhaps have made *Rilla* more locally specific than Montgomery wished, undermining the universality that would win it so much acclaim.

Likewise, if Montgomery wanted to document real PEI women's war work, she would have needed to incorporate the ways in which rural women responded to the presence and absence of specific resources in their communities. Rural Islanders were notoriously cash-poor even before the war, so large cash donations were difficult to acquire. Wool and eggs, on the other hand, they had in abundance, and these sorts of in-kind donations could either be sold (eggs) or used (wool) in support of women's war work.[35] Human resources played an important part, too: finding women with what Maud called "executive ability" could be challenging in small communities, and it was important to maximize women's strengths by finding them the right job within an organization or fund-raising venture. Montgomery provides readers with Rilla's internal dialogue on this subject as she dreams up her Junior Reds and assigns the various roles according to ability.[36] What Montgomery does not discuss, but we might read into the narrative, is Anne Blythe's relief at finally having an outlet for her own considerable abilities. With her children grown to young men and women, poor Anne lacks even the distractions of childrearing to fill her days. No wonder she throws herself so wholeheartedly into war work, swiftly organizing her senior Red Cross Society with Miss Cornelia, and attending Red Cross conventions in Charlottetown.[37] Her cleverness, social status as the doctor's wife, and relish for a chal-

6 Street, "Patriotic, Not Permanent," 149.
7 Rothwell, "Knitting Up the World," 136; Reznick, *Healing the Nation*, 3.
8 Quiney, "Bravely and Loyally."
9 Macphail, *Official History*, 342.
10 Glassford, "Marching," 268–9; Glassford, "Greatest Mother."
11 Tector, "A Righteous War," 80.
12 Montgomery, *Rilla*, 89, 275–6.
13 For three very different examples of this kind of work, see Norman, "In Defense of the Empire," Duley, "The Unquiet Knitters," and Wilde, "Freshettes, Farmerettes."
14 Montgomery, *Rilla*, 122–3, 282–4.
15 On mobilizing the home front for war charities, see Glassford, "Marching," 121–33; Morton, *Fight or Pay*, 57–9, 62–83; Rutherdale, *Hometown Horizons*, 194–9; Daley, *Volunteers in Action*, 8–18. On the CRCS and CPF during the war more broadly, see Glassford, "Marching," chap. 3–7, and Morton, *Fight or Pay*.
16 Montgomery, *Rilla*, 69; Glassford, "Marching," 134, 340–2; Glassford, "Bearing the Burdens"; Sheehan, "Junior Red Cross."
17 Glassford, "Marching," 154–5.
18 McKenzie, "Women at War," 326.
19 Montgomery, *Rilla*, 105.
20 Montgomery, *SJ* 2: 193–4; Scates, "Unknown Sock Knitter"; Montgomery, *Rilla*, 239.
21 Montgomery, *SJ* 2: 174, 238, 280; Glassford, "Marching," 280–4.
22 McKenzie, "Women at War," 338–43; Tector, "A Righteous War," 81.
23 Montgomery, *Rilla*, 108–10.
24 Ibid., 79–80; Glassford, "Marching," 283; Glassford, "Greatest Mother," 226–7.
25 Montgomery, *Rilla*, 202–3.
26 Ibid., 315.
27 Ibid., 193, 218, 266; Lefebvre and McKenzie, introduction, xiv–xv.
28 On conveying or concealing war-related details, see Acton, "Diverting the Gaze"; Acton and Potter, "These Frightful Sights"; Cook, "Documenting War"; Keshen, "All the News"; and Roper, *The Secret Battle*.
29 Mann, *Margaret Macdonald*, 167.

30 Ibid., 166–8; Glassford and Shaw, "Introduction" to *Sisterhood of Suffering*, 8–9; and Macleod Moore, *The Maple Leaf's Red Cross.*

31 Dr Blythe's medical practice is successful enough to support a full-time housekeeper, and although the Blythe children have all worked as teachers in order to earn money for college tuition, the family appears comfortably clothed and well fed and owns a substantial house and property.

32 MacDonald, *If You're Stronghearted*, 6; Kechnie, *Organizing Rural Women*, 79; Kinnear, "Women's Work," 149.

33 Public Archive and Records Office of Prince Edward Island (hereafter PARO), ACC 2990, Royal Edward Chapter, IODE (Charlottetown, PE) fonds, series 1, files 3 and 4, minute books covering 1913–18.

34 Women's Institute reports in the Reports of the Commissioner of Agriculture PEI, 1914 to 1918, in *Journal of the Legislative Assembly* (Charlottetown, PE: Examiner Publishing Co., 1915–19), www.peildo.ca, accessed 16–20 February 2014. See also the following minute books in PARO: ACC 4700, Cornwall WI fonds, box 2, PEIWI Minute Book, Cornwall–York Point Branch, 1916–18; ACC 4761, Crossroads WI fonds, PEIWI Minute Book, Macdonald Branch, 1916–20; ACC 3471, Maple Leaf WI, Travellers Rest fonds, series 1, vol. 1, PEIWI Minute Book, 1913–16; ACC 4403, Red Point WI fonds, PEIWI Minute Book, Red Point Branch, 1915–19; ACC 3472, New Annan WI fonds, file 3472/1, PEIWI Minute Book, New Annan Branch, 1915–20; ACC 3466/HF74.192, Meadowbank WI fonds, file 74-192-01-02, PEIWI Minute Book, Meadow Bank Branch, 1913–18; ACC 2887, YMCA Charlottetown, PE fonds, series 2, Ladies Auxiliary Records, file 1, "Minute Book, 1905–1920"; ACC 2990, series 1, file 3, 12 October 1915, and file 4, 11 November 1918.

35 MacDonald, *Stronghearted*, 80; author's aggregate databases drawn from PEIWI minute books and annual provincial reports. Red Point, Georgetown, and Ray of Hope Institutes are among those that reported spinning or carding bees.

36 Montgomery, *SJ* 2: 280; Montgomery, *Rilla*, 70.

37 Montgomery, *Rilla*, 57, 79.

38 Edwards and Litster, "End of Canadian Innocence," 32; McKenzie, "Women at War," 334.

39 Montgomery, *Rilla*, 140–8, 149–53.

40 Doyle, "Canadian Women Help," 32; Glassford, "Marching," 280–1.

41 "They Drown the Conversation," 6–7.

42 PARO, ACC 3471, series 1, vol. 1, PEIWI Minute Book, Maple Leaf Institute, 1913–16, Mrs H.P. McNeill, "Outline of the Doings of Maple Leaf W.I. Travellers Rest and Sherbrooke from July 25, 1913 to March 1921, November 1928," 3.

43 Montgomery, *Rilla*, 70.

44 For a sustained example of this social pressure on female undergraduates, see Quiney, "'We Must Not Neglect Our Duty.'"

45 McKenzie, "Women at War," 338–43; Tector, "A Righteous War," 81.

46 Edwards and Litster, "End of Canadian Innocence," 32.

CHAPTER 7

Across Enemy Lines: Gender and Nationalism in Else Ury's and L.M. Montgomery's Great War Novels

Maureen O. Gallagher

Peter Webb asserts that it can be difficult to distinguish between literature and propaganda in Canadian First World War writing.[1] The context of war heightened patriotism and called upon nationalism, valorizing homegrown participants and demonizing the enemy. For instance, Susan Baker, an elderly spinster and maid to the Blythe family in L.M. Montgomery's war novel *Rilla of Ingleside*, hears dreadful stories of German atrocities on the battlefields of Europe. Fearing that her own quiet island is about to be invaded by ruthless Germans, she is spurred to heroic resolve. Susan declares, "The Huns shall never set foot in Prince Edward Island as long as I can handle a pitchfork," and the narrator describes her "looking and feeling quite equal to routing the entire German army single-handed."[2] But through her characters, Montgomery's war novel also represents more diverse and complex attitudes about the war: like Susan, the novel's heroine, Rilla, throws herself into war work and enthusiastically supports Canadian participation. Montgomery shows the cost of war and its horrors through Rilla's grief and suspense when the men who enlist and go to war are wounded and killed. As Andrea McKenzie argues, Montgomery agonized over the war and "needed to find a correspondingly strong justification for it to balance the horror."[3] Both Susan and Rilla become that justification, representing the wartime spirit that Montgomery foresaw would create a unified Canada.[4]

However, such an outpouring of patriotism and nationalism was not unique to Canada or to Montgomery. German literature shows a similar chauvinism and a similar drive to unity, portraying Germany as the victim of European imperialism, a besieged country surrounded by British, French, and Russian empires eager for land and jealous and afraid of Germany's technological and industrial prowess.[5] At the outbreak of the war, Kaiser Wilhelm famously proclaimed, "I know no parties, I know only Germans," capturing the popular sentiment that the war would help Germans overcome contentious social divisions based on political affiliation, religious denomination, and class to finally complete the process of national unification begun in 1870. German writing from early in the war reflects optimistic hopes for the nation, a feeling that was known at the time as the Spirit of 1914.[6] German author Else Ury, like Canadian L.M. Montgomery, wrote with a heightened awareness of patriotism and nationalism. Both authors, however, undercut these bolstering narratives to provide more complex and nuanced visions of the war's impact on girls and women. Montgomery's heroine, Rilla Blythe, and Ury's Annemarie Braun, heroine of *Nesthäkchen and the World War*,[7] show striking similarities in their fictional life stories. Both girls are the youngest of their families. Born around the turn of the century, they enjoy idyllic childhoods, romping freely with their older siblings while their fathers work as doctors and their mothers keep house. Both are irrepressible, if a little immature, and well meaning, while always getting into scrapes and troubles. When the First World War breaks out, their childhoods come to an abrupt end as they say goodbye to their dearest loved ones, unsure if they will ever meet again. Through war, these two fictional girls shed their immaturity to become young women, a wartime womanhood defined by making sacrifices and doing their part in the war effort to help their imperilled homelands. Although Montgomery was on the Allied side of the conflict and Ury was on the German side, the novels they wrote cross enemy lines through their fictional heroines' lives.

The resemblances between these two texts are not coincidental. As Jennifer Redmann notes in her article on German and Anglo-American girls' literature from the First World War, similar social developments, including new printing technologies, the expansion of schooling, and the achievement of near universal literacy, as well as increased leisure time and the rising marriage age of women, led to a boom in the production of similar types of books for girls in Germany, Canada, Great

Britain, and the United States.[8] However, it is not only the nearly identical episodes and resemblances in characters and plot structure that make these two works fruitful for a comparative study, but also how both Montgomery and Ury simultaneously bolster and undercut wartime nationalist narratives. They construct gendered images of wartime nationalism, using young female figures as symbols that represent the hopes and futures of nations.

Bringing these two literary traditions of wartime writing into transatlantic conversation becomes a way of discussing both images of national unification and enthusiastic patriotism and where these images show cracks and begin to break down. The war novels of Montgomery and Ury are particularly fruitful for this type of comparative analysis because both link the transformative effects of war with a traditional coming-of-age narrative.[9] The coming-of-age story of an immature or spoiled girl who grows into a responsible or marriageable young woman gained national significance in wartime. Susan R. Fisher notes the importance that was placed on children's behaviour during the war; children were expected "to demonstrate that they were worthy of the sacrifices being made on the battlefields."[10] Rilla and Annemarie learn to embrace the duties and responsibilities of women in wartime; as Anne Blythe says to her daughter, "the war has made a woman of you too soon."[11] In growing up and becoming women, they make a contribution to the war effort and embody the next generation of Canadians and Germans who were supposed to lead their respective nations forward.

In showcasing young female figures who grow up in wartime, these works show the truth of the observation that "war must be understood as a *gendering* activity, one that ritually marks the gender of all members of a society, whether or not they are combatants."[12] War, particularly the types of "total war" seen during the First and Second World Wars, exerts profound cultural effects on men and women and on the relationships between them. Although wartime gender discourses rely on prewar conceptions of gender, war also "restructures gender relations."[13] The characters of Rilla and Annemarie show these tensions and how new understandings of gender brought on by war overlap, coexist, or create tensions with traditional or conservative definitions.

To allow for a thorough comparative reading of *Nesthäkchen* and *Rilla*, I will first offer a brief sketch of the publication history of Ury's *Nesthäkchen* books; more on the publication history of Montgomery's work can be found in the introduction to this volume. Ury's novel appeared among a flood of war literature directed at young Germans, both boys and girls, that emphasized the importance and greatness of contemporary times.[14] Beloved heroes and heroines of series books joined in the war effort, too. *Nesthäkchen and the World War* (1916) was the fourth of what became a ten-volume series about Annemarie Braun, called Nesthäkchen (literally, "little nest hook") because she was the baby of the family and, therefore, like Montgomery's Rilla, the last to leave the nest. The *Nesthäkchen* books, published between 1913 and 1925, chronicle Annemarie's childish misadventures and then her growing up, going to college, marrying, raising children, and ultimately becoming a grandmother. Like Rilla's mother, Anne Shirley of Montgomery's *Anne* series in North America, Annemarie was one of the most beloved figures from German children's and young adult literature in this period and remains well known today.[15] In the 1980s the *Nesthäkchen* series was the subject of a popular television adaptation in West Germany, just as Kevin Sullivan popularized Montgomery's Anne Shirley through a series of television films. Though Ury had initially planned to discontinue the series after Nesthäkchen's marriage in the sixth book, so many little girls wrote begging her to continue the series that she went on to write four more books chronicling Annemarie's life as a mother and grandmother.[16]

The First World War saw the mass mobilization of youth on both sides of the conflict.[17] In Germany, literature was part of a broad effort to mobilize young people for war, with these efforts grounded on an understanding of war itself as a powerful educational force that could shape youth, and young women in particular, into responsible German citizens.[18] The First World War initiated a new era of pedagogy into the German school system, with the traditional curriculum abandoned in favour of incorporating the war and other current events into lessons.[19] This aggressively nationalistic and jingoistic content was accompanied by widespread educational reform and, for the first time, the introduction of child-centred pedagogy, such as free writing activities, into German schools. The precepts upon which these reforms were based were popularized by Theobald Ziegler in his "Ten Commandments of War Pedagogy," of which commandment three is of particular note: "Thou shalt raise your schoolchildren to be citizens. You now have the best opportunity to do that because the war is a teacher of first rank."[20] With war itself serving as a teacher, the Great War becomes an opportunity to bring about the rebirth of the German nation through its youth, rejecting the shallow materialism of modern society to return to more traditional values.

The educational, social, and cultural effects of this totalizing war ideology were not unique to Germany. Canada similarly underwent a mass mobilization of young people for war, as Fisher has noted.[21] Canadian children and young people were drafted into the war effort, called on to collect scrap paper, knit, make gifts for soldiers, work the soil, be frugal, and collect money for war charities.[22] Canadian author and feminist Nellie McClung, too, referred to the war as a "great teacher," indicating that this understanding of the transformational power of war was a transatlantic phenomenon.[23]

Ury's novel captures the social and cultural changes wrought by the war. When Annemarie returns to school after the start of the war, she finds that much has changed: "The teachers taught their young pupils different things now: ardent love for the Fatherland, boundless willingness to make sacrifices for those fighting, the superior pride of being a German boy or girl, and the resulting obligation to do your bit in these difficult times in spite of your youth."[24] These changes reawaken the Braun children's interest in school; Annemarie's brother Klaus, a reluctant student, is particularly captivated by the new, modern pedagogy. Learned in school, this new understanding of their place in the world and their responsibility as German boys and girls transforms Annemarie and her brothers.

The educational force of the war can also be seen in Montgomery's novel but on a personal level rather than an institutional one. Heroine Rilla is uninterested in formal schooling, but the war nonetheless helps her mature into a more responsible young woman. Rilla reflects, "They have been two terrible years – and yet I have a queer feeling of thankfulness for them – as if they had brought me something very precious, with all their pain. I wouldn't *want* to go back and be the girl I was two years ago, not even if I could. Not that I think I've made any wonderful progress – but I'm *not* quite the selfish, frivolous little doll I was then."[25] While Anne Shirley's maturation from child to teenager to woman and mother occurs across several novels, Rilla's transformation is abrupt and immediate, as war becomes a sobering catalyst for maturity. Rilla's thoughts on the war years and her desire to find meaning reflect Montgomery's own views of the war and her desire to give meaning and greater purpose to the horrors of war. *Rilla* was written shortly after the war, when Montgomery hoped the horror and slaughter would prove justified by the creation of a better society following it, a view that gradually yielded to disillusionment in the 1930s and 1940s.[26]

In *Nesthäkchen*, Ury, too, emphasizes the importance of children in remaking German society. The Braun children imbibe patriotic sentiment in schools and then, in turn, pass it on to their elders. They are zealous in their duty, encouraging their grandmother not to hoard food, to stick to the bread ration cards, and to surrender copper kettles for use in munitions manufacturing. It takes the efforts of all three children to convince her to turn in her gold for paper money, but she eventually accedes to the children's requests: "She never would have thought she would ever give up her hoarded gold. But the intelligent, patriotic woman had realized that it was necessary to put the welfare of the people ahead of the welfare of the individual. 'Yes, yes, the world is all turned around, and now the old learn from the young,' she said."[27] For Ury, the war has a transformative effect upon young people, helping them to learn traditional German values and to become less selfish and more civic-minded, and in turn allowing them to help regenerate a German society that was implied to be degenerate. Young people like the Braun children offer a way of making sense of the horrific war by providing the foundation for a new, better society that will emerge in peacetime. In this, Ury's optimism mirrors that of other German authors swept up in the "Spirit of 1914" at the start of the war.

In both *Rilla* and *Nesthäkchen*, the authors offer decidedly female depictions of heroism, wherein traditional womanly activities such as knitting, cooking, housekeeping, and caring for babies are recast as having national significance.[28] Both Rilla and Annemarie learn to embrace traditionally feminine activities as a means of demonstrating their own patriotism, heroism, and support of the war effort. An-nemarie goes from wishing she were a boy "because then I could help in any other way than with this stupid knitting" to the most eager knitter in her class, finishing her sock before anyone else (even if it looks like it is meant for an elephant instead of a man).[29] Annemarie's favourite teacher, Miss Hering, jokes with the girls to motivate them when they tire of always knitting grey socks, saying "our soldiers can't very well march on Paris and Petersburg barefoot!"[30] When Anne-marie is frustrated, her grandmother reminds her, "Even children can make small sacrifices and do their bit. Nothing is too small, even the smallest stone that you contribute to the great structure of war work is valuable."[31] Similarly, Montgomery emphasizes Rilla's transforma-tion from girl to woman. Though when she first meets him, Rilla de-scribes Jims, her adopted war baby, as "an ugly midget with a red, distorted little face," she soon grows to tolerate and ultimately to love him and become a true mother figure.[32]

As many scholars have noted, Montgomery rewrites the traditional male combatant heroic narrative of war to include female heroism. Elizabeth Epperly argues in *The Fragrance of Sweet-Grass* that *Rilla* "shows how the struggles of the women and men at home parallel the deadly combat on the eastern and western fronts of Europe."[33] Montgomery's depiction of heroism is more romantic than Ury's, with the teenaged Rilla, a figure on the cusp of womanhood and marriage, carrying a greater symbolic weight as a representation of what Cana-dian men are fighting for.[34] Rilla strives to live up to the repeated phrase – "When our women fail in courage, / Shall our men be fear-less still?"[35] – in her work on the home front; the cooking, sewing, and taking care of her "war baby" provide the counterweight to the fighting in Europe. Montgomery herself called *Rilla* her only novel "written with a purpose" and referred to it as her "tribute to the girl-hood of Canada."[36] McKenzie reads *Rilla* as presenting a vision of "a new nation based on *shared* sacrifice and *shared* suffering, with women as the representatives of the nation-in-the-making."[37] For Montgomery, young people like Rilla offer new hope for the future. In the opening scene of the novel, Susan, Anne, and Mrs Marshall Elliott ignore the headlines about the growing troubles in Europe to gossip about love affairs and plot matches for all the young people.

These plans are interrupted when the war begins and so many young men travel to the battlefields of Europe, but the final chapter sees many of those same young people more sober and mature, preparing to pair off and create the next generation of Canadians, who will be responsible for "build[ing] up the new" world, one that must, in Jem's words, be "a better one than the old."[38]

The war both reifies traditional gender roles and subtly undermines them. *Rilla* and *Nesthäkchen* are full of domestic scenes that empha-size the value of the home and women in their roles as wives, mothers, nurturers, and caregivers. At the same time, historically, the war opened up new possibilities for women, for it was necessary for everyone to work and be active in the war efforts. In *Rilla*, girls and women take on greater roles in the social life of the community and in running busi-nesses, households, and farms as more men enlist or are drafted. Susan Baker, for instance, a figure who otherwise polices gender expression and advocates traditional roles and duties for men and women, goes to work in the fields to bring in the harvest when there are not enough men to do so.[39] Rilla herself embodies more traditional roles for women. Unlike her more studious brothers and sisters, she shuns fur-ther schooling and has no interest in attending college or training for a career – the war is her education. During the war she occupies her-self with corralling her Junior Red Cross society, organizing benefits, concerts, and charity work, and raising her war baby. Ury, although having *Nesthäkchen* perform traditional female war work such as knit-ting, also depicts a greater range of non-traditional female work. *Nesthäkchen* and her friends are amazed by the presence of female conductors, elevator operators, street sweepers, and even mail carriers. In one scene, Annemarie dresses like a boy in order to accompany her brothers on a rag-collecting expedition. This behaviour receives neither censure nor punishment from adults, indicating the greater leeway and flexibility regarding gender and women's roles that even young girls enjoyed in wartime.[40]

Just as there is a certain ambiguity in the representation of gender, there is ambiguity about the war and nationalism. Though the over-arching themes and stories of both novels show nationalistic over-tones and a general glorification of the war, they also undermine this nationalism in important ways. Annemarie, for example, constantly misinterprets the geopolitics of the global war and takes her patriotism too far, leading her to backtrack, apologize, and regret her behaviour. Early in the novel she assumes her neighbour is from Japan, one of Germany's enemies. In her childish eagerness to show patriotism, she spits out the chocolate he has given her and shouts indignantly, "I don't accept gifts from our enemies!"[41] When she learns he is actually from Siam (Thailand), she is ashamed of her behaviour, and regrets it, for even though she apologizes, she never receives a gift from him again.[42] Soon thereafter, she leads her classmates in a revolt against French class, telling her teacher, "I am a German girl and I don't wish to learn the language of our enemies."[43] For this she receives a stern lecture on the importance of languages not only as part of general education (*Bildung*) but also as tools to help the Fatherland. Yet, even after these two incidents, Annemarie has still not learned her lesson; when a young girl named Vera joins her class after being displaced from her home in the east, Annemarie assumes she is also one of Germany's enemies because she speaks Polish. Annemarie warns her classmates that being friendly to Vera constitutes "treachery to the Fatherland" and is very mean to her, making up only when Vera's father is killed in battle and Annemarie realizes he was fighting on the same side of the war as her own father.[44]

In making Annemarie such an overzealous patriot, Ury creates a caricature of Germany's unrelenting nationalism and jingoism. Ury writes that "*false* patriotism had hardened her [Annemarie's] heart against Vera," and notes that "Annemarie's little head was just as disorganized as her drawers usually were. Russians and Poles were so mixed up together she didn't know how to keep them separate."[45] These scenes are humorous, but in making Annemarie a figure of mockery, Ury is able to subtly undermine and counter the nationalist images ever-present in German literature from this period. Annemarie's nationalism, rather than being presented as heroic, is constantly being corrected and revised by authority figures. Her ideas, attitudes, and actions are often presented as incorrect and harmful, and she comes to deeply regret her behaviour.

Montgomery's use of the comedic, yet thoroughly patriotic, figure of Susan offers a sharp contrast to the humour of Ury's novel. While

Ury subtly pokes fun at Annemarie's jingoism and patriotism, Montgomery makes Susan into a heroic figure for her staunch support of the war. Though Susan herself is a figure of fun, her embrace of the war effort is no laughing matter. In contrast, Rilla's brother Walter is a heroic figure who nonetheless dwells on his horror of the war and the fear that prevents him from enlisting, giving a much more frank and serious voice to scepticism about the war than is found in Ury's novel. And even though Montgomery's characters roundly condemn the pacifism of Whiskers-on-the-Moon, the inclusion of this character in the novel nonetheless gives voice to counter-arguments to the war. These tonal differences can be attributed, in part, to the different ages of the target audiences of the novels and the main characters. Different behaviours are expected of pre-teen Annemarie and teenaged Rilla, who is almost a grown woman.

Montgomery and Ury both blend national and familial concerns in a way that emphasizes the disruptive nature of war. Kenneth Ford, Rilla's sweetheart, sees enlisting as his duty because the war is "a family affair."[46] For him, going to the aid of England is as natural as helping your brother in a fight, but in leaving to do what they consider their duty, Jem, Kenneth, and in particular Walter break Rilla's heart and tear her family apart. The war disrupts Annemarie's normal family life, too. Her father, a doctor, spends most of the war away at the front, and her mother, who was in England visiting relatives when the war broke out, is unable to return for almost two years. Annemarie and her brothers are left in the care of the cook, a nursery maid, and their grandmother. For this last figure, her individual, familial worries mirror national concerns and compel her to choose her loyalties: "the old woman magnanimously placed these worries about her daughter behind her general concern for the threatened Fatherland."[47]

With Annemarie and Rilla at the centre of their respective narratives, the emotional pain they experience by being separated from beloved family members during the bulk of the war takes centre stage, eclipsing any portrayal of the noble sacrifice of those family members who left. With her father at the front and her mother trapped in England, Annemarie spends most of the war desperately worried for their safety, particularly for her mother, who was imprisoned as a suspected

spy and not allowed to write to her children. In the same way, Montgomery's narrative, with its focus on the home-front lives of women
and the inclusion of Rilla's diary, could be read, as Epperly argues, as
a psychological study of the effects of war on those left at home.[48]
The novel focuses on Rilla's emotional state while she misses her
brothers and worries about them; thus, the role of war as a bringer of
fear, worry, and loss takes precedence over the image of war as noble
and courageous. While Walter's death plays a prominent role, the novel
remains centred on Rilla and her reactions to his death, again placing
the feelings of the women left behind in the foreground.

In *Rilla of Ingleside* Montgomery masterfully contrasts idyllic life
in Glen St Mary with the brutality of trench warfare. Amy Tector
notes, "By juxtaposing the pastoral safety of Ingleside with the chaos
of war, Montgomery is able to give readers the sense of dislocation
and terror that the war evoked, without alienating them from the
story."[49] The sun-dappled childhood Rilla enjoys, her greatest worry
the indignity of being left behind and having to slather her heels in
goose grease after her first dance, is abruptly shattered on the outbreak of the war. Even though the novel ends on a hopeful and nos-
talgic note, with Rilla's lisping "yeth" in response to Kenneth Ford's
marriage proposal, we are left with the enduring sense that something
has fundamentally changed, that the world of 1914 is gone and, in
Nan's words, "Nothing can ever be quite the same for any of us
again."[50] *Rilla of Ingleside* is decidedly darker than *Nesthäkchen*.
When Rilla learns Walter has enlisted, she immediately thinks that
she can't bear it, but "then came the awful thought that perhaps she
could bear it and that there might be years of this hideous suffering
before her."[51] The novel dwells on Walter's horror of war, and even
Jem's joking tone cannot fully disguise the uglier aspects of life in the
trenches – the standing water, the cold, the hunger, the lice and vermin.
Letters from Walter and Rilla's diary passages about her fears for him
ramp up this atmosphere until his tragic death. In his last letter to
Rilla, he is so overcome by the ugliness and brutality of war that he
seems to long for death, writing, "I shall never be afraid of anything
again – not of death – nor of life, if after all, I am to go on living. And
life, I think, would be the harder of the two to face, – for it could
never be beautiful for me again. There would always be such horrible

things to remember – things that would make life ugly and painful always for me. I could never forget them."[52] Here, Montgomery employs a strategy of "realism and romance," to borrow one of her own chapter titles. She presents a realistic scene of the horrors of war and the emotional pain of those waiting at home, followed by a more romantic image that glorifies war and sacrifice. In the above passage, this occurs when Walter asserts that in fighting he has "helped to make Canada safe for the poets of the future."[53] Rilla's words, too, when she reflects on the four years of war and her lost youth, echo this pattern: "I expected that these past four years would be the most delightful years of my life and they have been years of war – years of fear and grief and worry – but I humbly hope, of a little growth in strength and character as well."[54] A glimpse of the horror and pain of the Great War is immediately contrasted with a redemptive image that presents war as a kind of noble sacrifice.

Montgomery's war novel, with its large and diverse cast of characters, offers a polyphonic commentary on the war, presenting multiple perspectives on the First World War, from Jem's enthusiasm to Walter's fear and worry and Whiskers-on-the-Moon's pacifism.[55] Characters express nationalist fervour and the desire to make a glorious sacrifice, but Montgomery also dwells on the fear and worry of those at home and the disgust and revulsion at the ugly realities of trench warfare. She includes voices and characters that question the utility of war and whether the cost is worth it, such as Cousin Sophia and her unrelenting pessimism: "All the boys were going to be killed in the long run, so Cousin Sophia felt in her bones, but they might better die with warm feet than cold ones, so Cousin Sophia knitted faithfully and gloomily."[56] While Montgomery's text is not anti-war, it shows, at times, as Peter Webb notes, "a mildly skeptical countercurrent against jingoism."[57] Bruce Meredith's pain is represented several times, in his horror over the idea of babies starving in Belgium or drowning on the *Lusitania* and in his action in killing his favourite cat, Stripey, in order to bring Jem home safely – an ultimately senseless death. For Owen Dudley Edwards, this scene shows Montgomery's resistance to an uncritical pro-war stance: "if Walter's story can leave readers in tears, the kitten story seems deliberately designed to make them ill."[58] With the inclusion of such scenes alongside images of glorious sacrifice and sunny patriotism, Montgomery offers a range of experiences of the war, presenting a complex picture of the global conflict and its impact on all participants.

Ury's text, written during the war for a younger audience than *Rilla*, offers a simpler worldview and impression of the war, in keeping with the age of Annemarie and her child's perspective.[59] Annemarie's lack of knowledge of geography and global geopolitics provides humour and madcap adventures in the novel, but also offers Ury the opportunity to use the figure's childish innocence to question German nationalist narratives. Take, for example, a scene early in the novel:

> Nesthäkchen lay in bed and prayed from the bottom of her heart: "Dear God, let mother come back to Berlin soon, but not the old Russians. And also protect my father in the war. And Uncle Henry and all the other soldiers. And please send us another nice victory like today? Please help us Germans, dear God." Suddenly it occurred to Nesthäkchen that French and English children might also be begging God for His help at the same time, so she quickly added: "And if You don't want to help us, then please don't help the others either. At least stay neutral, dear God. Amen."[60]

This scene is humorous and endearing, and we laugh at Annemarie's childish nationalism, but its inclusion is remarkable in a wartime German novel. Young Annemarie, the ardent nationalist and patriot, nonetheless envisions an international community of children, on both sides of the conflict, praying to the same God. This is a powerful image that transcends the partisan conflict and nationalist overtones that otherwise permeate the novel.

For all their similarities, the books' reception in the decades after their publication differs greatly. Much like Anne Shirley Blythe, Annemarie Braun became a beloved figure known to and read by generations of young people. In the decade after its initial publication, *Nesthäkchen and the World War* remained very popular and outsold the other volumes in the series. Montgomery's novel, which she intended as a decisive end to the *Anne* series, was slightly less popular than its predecessors, which she attributed to the public being sick of hearing about the war, but it has had a long and illustrious afterlife.[61] As McKenzie points out, *Rilla of Ingleside* stands alongside John McCrae's "In Flanders Fields" as one of the few Canadian First World War texts to be continuously read and to retain its importance to Canada's cultural memory of the war.[62] By contrast, *Nesthäkchen and the World War*, though by far the most popular volume of the series when it was first published, was excised from the series following the Second World War, when the nationalism and patriotism it expressed became politically unpalatable.[63] It has only recently been republished in Germany.[64]

Reading *Rilla* and *Nesthäkchen* together offers a transnational window on the relationship between nationalism and gender in wartime. Even though Canada and Germany were pitted against each other in bitter conflict, they nonetheless offered strikingly similar reading material to their young people. The novels both show how gender roles are made and re-made in wartime. Montgomery and Ury capture societies and gender roles in flux; the war has disrupted traditional familial structures, and the novels valorize both traditional female activities (knitting and caring for babies) and non-traditional gender roles when women take over traditionally male occupations. Montgomery and Ury show the symbolic weight that was placed on young people – and young women in particular – to be good, to display home-front heroism, and to prove themselves worthy of battlefield sacrifice, even though these authors undermine overzealous jingoism.

Comparing the afterlives of *Rilla* and *Nesthäkchen* and the very different fates of the two novels offers another window into nationalism and nationalist narratives. Like Anne and Rilla, Nesthäkchen was and remains a beloved cultural icon. However, the war volume was all but erased from the series after the Second World War, banned by the Allies for representing a dangerous kind of German nationalism, a sad irony for a book written by a German Jewish author who perished in Auschwitz.[65] Montgomery's work, on the other hand, valorized Canada's emerging national identity and new prominence on the international stage and became an important part of Canada's cultural memory of the First World War.

Montgomery and Ury capture the patriotic and nationalistic sentiment of the times but also offer subtle revisions of it. Although both heroines embrace war work and demonstrate their patriotism, neither author offers an unambiguous portrayal of the war as a righteous and glorious cause. Montgomery's and Ury's novels cross enemy lines to capture diverse, sometimes contradictory, perspectives on the war, from depictions of glory, sacrifice, and national unity to the pain, ugliness, horror, and futility that war causes. Montgomery and Ury, writers, women, and wartime enemies, ironically capture many of the same ambiguities and grey areas that haunt global warfare.

NOTES

1 Webb, "A Righteous Cause," 32.
2 Montgomery, *Rilla*, 305.
3 McKenzie, "Women at War," 326.
4 Gammel and Epperly, Introduction to L.M. *Montgomery and Canadian Culture*, 7. See also Edwards and Litster, "End of Canadian Innocence," for more on the First World War in Montgomery's novels. McKenzie makes a similar assertion in "Women at War."
5 For more on how German literature portrays Germany's relationship to the rest of the world during the First World War, see Gallagher, "Young Germans in the World."
6 The support of the war by the Socialist Party resulted in an unhoped-for unanimity in an otherwise politically, socially, and class-stratified German society. For more on the "Spirit of 1914," as the outpouring of enthusiasm that occurred after the outbreak of the war is generally referred to, see Verhey, *The Spirit of 1914*.
7 Else Ury (1877–1943) was one of the most popular authors in Wilhelmine and Weimar Germany, producing more than forty works for children and young adults, including two popular series – *Professors Zwillinge* (The Professor's Twins) and *Nesthäkchen*. After 1938 she was forbidden to continue her literary career because of her Jewish origins, and she later perished in Auschwitz. Most biographical and scholarly work on Ury is in German, but a good English-language biography can be found in Fox's "Else Ury: A Life in Hitler's Time."
8 Redmann, "Doing Her Bit."
9 German literature for girls in the period immediately before the First World War was highly formulaic, generally portraying a rebellious

adolescent girl who undergoes a transformation into a well-behaved, marriageable young woman. For more on literature for girls in this period, see Askey, *Good Girls, Good Germans*.

10 Fisher, *Boys and Girls*, 31.

11 Montgomery, *Rilla*, 233.

12 Higonnet et al., introduction to *Behind the Lines*, 4.

13 Ibid.

14 These novels had titles such as *At Home in Great Times* (*Daheim in großer Zeit*), *In a Holy Struggle* (*Im heiligen Kampf*), and *German Girls in Great Times* (*Deutsche Mädel in großer Zeit*). For a comprehensive German-language overview of literature for girls from the First World War, see Wilkending, "Mädchen-Kriegsromane im Ersten Weltkrieg." Donson, "Models for Young Nationalists and Militarists," gives the best English-language overview of German wartime literary production for young people, focusing primarily on literature for boys.

15 Redmann offers an overview of the *Nesthäkchen* series and contextualizes its popularity in Weimar Germany in "Nostalgia and Optimism in Else Ury's *Nesthäkchen* Books."

16 As the introduction to this volume observes, Montgomery intended *Rilla* to be the final book in the *Anne* series. However, she returned to the series in the 1930s, publishing *Anne of Windy Poplars* and *Anne of Ingleside*.

17 For an overview of how Germany mobilized youth for war, see Donson, *Youth in the Fatherless Land*.

18 The German term for this phenomenon is *Krieg als Erzieher* (war as educator).

19 For more on these pedagogical changes see Donson, *Youth in the Fatherless Land*, and Kay, "War Pedagogy."

20 Translated in Donson, *Youth in the Fatherless Land*, 243–4.

21 Fisher, *Boys and Girls*.

22 Fisher meticulously documents how Canadian children were called on to participate in the war effort, in particular in the first chapter of her book, "Doing Their Bit," *Boys and Girls*, 31–50.

23 Quoted in Coates, "The Best Soldiers of All," 69.

24 Ury, *Nesthäkchen*, 36. All translations are my own.

25 Montgomery, *Rilla*, 238.

26 McKenzie, "Women at War," 344–5.

27 Ury, *Nesthäkchen*, 135–36.

28 As Redmann shows in "Doing Her Bit," this was common not only to Canadian and German books, but also to British and American texts for girls from the First World War.

29 Ury, *Nesthäkchen*, 7. Annemarie's eldest brother undergoes a transformation that is presented in a much more ambiguous manner than Annemarie's positive change. Hans suffers silently with worry about his mother in England (who is briefly detained there on suspicion of espionage), finally bursting out with, "If only father would allow me to enlist; two of my classmates are already in the battlefield. If I could just fight against England! They should pay in blood for every tear mother has shed!" The narrator continues, "Grandmother looked with shock on the agitated boy. What the war had made out of that gentle boy!" (150). Hans enlists the following year.

30 Ury, *Nesthäkchen*, 34.

31 Ibid., 2.

32 Montgomery, *Rilla*, 81, 89.

33 Epperly, *Fragrance of Sweet-Grass*, 112.

34 Ibid., 114.

35 Montgomery, *Rilla*, 54. Montgomery repeatedly lionizes women's sacrifice, with characters repeatedly insisting that women have a harder time than men in war: "'*Our* sacrifice is greater than *his*,' cried Rilla passionately. 'Our boys give only *themselves. We* give them.'" (156).

36 Quoted in Tector "A Righteous War," 72.

37 McKenzie, "Women at War," 326.

38 Montgomery, *Rilla*, 348.

39 Susan's policing of Walter's gender expression is discussed in detail in Lefebvre, "Walter's Closet."

40 In *Youth in the Fatherless Land*, Donson writes extensively about the impact on German society of the deployment of so many husbands, fathers, teachers, and male authority figures.

41 Ury, *Nesthäkchen*, 46.

42 Ibid., 47.

43 Ibid., 50.

44 Ibid., 98.

45 Ibid., 115 (my emphasis), 98.

CHAPTER 8

The Shadows of War: Interstitial Grief in L.M. Montgomery's Final Novels

Caroline E. Jones

L.M. Montgomery's life spanned the transformative modern conflicts of the First and Second World Wars; each of these events, and her lived experience of them, is reflected in both her life writing and her fiction. Her First World War and postwar novels offer a spectrum of sensibilities and realizations about the ideals and costs of war, and about the hope and despair that characterize human nature. In *Rainbow Valley* (1919) and *Rilla of Ingleside* (1921), war is depicted as a tragic but necessary evil, a mechanism that will ultimately render itself obsolete and bring forth a new era of humanity. Yet, in the 1930s, as Montgomery watches the world moving inexorably *back* into war, her novels, though they do not deal with war topically, reflect hopelessness at the futility of the sacrifices and loss of the First World War. *A Tangled Web* (1931), *Anne of Windy Poplars* (1936), *Anne of Ingleside* (1939), and *The Blythes Are Quoted* (submitted for publication in 1942, though not published till 2009) all carry currents of discord and discontent under the conventional optimistic tone Montgomery generally assumes in her work. Similarly, Montgomery includes veterans as supporting characters in *Mistress Pat* (1935) and *Jane of Lantern Hill* (1937), and, even in novels where there is no explicit mention of war, Montgomery's themes are darker, and her characters often engage in futile and absurd conflicts. As Benjamin Lefebvre notes in "'That Abominable War!' *The Blythes Are Quoted* and Thoughts on L.M. Montgomery's Late Style," Montgomery's final book "takes up such topics as adultery, illegitimacy, misogyny, revenge, murder, despair, aging, hatred, and death," a seeming culmination of the grief and depression of Montgomery's final years.[1]

The shadowed themes and personalities of this "late work"[2] reflect Montgomery's own sense of hopelessness. She occasionally expresses her increasing depression over the state of the world in her letters and journals. In 1935 she writes in her journal: "The war scare in Europe continues. War! God in heaven, can anyone who lived through the Great War ever dream of making or provoking war again?"[3] Three years later, she re-emphasizes her own incredulity: "The war situation darkens every day ... War! The mere word sends a shudder down my spine. Those awful four years! Who that lived through them could ever dream of appealing to the God of Battles again! But to the young generation 'the war' is as a tale that is told."[4] Letters to George Boyd MacMillan and Ephraim Weber echo her journals: on 27 December 1936 Montgomery writes to MacMillan, "Since 1914 the world has been a nightmare. Sanity seems to have departed from it."[5] In a letter to Weber dated 8 May 1939, she declares, "I am *not* going to say *anything* about the situation in Europe. It is not fit to be written of ... The whole world seems mad with fear and suspicion and hatred."[6] In her final letter to MacMillan, dated 23 December 1941, she reveals, "This past year has been one of constant blows to me," referencing several difficulties in her personal life. She concludes, devastatingly, "The war situation kills me along with many other things. I expect conscription will come in and they will take my second son and then I will give up all effort to recover because I shall have nothing to live for."[7]

Paul Tiessen, in "Opposing Pacifism: L.M. Montgomery and the Trouble with Ephraim Weber," explores this candour about her disillusion about war. In the early years of the Great War, Montgomery spiritedly defends her support of the conflict and her idealized perceptions of its purpose and outcome, but, as Tiessen notes, "in 1933 she ... confessed to [Weber] ... that she had lost the naïve enthusiasms of her youth ... Now, she stated firmly to him, war must be got rid of altogether."[8] This "firm" and assertive language of her personal correspondence shifts in her fiction, sometimes wavering, sometimes manifesting as bitterness or pain, but occasionally still emerging as an urgent and patriotic call.

Sarah Cole outlines a framework for understanding the language of violence in literature: enchantment and disenchantment. Enchantment, she suggests, is "violent death as a sign and precipitator of sub-limity (in a person, community, or nation)," while disenchantment, "conversely, [offers] violent death as a sign and precipitator of total degeneration and waste."[9] From the First World War to the Second, Montgomery's personal war rhetoric shifts: her writings about and during the Great War reflect a sense of collective sacrifice for the greater good of the world. By the 1930s, she has lost her idealized belief that the First World War would not only save Europe from the tyranny of dictators but would also eradicate violence as a means of resolving human conflicts. Her rhetoric becomes imbued with disenchantment, focused primarily on the uselessness of war, the absurdity of moving back into it, and the scale of her own personal losses.

From 5 August 1914, when she records, "England has declared war on Germany!" through 1 December 1918, when she announces, "The war is over!" news of the Great War permeates Montgomery's published journals.[10] She writes of dreading the mail ("it is a torture every day to get the mail – but it is a worse torture *not* to get it"), of obsessing over battles and civilian casualties, and of intense emotional affiliation with the war's progress.[11] Her struggle to find enchantment in the midst of disenchantment is evident throughout her reflections about the war; for instance, she wonders in January 1915, "Will some great blessing, great enough for the price, be the meed of it? Is the agony in which the world is shuddering the birth pang of some wondrous new era? Or is it all merely a futile 'struggle of ants / In the gleam of a million million of suns?'"[12] Throughout the war, Montgomery clings to a desperate belief that the war must mean something, must have an outcome greater than itself, a transformative reconstruction of humanity and its conflicts.

The novels Montgomery wrote during the First World War – *Anne of the Island*, *Anne's House of Dreams*, and *Rainbow Valley* – echo this struggle to find enchantment in the midst of disenchantment, to give meaning and purpose to the very real horrors and sacrifice that the war caused. Owen Edwards and Jennifer Litster suggest that Montgomery was working under and with a variety of contradictory attitudes and motivations: that she was extolling the necessary sacrifices of a just war, even as she seems "quite deliberate in her intention of conveying the full horror of war by visiting its ravages on a heroine associated in the public mind both with the isolated regional idyll and peaceful pastoralism."[13] In early 1916 Montgomery reinforces this idea of the war as just, characterizing (to Ephraim Weber) the conflict as "a death-grapple between freedom and tyranny, between modern and medieaval [sic] ideals ... between the principles of democracy and militarism. I believe that it is the most righteous war that England ever waged and worthy of every drop of Canadian blood."[14] She adds that she truly believes that if then five-year-old Chester were old enough, "I could and would say to him 'Go,' though it would break my heart. And if he fell I would believe that he perished as millions more have done, cementing with his blood the long path to that 'far-off divine event' we all in one way or another believe in!"[15]

These patriotic perceptions infuse her First World War novels with a dark and realistic, yet ultimately noble and necessary, sense of conflict and loss. Yet as the world moves into its second global conflict and Montgomery comes to understand how little its political leaders seemed to have learned from the First World War, her personal writings and novels shift from a sense of the grim yet noble heroism of the Great War (enchantment) towards a cynicism that questions the value of Canada's sacrifices (disenchantment). Shadows come through clearly, albeit indirectly, in these later novels.

As Heidi MacDonald notes in "Reflections of the Great Depression in L.M. Montgomery's Life and Her *Pat* Books," "Montgomery was very affected by events in the world, her community, her church, and her own family."[16] The Great Depression of the 1930s infused, as did most "external factors," Montgomery's "anxiety," moods, and writing.[17] This sense of greater social and economic instability in the world, coupled with her recognition of the inexorable descent into a war that promised even more destruction and loss than the Great War, deeply informs Montgomery's work of the time. These later novels foreground conflict, offering happy endings that do not always overcome the notes of futility that Montgomery, consciously or otherwise, incorporates into her plots.

Similarly, we see a great deal of conflict – often absurdly exaggerated – in most of Montgomery's novels of the 1930s: *A Tangled Web* (1931) centres on an enormously disproportionate family conflict over an heirloom jug. The ongoing crisis prompts many life changes and attitude adjustments, some superficial, others genuine, but, in the end, when the jug disappears and the clan factions are left with nothing, Montgomery parallels, perhaps, the "sound and fury, signifying nothing" that the outcome of the First World War was proving to be. While the novel is ultimately comedic, the loss of the central artifact is significant: "what," Montgomery seems to ask, "was the point of it all?"[18]

In *Anne of Windy Poplars* (1936), the entire community of Summerside wages myriad ongoing battles: over the choice of Anne Shirley as principal of the high school; over social status and standing; over family secrets inadvertently outed. Anne's presence, unsurprisingly, proves a balm and panacea to these various feuds: the Pringles "capitulate" to Anne's charm, via her knowledge of a certain tidbit of family history; little Elizabeth and her father are reunited through Anne as *deus ex machina*; crotchety, stubborn old men are soothed, couples are brought together, and lonely people find home through relationship with friends, lost family, or lovers.[19] But the tone of *Windy Poplars* is somehow "off," its myriad happy endings undermined by the Valentine Courtaloes and Minerva Tomgallons, revelling not in the happy lives of deceased townspeople or the noble history of a founding family, but in the gruesome deaths and macabre relationships of those "dearly" departed. Anne Shirley had come to embody the values of hope and optimism in Canadian culture – in fact, in western culture more broadly by this time – and Montgomery, pressed for financial success and cognizant of the public's expectations, created a story that can arguably be defined more by its undertones than its surface. While some of the premises are patently absurd – the would-be-bride too indecisive to elope, for instance – Anne's walks through the graveyard and her night at Tomgallon House overshadow her social and professional success. Montgomery, feeling bound by her public's demands, creates an Anne novel that fills in a significant gap in the beloved heroine's life, with enough sly humour and quirky characters that the underlying thematic shadows can be overlooked. A McClelland and Stewart advertisement for *Windy Poplars* promises, "A new romance of the beloved heroine, Anne Shirley, that will delight all readers, old or young," though it fails to mention the deaths, thwarted hopes, and perverse satisfaction in others' misery that also abound.[20]

On the other hand, Montgomery characterizes *A Tangled Web* as "a humorous novel for adults"[21] and thus allows herself to include more dark secrets, more cynicism, and a greater degree of negative emotional complexity despite – or perhaps because of – the novel's humour. Because it is not meant for children, Montgomery can more overtly mock the absurdities of adult hypocrisy and comically demonstrate the failings of pompous, self-aggrandizing characters. Importantly, she uses this novel to call into question the merits of relying on tradition to make decisions, and to highlight the perils of never thinking beyond one's own experience. In it, we glimpse the contradictions and conflicts that become part of Montgomery's reflective response to the First World War.

Montgomery more overtly invokes the Great War in *Mistress Pat* and *Jane of Lantern Hill*, published in 1935 and 1937 respectively, when she includes veterans as characters who play significant roles in both thwarting and advancing the characters and plots. David Kirk in *Mistress Pat* and Andrew Stuart in *Jane of Lantern Hill* are both depicted as engaging individuals, who harbour cynicism or bitterness that colours their interactions with the primary characters of these respective novels. Montgomery describes David Kirk, a widower and a veteran, as a "quite old [man] ... forty if a day,"[22] who was "shell-shocked somewhere in France."[23] He is an intellectual and whimsical conversationalist, but the narrator notes "a flavour of mockery in [his] laughter and a somewhat mordant edge to his wit."[24] Tragedy has marked him, through both the loss of his wife and the grief of the war. Twice Montgomery has Pat use the descriptor "bitter" for him, and twice has her find that bitterness appealing: she first notes something "stimulating and pungent about his bitterness,"[25] then admires the "stimulating pungency of his bitterness," likening it to choke cherries: "They puckered your mouth horribly but still you hankered after them."[26] However, Pat's "hankering" is markedly reserved, even after she has agreed to marry David, and he ultimately breaks off the engagement because the friendly affection she can give is not enough. David is thwarted in his desires, guaranteeing that the bitterness (and grief) Montgomery has given him will linger, even as he slips out of the story.

Andrew Stuart, in contrast to David Kirk, has charm, and he appeals to young protagonist Jane when she first sees his picture (under a pseudonym) in a newspaper. She is inexplicably drawn to his face, seeing in it stricture (a "firm mouth" and "slightly stern eyes"), humour ("jolly wrinkles" at the corners of the eyes), and familiarity (a "square, cleft chin" that "seemed like an old friend").[27] First, Montgomery calls upon an appearance that engages, then an emotional, perhaps even psychic, connection not simply of blood to blood, but of kindred to kindred. Although he is Jane's father, Andrew Stuart is anathema for the Kennedys – the family of his wife, Robin. In fact, they have allowed Jane to believe he is dead. Andrew is considerably older than Robin (Jane's mother), he fought in the war, and he must work for a living instead of inheriting wealth as his wife's family has, but, when meeting him face to face, Jane (perversely in the eyes of the Kennedys) loves him immediately: he is the home she has not known she lacks. He is easy-going, charming, and pleasantly impulsive in all things. However, when Jane discovers his Distinguished Service Medal, marking him as not simply a veteran, but a hero, grief emerges through the joy of reunion: his face goes "strange" and his voice takes on an "oddly savage" tone as he tells her, "Once I was proud of it. It seemed to mean something when ... throw it out."[28] She tells him she will not do that, and he compromises with, "Well, don't let me see it."[29] Later in the novel, as Andrew tells Jane how he fell in love with her mother, he describes his war experience quite simply: "I was just out of the mud and stench and obscenity of the trenches, and I thought she was a creature from another star."[30] The marriage, born of Andrew's idealization of Robin, and never given a chance to establish itself on its own merits, inevitably fails, eerily parallelling the world's honeymoon period of peace in the 1920s. Montgomery's contrast of Andrew Stuart with the idealistic, hopeful Jane emphasizes the transition from innocence to experience of the Canadian people. This indicates, perhaps, Montgomery's own desires, futile though she might find them, for a cultural return to innocence.

Cole suggests that "writers of all political positions tended to filter expressions of violence through the enchanted-disenchanted lens," and that, in the First World War era, "England was looking for ... a language that would frame the war's oncoming violence in terms of fruitfulness."[31] This is something Montgomery clearly sought for Canada, as we see in the First World War novels, and for herself, as we see in her journals and letters of that period. Yet, as the Second World War approaches, her linguistic framework for war shifts from the themes of necessity and "fruitfulness" to a sense of horrified disbelief. In fact, the novels incorporating veterans may be Montgomery's attempt to warn "the young generation," which, as she noted in her journal, seems disengaged from the Great War, of the perils of forgetting the lessons of history, and thus negating the sacrifices of an older generation.[32] Thus, in both a novel appealing to older readers (*Mistress Pat*) and one intended for children (*Jane of Lantern Hill*), we see First World War veterans as characters significant to the protagonists, who make them aware of the bitterness and cynicism that war service causes.

Interestingly, Montgomery offers both of her veterans the outlet of professional writing. Both David Kirk and Andrew Stuart are journalists. In addition to his newspaper work, David has written a history of the war, but Andrew is more eclectic: his repertoire includes poetry, political essays, even a novel. While David finds professional success and acclaim with relative ease, Andrew's novel is rejected, and, to keep himself fed and housed, he relies on newspaper commissions; notably, the first of these that Jane encounters is called "Peaceful Readjustment of International Difficulties."[33] However, Andrew's ending, in contrast to David's, is idyllic: he is offered a steady salary as an assistant editor at a weekly magazine, his novel is accepted by an American publisher, and he gets the girls – both his daughter and his estranged wife. While David's book is critically acclaimed, and he's offered a newspaper editorship, he refuses to marry Pat, because she does not love him romantically. The similarities in these veteran-writer characters are striking, but their endings, and the tones with which Montgomery portrays them, are telling and poignant. Essentially, Montgomery demonstrates that happiness is arbitrary: Andrew had Jane, an instigator of progress and change, to resolve his stubborn bitterness, while David had the misfortune to fall in love with Pat, whose affections were claimed entirely by a home with which he could not compete. As MacDonald notes, "Pat's overarching desire is to avoid change ... The heightening dread that characterizes the second *Pat* novel, in particular, parallels Montgomery's despair while writing it."[34] Rather than the optimistic, hopeful tone of Anne Shirley's sense of change and possibility – the proverbial "bend in the road"[35] – Pat, perhaps reflecting Montgomery's own fears about the world and its possibilities, dreads nothing more than change.

The smaller theatre of Montgomery's grief is present in her fiction as it is in her letters and life writing. The past and impending wars are similarly arbitrary – people are casualties, whether through combat or circumstance, and they can do nothing to prevent the recurrence of the atrocities. The contrast between the novels of 1908 and 1935 are striking: Anne's changes are positive, full of opportunities for growth, while Pat's all signify some sort of loss. Anne will save her home and family, earn money and gain experience as a teacher, and continue her education on her own terms. Pat loses her brother to May Binnie, her mother to (ironically) her own restored health, Judy Plum to death, and Silver Bush to fire. In light of all this loss, the return of her old friend Jingle as romantic hero seems poor consolation.

On 12 September 1938, Montgomery writes in her journal: "On this hot dark muggy day I sat me down and *began to write Anne of Ingleside*."[36] This moment is an epoch for Montgomery, as she had not written "a single line of creative work" in "a year and nine months."[37] Despite Montgomery's reluctance to return to Anne again and again, her delight and relief at "*still*" being able to write, and at losing herself "*in [her] own world*" speak volumes about her state of mind to this point. She says, "It was like going home," and the writing of the novel sustains her through the end of the year.[38] The novel focuses on Anne as much as on her children, indicating an audience of adults who know Anne and want the last gap of her literary chronicle filled. With this book, Montgomery was able to nostalgically return to the idyllic days of Rainbow Valley, when Anne's and her own children were young and the world was "innocent." She incorporates elements of Avonlea and visits from folks of the Windy Poplars years into the novel. Yet, she cannot fully immerse herself in innocence: Edwards and Litster remind us that "Montgomery was widening the parameters of her fiction to include the new reality and the new Canada that war had created,"[39] and we see that, even in a deliberate retreat into the past, Montgomery is unable to forget that. Anne nearly dies of pneumonia; Gilbert has a dangerous bout of influenza; Gilbert's aunt Mary Maria arrives and stays, tainting Ingleside with her own bitter world view; the family loses a series of pets; and the children encounter malicious "friends" and learn about boundaries of class and social status. Finally, Anne feels estranged from Gilbert, experiencing an uncharacteristic bout of jealousy over a visit from Christine Stuart. Elizabeth Waterston suggests that these off-kilter elements, particularly Aunt Mary Maria's self-involved interference in the life of the family, reflect both Montgomery's own self-involvement and the cratering of the world that the Great War had been meant to build. Montgomery also incorporates several bits of "foreshadowing" concerning Walter's death – Waterston characterizes them as "embedded awareness of the horrors awaiting happy boys."[40] About Walter, Leslie Ford reflects that, "Earth was not his habitat," and the novel's happy ending is touched by the reader's (presumed) knowledge of Walter's death at Courcelette, as Anne sees the moon "casting a clearly defined shadow of a cross on the wall" above the sleeping child's head. Montgomery sidesteps this grief by noting, "tonight it was only a shadow … nothing more."[41]

Awareness of Walter's death in war infuses both *Anne of Ingleside* and Montgomery's last book, *The Blythes Are Quoted* (2009). *The Blythes Are Quoted*, an intriguing exercise in form, is in two parts: "The first half of this book deals with life before the First World War. The second part deals with life after the war."[42] In this work, Montgomery melds short stories (in which the Blythe family makes cameo appearances) with scenes of the Blythes' family circle. In these scenes, Anne reads a selection of her poems (and Walter's, in Part 2) to the family; each poem is followed by familial commentary, framed with little to no narrative. Part 1 ostensibly recalls the pre–First World War era that Montgomery was so relieved to return to when she began *Anne of Ingleside*, but it nonetheless feels haunted by the melancholy and grief instilled in her by that war. The stories all have happy endings, yet those endings seem insignificant beside the characters' circumstances: lonely children, fallen men, women on the verge of insanity. The poems are likewise imbued with melancholy, and the family dialogues in which Montgomery includes Walter carry out the same "foreshadowing" that we see in *Ingleside*. Thus, the author – unconsciously or otherwise – brings into Part 1 the war and the toll it will take at Ingleside and in Glen St Mary.

Part 1 opens with "The Piper," a poem mentioned in *Rainbow Valley* and *Rilla of Ingleside*, but not written until much later. Montgomery introduces it by saying, "It has been written recently, but seems even more appropriate now than then."[43] Rather than the noble and patriotic spirit implied in *Rilla*, the poem conveys a sense of loss and grief – necessary, perhaps, but neither noble nor great, casting even the prewar part of this novel under the shadow of war. As Benjamin Lefebvre discusses in his afterword to *The Blythes*, the reality of "The Piper" "feel[s] far more conflicted than the poem alluded to in *Rilla of Ingleside*."[44] The other poems in Part 1 seem primarily happy, but many contain a note of sadness or loss: "Farewell to an Old Room" acknowledges the loss of a cherished place and the pain suffered there as well as the joys celebrated.[45] "Song of Winter" laments the giving over of the world to frost and ice in the first and third stanzas, but counters those laments with "but" phrases: "But at twilight we foregather by the red and purring flame."[46] "Night" dwells on the healing powers of darkness and solitude, as the final stanza exemplifies:

> The world of day, its bitterness and cark,
>> No longer have the power to make me weep ...
> I welcome this communion of the dark
>> As toilers welcome sleep.[47]

These poems offer readers an Anne Shirley Blythe both familiar and with previously unrevealed depths of shadow. In these poems she explores ideas familiar from previous *Anne* novels – home, welcome, nature, and friendship – but she also includes the bittersweet themes of change and loved ones lost, and more sinister and worldly themes such as jealousy and "success."[48] Montgomery also adds authorial shadows (and foreshadowing). For instance, in the dialogue following "To a Desired Friend," Walter silently hopes to someday have such a friend, and he is answered by "A VOICE NO ONE HEARS" saying, "You will. And his name will be death," followed by Susan Baker's thought, "I wonder why I shivered just now. My old Aunt Lucinda would say someone was walking over my grave."[49] Montgomery, despite her fervent desire to return to prewar realities and sensibilities, knows she cannot; moreover, she cannot maintain the pretense even in an ostensibly prewar literary world.

Part 2 is overtly darker. There are fewer stories in this section: two are typical Montgomery stories in style, relying on misdirection and miscommunication before bringing the romance plot to successful conclusion. But "Brother Beware" features a demurely manipulative woman, and "The Road to Yesterday" highlights a woman's curious attraction to a man she remembers with fear and distrust. Carole Gerson points out that, "all her life, Montgomery admired and asserted female agency,"[50] and Miss Alma Winkworth of "Brother Beware" is no exception. She is engaging and genteel, well liked in the Glen St Mary community – and has the Blythe seal of approval, as she sits in their pew at church.[51] Timothy Randebush, so intent on protecting his brother from Miss Winkworth's charms, fails utterly to protect himself, and Miss Winkworth placidly carries the day, winning Timothy (according to one character, the better-looking brother) without lifting a finger.[52] And the "Dick" who greets Susette on her trip down memory lane in "The Road to Yesterday" turns out to be his cousin, Jerry, a kinder and more virtuous person altogether. Nonetheless, these stories each have discordant notes to mar the conventional sentiments. Timothy Randebush is so worried about change ensuing from his brother's possible remarriage that he almost fails to seize his own chance at matrimonial happiness. Susette's memories of Dick's past cruelties, not to mention the fact that he is on leave from the war, haunt her story almost more powerfully than the resonance of her happy ending.

The other two stories are more unusual, both structurally and thematically. "Here Comes the Bride" adopts multiple points of view as a congregation gathers for a wedding. Readers learn, with Susan Baker, the true story of the couple's courtship and, incidentally, of the bride's sister's romance – both the subjects of much community speculation – but we also see uniquely from the perspectives of individuals within that community. By this device, Montgomery can explore less admirable, but more interesting characters with contradictory views: for instance, Prue Davis, bitter about being on the verge of spinsterhood, tells herself to "Throw back your head and look as if you were sitting on top of the world," while another guest savvily notes, "Poor Prue Davis ... smiling with her lips but not her eyes ... hope deferred maketh the heart sick."[53] Gossipy Toronto cousin Barbara Morse condescends to the country affair; Aunt Helen Bailey worries about her own three unmarried daughters and assumes the bride's mother must be heartbroken that the groom is only a professor, not the millionaire she had hoped for; and Uncle Douglas March reminisces about the good old days and laments the thinness of modern women. We hear bits of the story from five outsiders, then have strong emotional responses from five principal players, followed by the full story from Mary Hamilton, the family's cook and the *deus ex machina* who brought about the marriage. This story allows Montgomery to play with form and perspective as she provides Austen-esque insights into the mores of rural Canadian society.

"A Commonplace Woman," the penultimate story in the collection, is set during the deathwatch of the titular character, a woman whose passing will be mourned only by her dog. The family waits impatiently for death, reflecting on the insignificance of Aunt Ursula's life, and the inconvenience of her prolonged dying. Ursula Anderson herself welcomes death and spends the time awaiting it "living over her whole life," reflecting on her secret joys of a lover and a daughter.[54] While a child born out of wedlock might seem out of keeping with Montgomery's more popular work, Ursula herself is the most striking element of the story. She is unrepentant about her actions and celebrates her life rather than regretting it. The last section of the piece, in which Ursula recalls her lover, her daughter, Isabel, whom she gave up for adoption, and her seemingly peripheral role in Isabel's life, counters the pettiness and superficialities of her relatives, giving the story an unusual depth and complexity that reflect Montgomery's loss of hope as the Second World War loomed. When Ursula recalls her criminal – and heroic – act of pushing her daughter's drunken and abusive husband down the stairs, she reflects, "I am not sorry for anything ... not even for killing Geoff Boyd." She dies with the declaration, "I ... I ... I have been the one who has lived. I have sinned ... so the world would say ... I have been a murderess ... so the world would say ... but I have lived!"[55] While the truths of Ursula Anderson's life die with her, her family members continue their lives undisrupted by the truth – that Ursula, whom they consider the most insignificant among them, contains all of the depths and complexities that they themselves lack. Montgomery lets her character go unlamented – except by the dog – and does nothing to disabuse those left of their own pitiable complacency.

Montgomery's conflict with her own ethos about war becomes evident in the character of Ursula: Ursula unrepentantly commits murder in the noble cause of protecting her daughter, and does it unsung and unrewarded, recalling Montgomery's early defences of the First World War. Yet, Ursula's family remains untouched by her sacrifices: first, in giving up her child to a better life, next in killing a man to protect that child, and finally in losing that child – again – to the better life Ursula had wanted for her. The family left behind only marvels at the drudgery that seemed to be their aunt's lot and wonders why she is taking so long to die. Her sacrifices, like those of the survivors of the Great War, are disregarded by the next generation.

As challenging as these stories are, the most intriguing part of the book, by far, is the final poem, "The Aftermath," attributed to Walter, and containing a horrific description of the narrator bayonetting another man. The poem is a lament and a caution, not a patriotic paean to the necessities of war. Clearly, Walter, in the trenches, already knows the futility of his war, regardless of its outcome. The poem concludes with these lines:

> The wind has voices that may not be stilled ...
> The wind that yester morning was so blithe ...
> And everywhere I look I see him writhe.
> That pretty boy I killed![56]

Although Jem assures his mother in the final dialogue that "Walter never bayonetted anyone, mother," Anne echoes Rilla (in *Rilla of Ingleside*) in saying that she is glad that Walter did not come back. She understands, from that poem, that "He could never have lived with his memories ... and if he had seen the futility of the sacrifice they made then mirrored in this ghastly holocaust ..."[57] Anne's thought is unfinished, but Montgomery's is clear. As other authors in this volume have mentioned, Montgomery offers, through Walter, not a prescience about the war to come, but an understanding of the "futility" of *all* wars – including his own – in transforming the world.[58]

Interestingly, Montgomery's editorial notes suggest that she had doubts about including "The Aftermath" and its narrative in the finished volume. In the "entire typed" manuscript of *The Blythes*, "Poem Four" is crossed out by hand, and there is a blue ink "X" over the remaining text on the page, stanza one of "The Aftermath."[59] Lefebvre notes this in his afterword, characterizing Montgomery as "highly ambivalent" about the poem.[60] She undoubtedly recognized that it would prove difficult for her readers, and perhaps was reluctant to publish her own flagrant despair at the emptiness of the sacrifices of the First World War in light of the Second. This editorial and authorial "ambiguity" offers the clearest sense of Montgomery's struggle between enchantment and disenchantment, between hope and despair, and between the truth she experienced and the truth she so desperately longed for.

Grief is an ongoing part of Montgomery's milieu: even her earliest fiction acknowledges the grief and tragedy of both child and adult life. Yet the final books of her life address grief differently, almost more resignedly, as if she feels that grief is less contained, less confined to occasional tragedies and more a part of the everyday world. As her life and her world gradually became less and less what she felt they should be, and slipped more and more from her control, the grief that permeated her world increasingly infused her work. These final novels seem almost more poignant and more painful than those that deliberately explore themes of grief, loss, and sacrifice. Montgomery's role as a documenter of the First World War is solidified not simply in her novels of that war, but in the novels that followed, and in the work that reflects not the events of war, but the shadows it leaves in its aftermath.

NOTES

1 Lefebvre, "That Abominable War," 112.

2 Ibid., 114.

3 Montgomery, *SJ* 5: 39.

4 Ibid., 278.

5 Montgomery, *My Dear Mr. M*, 184.

6 Montgomery, *After Green Gables*, 247.

7 Montgomery, *My Dear Mr. M*, 204.

8 Tiessen, "Opposing Pacifism," 137.

9 Cole, "Enchantment, Disenchantment, " 1632.

10 Montgomery, *SJ* 2: 150, 270.

11 Ibid., 179.

12 Ibid., 160.

13 Edwards and Litster, "End of Canadian Innocence," 32.

14 Montgomery, *After Green Gables*, 61.

15 Ibid.

16 MacDonald, "Reflections," 142.

17 Ibid.

18 Montgomery, *A Tangled Web*.

19 Montgomery, *Anne of Windy Poplars*.

20 L.M. Montgomery Online, "Montgomery Ad 2."

21 Quoted in Waterston, *Magic Island*, 162.

22 Montgomery, *Mistress Pat*, 103.

23 Ibid., 105.

24 Ibid., 106.

25 Ibid.

26 Ibid., 128.

27 Montgomery, *Jane of Lantern Hill*, 34.

28 Ibid., 94.

29 Ibid., 95.

30 Ibid., 131.

31 Cole, "Enchantment, Disenchantment," 1632, 1635.

32 Montgomery, *SJ* 5: 278.

33 Montgomery, *Jane of Lantern Hill*, 34.

34 MacDonald, "Reflections," 151.

35 Montgomery, *Anne of Green Gables*, 245.

36 Montgomery, *SJ* 5: 278. Italics in original.

37　Ibid.

38　Montgomery, *SJ* 5: 277–9, 281, 284, 286, 295. Italics in original.

39　Edwards and Litster, "End of Canadian Innocence," 43.

40　Waterston, *Magic Island*, 210.

41　Montgomery, *Anne of Ingleside*, 87, 276.

42　Montgomery, *Blythes*, epigraph to Part 1, n.p.

43　Ibid., 3.

44　Lefebvre, afterword, 519.

45　Montgomery, *Blythes*, 208–9.

46　Ibid., 214.

47　Ibid., 92.

48　Ibid., 94, 253–4.

49　Ibid., 145.

50　Gerson, "L.M. Montgomery and the Conflictedness of a Woman Writer," 70.

51　Montgomery, *Blythes*, 380.

52　Ibid., 382.

53　Ibid., 411, 417.

54　Ibid., 460.

55　Ibid., 473.

56　Ibid., 510.

57　Ibid.

58　See the chapters by Fisher, Robinson, and McKenzie.

59　Montgomery, typed ms. of *The Blythes Are Quoted*, University of Guelph Archives, Montgomery Collection, XZ1 MS A1000002, box 001A.

60　Lefebvre, afterword, 519.

CHAPTER 9

Women at War? One Hundred Years of Visualizing *Rilla*

Andrea McKenzie

Gunther Kress and Theo van Leeuwen, in their theory of visual grammar, argue that "visual language is not – despite assumptions to the contrary – transparent and universally understood; it is culturally specific."[1] They refer to the conventions of creating and reading images, and how different cultures may, for instance, read colours or the composition of images in different ways. Within cultures, variants may appear, too, and conventions can change with time and trends. In other words, the "language" of images reflects national and cultural experiences at given moments in time, reflecting creators' personal experiences and interactions and the cultural and artistic values of the time – though artists and readers are free, of course, to rebel against these values. Book covers, of course, are marketing tools that try to draw prospective readers into the text, and so tend to reflect what the publisher considers to be influential or popular values of the time.[2]

L.M. Montgomery's *Rilla of Ingleside*, published in 1921 and depicting a Canadian community's experiences during the First World War, has been continuously in print in multiple languages, countries, and editions for almost a century, its popularity enduring through the global and local wars of the twentieth and twenty-first centuries. Yet our understanding of the First World War and our cultural memories of it have undergone changes that are specific to nation, time, and new perceptions. As I observed in an earlier paper and as Jay Winter and Antoine Prost claim, each nation involved has its own distinctive "myth," or cultural understanding, of the First World War.[3] In postwar Britain, for instance, the anti-war attitude cultivated by writers such as Siegfried Sassoon, Wilfred Owen, and Edmund Blunden, all of whom questioned the meaning of the war's sacrifices, was not necessarily shared by the majority of Canadians. Indeed, the dominant Canadian postwar myth was of the First World War as a watershed event that unified Canada as a nation and gave it independence from Britain in international affairs.[4]

What was common across postwar nations for decades was the forgetting or devaluing of women's war writings and wartime contributions. Women's war scholars, however, have successfully challenged the privileging of male combatant experiences and writings, especially since the 1978 watershed republication of British writer Vera Brittain's *Testament of Youth*.[5] This new printing resulted in a burgeoning field of studies in war and gender. For instance, Margaret Higonnet's pioneering 1993 work neatly depicts the artificial divide created in traditional male-oriented scholarship and in male soldiers' war writing as "civilian propaganda set against the soldier's truth," demonstrating how male combatants' voices have come to be seen as more legitimate than those of civilians – especially civilian women. "Where *men* fight," Higonnet continues, delineating one of the barriers that women must overcome to "[trespass] onto the territory of war fiction, … *wom[e]n* should be silent. They cannot be permitted to speak, because their knowledge has no official standing" in such a battle-based world.[6] Her reading of women's war writings elegantly overturns these clichés, challenging traditional assumptions that war is men's sacrosanct territory and showing that women's voices and language elide the "oppositions between battlefront and home front, public and private, war and peace, men and women." She thus reconceptualizes the "definition of war."[7] More recently, Janet S.K. Watson has argued that the First World War was depicted as a "communal" effort while the war was ongoing. Both men and women were deemed to be actively involved, much as Montgomery depicts the war in Canada in *Rilla of Ingleside*. Watson, delving into how the artificial and divisive binary categories of "battle front" and "home front" came into being, theorizes that "trench warfare" became "the primary symbol of the conflict" partly because of its "novelty," resulting in "women and non-combatants [being] pushed out of the history of the war, which became exclusively a 'soldier's story,' incomprehensible to everyone else."[8]

L.M. Montgomery's *Rilla of Ingleside*, her tribute to girls' and women's contributions to the First World War, has influenced successive generations of readers with its complex perceptions about war and women's active and influential part in it. Instead of depicting a divide between the men overseas and the women at home, Montgomery creates a Canadian community whose members, male and female, share their war experiences and their knowledge, and whose women are considered as active as its men. The visual art of the covers, then, should reflect changing attitudes about women's roles in wartime at specific moments in time in specific cultures. Through the cover art of *Rilla of Ingleside* across time and cultures, this chapter explores visual narratives about women in wartime. Do such images contradict or uphold Montgomery's complex, sometimes ambiguous attitudes towards the First World War? And do these visual narratives reflect the changing perceptions of women in wartime?

Rilla of Ingleside: Grief in Wartime?

On the original 1921 cover of *Rilla of Ingleside* (fig. 9.1), Rilla Blythe, L.M. Montgomery's First World War heroine, sits upright, clasping a letter to her bosom with both hands, gazing ecstatically into the distance.[9] The vivid flame-red of her coat exactly matches that of the maple leaves in the trees and those fallen on the grass around her, thus connecting her to the beauty of nature and a seemingly Canadian landscape. But this colour, a contrast to the virginal white of her dress, also suggests passion. We can assume, then, that the letter, white like her dress, is the cause of her rapture, a love letter that holds the potential for changing the virginal to the passionate. Nature becomes an idyllic setting for romance. Only the letter Rilla holds indicates absence and distance, and her ecstatic expression promises a happy ending. Not shown is the cost of the war for those at home and those abroad: the emotional suspense and grief, or the missing, wounded, and dead soldiers, all of which Montgomery foregrounds in her text.

As Jonathan Vance observes in *Death So Noble*, Canadian historians have articulated "a vision of the war as a nation-building experience of signal importance. Canada's progress from colony to nation

9.1
Cover, first edition of *Rilla of Ingleside*, Stokes, 1921,
illustrated by M.L. Kirk.

by way of Flanders ... has become the standard method of judging
the impact of 1914–18."[10] Vance emphasizes specific aspects of the
myth, including the Battle of Vimy Ridge, as symbolically unifying
the country. Yet, given Vance's perception, the workings of Canadian
cultural memory about the war have also led to women's roles in the
First World War being largely omitted or marginalized in both popular and "official" Canadian narratives of the war.[11] Such a battle-
centred myth focuses on the soldiers who fought, thus eliminating
women from nation building. Montgomery's text, however, subverts
male-centred myths, transforming them to enhance women's roles –
especially those of Rilla and Susan Baker – as upholders of Canadian
freedom and the fundamental builders of the future nation.[12]

    But the original cover, by American M.L. Kirk,[13] deprives Rilla of
an active wartime role. The *New York Times Book Review and Magazine* describes this illustration as "a dainty bit of work ... [that
shows] Rilla in the woods with her love letter pressed to her bosom."[14]
For Americans, the maple leaves become merely part of nature, albeit
a reflection of Montgomery's loved Prince Edward Island setting.
Canadians of the time, having been immersed in the war for more
than four years, with the song "The Maple Leaf Forever" played as
troops and medical staff left home on trains and ships to go overseas,
would probably have read the maple leaves as a distinctive symbol of
Canada.[15] But as Vance also observes, the myth of the war as uniting
Canada to forge a true nation, thus justifying the war's sacrifices, did
not become prevalent for several years afterwards, with Montgomery's novel helping to shape this commemorative perspective.[16]
For Canadian readers of the time, then, this cover would have placed
Rilla as a proud Canadian, but without any reference to her textual
role as a nation builder. Montgomery's text enables women to act on
and speak out about war, but this first cover fixes women in a gender-
appropriate role: waiting passively (and silently) at home for their
men to return.

    The British Hodder & Stoughton (H&S) edition of *Rilla of Ingle-
side*, published in 1924, would have had universal appeal for girls and
women who had, like Rilla, waved goodbye to a sweetheart, a son, a
brother, or a father during the war.[17] Instead of sitting passively in
Rainbow Valley as on Kirk's original cover, this Rilla is active, lean-

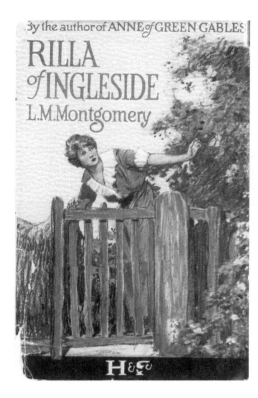

9.2
Cover, *Rilla of Ingleside*,
Hodder & Stoughton
(UK), 1924.

ing far over the garden gate to get that last glimpse of the person leaving (fig. 9.2). Unlike the original cover, the colours are subdued. Rilla's
lavender dress reflects half-mourning, and the bright flowers to the
left and on the bush above her shade to white and grey on the bottom
right: the potential for death and loss is apparent, but is somewhat offset by the brilliant yellow of the background and those few bright
flowers. Rilla's figure forms the bridge between the established world
of home and the path to war, for she gazes to the right, to what Kress
and van Leeuwen call the new. We, having read the book, know that
Rilla is waving goodbye to her sweetheart, but new readers of the time
would not know so: they would be able to read in their own sweetheart or brother or father. This specific cover transcends national
boundaries, though it also reflects Britain's growing postwar bitterness; in a world war, Rilla's farewell and sense of impending loss
would indeed be universal. But this cover is unusual in its depiction

of potential loss; it is the only one I could discover that pictures women's sacrifice and their anxiety. This cover speaks to what Carol Acton calls "consolatory rhetoric," where anticipating loss makes suspense easier to bear.[18]

Noticeably, both Kirk, the artist of the original American and Canadian cover, and the unknown illustrator of the H&S version focus on a romantic moment with Rilla's sweetheart, Kenneth Ford. Yet the difference is striking: Kirk depicts Rilla's ecstasy at receiving her first love letter, a moment that promises happiness without portraying suspense or tension; the British cover, in contrast, emphasizes the moment of farewell, of impending loss. Yet both speak to romance, though the first omits potential loss and the second accentuates it.

Jane Potter, in discussing British popular wartime romance novels, comments that "such novels, in providing encouragement in the face of loss and uncertainty, were, in effect, vehicles for the dissemination of patriotic ideals and models of appropriate wartime behaviour."[19] "Appropriate" usually meant abandoning modern decadence and returning to traditional values of hearth and home in a variation of what Samuel Hynes calls the purging and cleansing myth, but it also meant standing by your (appropriately wounded in a safe body part) man in his absence.[20] Sharon Ouditt, in *Fighting Forces, Writing Women*, argues that "Many of the popular songs, posters and postcards of the war reveal that romance was necessary as a life-enhancing counterpoint to the brutalities and degradations of war: if women were to keep the home fires burning, that fire was to be as alive in their hearts as it was in their hearths. Romantic love seemed to offer both soldiers and civilians some continuity and order to their lives."[21] Perhaps this is why Rilla's more peripheral romance with Kenneth appears so often on the book's cover, rather than her intense relationship with her brother Walter, which is the heart of Montgomery's text: romance promises distraction from war and affirms both a happy ending and women's traditional role, whereas the death of Walter in battle affirms war's brutality and grief. Owen Dudley Edwards writes that Montgomery "saw no reason either to shield her child readers from the existence of Death or to wallow in it. Death to her wartime readers, child or adult, was a fact, and she invited them to face it with a sympathetic but not schmaltzy eye."[22] He continues, "Death pervades

[*Rilla of Ingleside*], because we know we are waiting for one death, in which Canada's 50,000 dead will be subsumed."[23] For Edwards, Walter represents Canadian soldiers who died, but for any country involved in war, he represents their personal dead. Grief in wartime may, as Carol Acton writes, be "glamorised" in images, because by "elevating" women's sacrifice in giving up their men "to the war, and possibly to the 'supreme sacrifice' of death, [the woman] is persuaded that she can participate equally in the mythology of her country."[24] This mythology helps to keep the war going, to keep more soldiers enlisting, and more women supporting them. Certainly *Rilla* does subscribe to this mythology and to the abstract concepts of honour and self-sacrifice, and by that measure Montgomery seemingly upholds the prescribed script for women in wartime. Yet Montgomery's perspective is more complex, because she places grief prominently before us, showing the pain and disruption that death and loss cause for women: the pain of Rilla and her mother, Anne Blythe, is not hidden, but present and permanent.

But with the exception of the 1924 British cover, sacrifice, self-sacrifice, and death are absent from illustrators' depictions of Rilla; not even "glamorised" grief is shown on most of its covers. Instead, Rilla is, as many women's images were during wartime, confined to her romantic role. Potter notes, rather sardonically, that wartime postcards demonstrate that "when they are not being embraced, or looking longingly at their men or imagined versions of them, everyday heroines stare into space"[25] – as many Rillas do on many book covers across the century. But during and immediately after war, the population affected by it would have known that the images of women gazing at men or into "space" signified faithfulness, longing, and enduring love – that "continuity" amidst chaos that Ouditt mentions.

For instance, the 1947 Cavendish Library edition (fig. 9.3), like the first edition cover, does indeed have Rilla gazing off into the distance, clasping a letter in her hands, but it does, in a sense, contradict Potter's statement.[26] In 1947, the Second World War had been over for a bare two years. During this war, letters were again the main form of communication between those overseas and those at home. Yet unlike the British H&S cover, where Rilla's sense of loss is clearly felt, the expression of the North American Cavendish Library's Rilla indicates

strength and purpose. Her salience – her size, high above the landscape, her windblown hair, and her firm lips – speaks to independence and the strength to stand alone. The flowers in her hair highlight
romance, and the green of her dress connects her to the landscape in
which she stands. This Rilla is not passive, but the active, energetic,
staunch Rilla of the text. She reflects the public images of women dis-
seminated during the Second World War.[27] But the jacket text emphasizes that Montgomery's story is "a lively and an accurate picture
of a time that has passed – a time in which people lived, loved and suffered without the advantages of radio, aeroplane or the various im-
provements evidenced in the Atomic Age."[28] Montgomery's work has
become a historical document, a reminder that war is past and over –
even though, in 1947, the threat of the Atomic Age was most certainly
present. But showing war as over and done with, and presenting Rilla
as an attractive young woman, does provide stability after chaos, continuity in a world where atomic bombs had wreaked havoc and bomb
shelters continued to be built.

A Complex Complicity

During the First World War, images of women could be divided into
two categories: roles imposed on women in the home, and roles imposed on women when workplace recruiting was being performed. As
various scholars have noted, images of women in the home were used
to reinforce traditional gender roles, such as motherhood (including
future motherhood) and domesticity.[29] Many recruiting posters featuring women showed them either in need of protection – thus persuad-
ing soldiers to defend their homes from the "Huns" – or as staunch
recruiting agents themselves, standing behind their soldier men. Both
of these roles can be seen in what is perhaps the most famous war
poster that features women: "Women of Britain Say – 'GO!'" (fig. 9.4).[30]
Mother, wife, and children are foregrounded, standing before the door-
way of their home, with a column of soldiers marching to war to their
left, away from home and family. The women's grief is shown, but also
their strength: the mother looks after the soldiers with her head lifted

9.3
Cover, *Rilla of Ingleside*,
McClelland and Stewart
(Canada), Cavendish
Library edition, 1947.

high, showing staunchness and pride. Soldiers go to war to defend these women, while the women's role as supporters of soldiers is glamorized. Women are also frequently depicted as victims of German brutality: a semi-nude young woman flung over the shoulder of a gorilla in a German helmet, with the caption "Destroy this mad brute: ENLIST";[31] a drowned woman and child depicted after the German sinking of the *Lusitania*;[32] a Belgian refugee mother with her head buried in her arms, her child staring directly at the viewer in a demand for aid.[33] Canadian and American posters also depict women as fighters on the kitchen front, showing them preparing food without waste, and adhering to rationing.[34]

Montgomery clearly responded to such wartime propaganda: Rilla, like the women of Britain who tell their men to " GO!", recites at recruiting meetings to persuade young men to enlist, while Walter uses the reports of Belgian atrocities – young women brutalized by

9.4
E.J. Kealey, *Women of Britain Say "GO!"* Parliamentary Recruiting
Committee poster, 1915.

German soldiers – to convince Rilla that his enlisting is necessary. The Blythe household conforms to rationing in the kitchen, too, albeit Rilla's cooking remains at the level of candy and shortbread, sweet treats to send the men overseas. But Montgomery's attitude about war remains complex and ambivalent. Popular posters such as these dictated that women should respond with disdain to "shirkers" who resisted enlisting; young men who did not fight to defend their country and protect their women and homes were supposedly cowardly, unworthy of becoming sweethearts and husbands. Montgomery, however, depicts more ambiguity and complexity in her heroine Rilla's emotions when her brother Walter calls himself a "coward" for not enlisting. Instead of disdain, Rilla reaches out to Walter, telling him, "You feel things before they really come – feel them all alone when there isn't anything to help you bear them."[35] In doing so, she becomes the person who alleviates his aloneness, a staunch ally who will help him bear his imaginings. In this moment, "they comforted and strengthened each other," becoming confidantes and equals.[36]

Montgomery also uses Walter to foreground both men's and women's burden. Fighting is not an impersonal act, but the killing of, as Walter says, "some woman's husband or sweetheart or son – perhaps the father of little children."[37] As Walter realizes, each death causes grievous loss to a family. Subtly, his words reinforce the women's perspective, in which the men "give only *themselves*. *We* [the women] give them."[38] In this way, war becomes personalized and individualized; instead of faceless casualties in battle, each man killed becomes some woman's or family's personal loss and cause of grief.

Tellingly, Walter's words to Rilla also make her conscious that the cost of war is not just the potential loss of her brothers and male friends on the battlefield, but the psychological damage done to these men by the ugly and horrifying act of killing. Brother and sister become equal in their understanding. Walter's reluctance to go to war and Rilla's reluctance to have him go are thus justified; it is not cowardice on his part but considered reflection about the human cost of war for both the men who kill and the women who suffer loss. Alone of the men, only he recognizes the full significance of enlisting.[39] Driven to desperation by his own conflicting feelings and the public pressure to enlist, Walter "could not have lived through" this time "if it had not been for [Rilla's] little loving, believing heart."[40] Rilla becomes her brother's lifeline; he cannot survive without her and her staunch support. And yet, as Laura Robinson points out in chapter 5, that small "sore spot" in Rilla is relieved when Walter does enlist, because "no one" can call him "a slacker now."[41] Rilla's emotional response to Walter's dilemma demonstrates the depth of suffering and the complexity of women's response to war: Rilla believes that the cause is just, but her agony over Walter shows the personal cost of her support of that cause. But images of war, including illustrations of Rilla, seldom reflect complexity, confusion, or agony. Given the need to generate and sustain support for a war, only the positive aspects are usually emphasized: comradeship and heroism for male soldiers, and – as most of the covers of Rilla demonstrate – romance for women.

Motherhood, Home, and War

If romance provides "order" in a wartime world, with its potential for future stability through marriage, then the concept of a united family with children becomes the ultimate bedrock of continuity and a fruitful future life. During the First World War, "motherhood," as Susan Grayzel observes, "provided a means by which to target and unify all women, to make them feel that they, too, had an essential part to play in supporting the war."[42] Grayzel's comment appears to be applicable during wars other than the First World War. For instance, the 1938 American Grosset & Dunlap (G&D) cover of Rilla (fig. 9.5)[43] appears to emphasize romance and farewell, but in a much less serious fashion than the 1924 H&S edition. On the G&D cover, a stylized Rilla in an elegant long party dress waves goodbye to a soldier off in the distance. But her size dwarfs him; he is barely noticeable, given her slim elegance, the large flowers beside her, and the title text that seems to bend towards her. Even the trees' shadow points to Rilla, though its dark colour is slightly menacing. And right beside the soldier, as though to further distract our attention from him, is the text, "By the author of Anne of Green Gables." It is as though the mere appearance of a soldier who represents war is threatening, and so the illustrator must diminish him – through size, through distracting text, and through a Rilla

9.5
Cover and spine, *Rilla of Ingleside*, Grosset & Dunlap
(U.S.), 1938.

who is far larger, more active, and colourful than he is. Even his shadow
points away from her. The low modality, or lack of realism, lowers
any potential menace even further; this soldier is a toy soldier, perhaps
a cartoon, painted in far less detail than Rilla. This cover was created
when war threatened. However, should potential readers feel uncertain of a happy outcome, the spine would provide reassurance: a cute
little baby gazes directly at us and reaches one hand towards us, de-
manding our immediate attention. The soldier on the cover, then, will
return, and the family will be completed. And if we are still uncertain,
a glance inside the front cover at the end papers shows the couple in
elegant civilian clothes, with a reassuring group of children reading
and looking at birds in the peace of the woods. No soldiers or warriors
here, and no shadow of a cross or of grief; just a regular couple and a
regular group of kids pursuing regular lives.

The poorly worded inside jacket text constructs *Rilla* as a model for how girls should bear their wartime lives: "At sixteen, a tip-toe with romance and eager for Life's experiences, Rilla finds herself plunged into the realities of 1914. How she faces the problems of the American girl at home in wartime – with the same courage that the young Anne had faced the less trying problems of *her* young womanhood – and how she is fitted for a happiness greater than her dreams, makes the story." Putting aside the factual errors in jacket text,[44] war has become a means to attain a successful romance, with Montgomery's novel urged as an approved script for girls who must live with war and try to find a happy ending to it.

A 1956 Australian edition depicts a complete family group on the cover, instead of relegating the traditional family to the spine or the end papers.[45] In a rare close-up, we see Ken in uniform and Rilla holding a baby. In Montgomery's novel, this scene depicts Rilla's poignant and hilarious last farewell before sweetheart Kenneth leaves for overseas. In the text, Rilla's adopted war baby, Jims, howls upstairs until Rilla, in desperation, brings him downstairs, feeling that the baby is a ludicrous addition to what should be a romantic farewell. Rilla, dressed in virginal white, appears to Kenneth as a Madonna and, at this moment, he realizes that he loves her. In contrast, on the Australian cover, Rilla looks neither virginal nor romantic: the pinkish-red of her dress suggests sexuality, while the baby she holds emphasizes maternity. New readers, in fact, would assume that Ken and Rilla are married, and that the baby is theirs. Ken, dressed in uniform, gazes up at Rilla; motherhood becomes the most powerful element in the picture. Romance is complete, and the suspense of the text is alleviated.

On these covers, motherhood is uncomplicated and uncontested. Yet in her novel, Montgomery presents two portraits of motherhood: Rilla, who adopts a war baby, and Anne Blythe, mother of Rilla and her soldier brothers. Both portraits show the cost of motherhood: Jims, Rilla's adopted war baby, almost dies of croup; though he survives, her despair and her grief at impending loss echo her mother's emotions when Walter is killed on active service. Anne Blythe, as Elizabeth Epperly rightly argues, "serves as a reminder ... of the millions of quiet, nameless women who watched their sons and brothers and lovers and husbands and friends go to the front. And Montgomery makes it clear that for this she is heroic, for this and for running the Red Cross and carrying on her daily life."[46] Yet Epperly also argues that Anne "has finally been absorbed completely by the roles conventionally prescribed for her."[47] Owen Dudley Edwards and Jennifer Litster go further, calling Anne's "shadowy presence and near neurasthenic condition in this novel ... indicative of her comparative uselessness and inappropriateness."[48] Yet I read Anne Blythe differently. According to Carol Acton, "While private individuals often wrestled with contradictory feelings around the death of a loved one in combat, public narratives erased ambivalence"; "stoic acceptance and pride was the public face of grief."[49] Montgomery uses Anne Blythe to show the cruel impact of daily suspense and anxiety and grief on mothers. When Jem, Jerry, and Walter are transferred to the Somme front in the fall of 1916, "Mrs. Blythe's spirit failed her a little," yet she begs to keep on working because, she says, "While I'm working I don't think so much. If I'm idle I imagine everything – rest is only torture for me."[50] Imagination has become a means of seeing "terrible things – terrible years to come."[51] The sanctuary of Ingleside is threatened, and its chatelaine's eyes, "that had once been so full of laughter ... now seemed always full of unshed tears."[52] Anne Blythe's behaviour contradicts the dominant script for women's behaviour. Instead of being stoic and stable, accepting the prescribed script of self-sacrifice as Rilla does, she "lay ill from grief and shock ... for weeks" after Walter's death.[53] Her spirit has been permanently diminished by her son's death;[54] Anne has become a casualty of war as much as her dead son.

Motherhood in wartime is a complicated and often trying experience, but, as multiple nations emphasized, it was also a way of contributing to the war effort by bearing future soldiers who would help the nation. The covers of *Rilla* that include children erase the anguish and grief that many mothers felt during the war; romance, instead, naturally leads to stable, safe families in stable, safe homes.

Unlike the book covers we have seen so far, which depict "home" as an enclosed or limited space, Montgomery's text exponentially expands the concept of home. Jem, for instance, equates the "garden at

Ingleside" with the gardens of Europe, which hold "the beauty of centuries" that have been "mangled" and "desecrated" by the Huns in the equivalent of rape.[55] The men, too, bring the landscapes of war to Ingleside through their descriptions of trenches and mud. But if the men who fight bring the landscapes of war to Ingleside, "juxtaposing," as Amy Tector observes, "no-man's land" with the "pastoral" landscapes of Ingleside,[56] then the women provide an alternate world to that of the trenches, one that enables the soldiers to emotionally survive their circumstances. Jerry, for instance, when he wakes on the battlefield, sees Nan Blythe holding out her hands to him across the well in Rainbow Valley; and on the evening before he dies, Walter sees his sister Rilla and the gardens of Ingleside and Rainbow Valley as his last vision of beauty, for which he is willing to sacrifice himself.[57] Montgomery thus makes the division of "home front" and "battle front," in Susan Grayzel's words about the actual war, "porous."[58]

But few covers attempt to illustrate this connection or the expansion of local to global. One that does, from Australia, foregrounds Rilla, with her portrait spilling out of the frame, placing her in our world.[59] The letter she holds is the connecting link to the soldiers who are silhouetted in the background. Rilla is physically at home but mentally immersed in the battlefield: trenches and home are inseparable and entwined, with Rilla forming the bridge between them. In theme, this cover is derived from the postcards Potter described, but with a modern twist. The soldiers are unidentifiable and uniform; they do not fight, but march across a dark landscape that, by the 1980s and 1990s, had become emblematic of the First World War. The lack of identifying features means that these soldiers could be anyone's sons, sweethearts, or brothers. Like the 1924 H&S cover of Rilla waving goodbye at the gate, this cover has universal appeal for any potential reader who has or has had someone absent due to war. But covers that include war in this way, with a direct connection between women and men, fighting overseas and fighting at home, are rare. And even these covers, like the others, soften the impact of war; on the Australian cover, war is glamorized by the haze of pink in the sky surrounding Rilla and the soldiers.

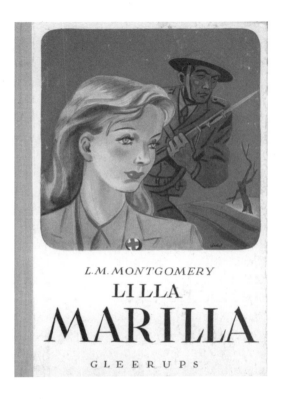

9.6
Cover, *Lilla Marilla*,
Gleerups (Sweden),
1947, illustrated by
Nils Wedel.

Women at War?

In startling contrast, post–Second World War Scandinavian covers of *Rilla* emphasize war's brutality and highlight the importance of local circumstance. The 1947 Canadian Cavendish Library edition emphasized Rilla's strength and endurance, but the jacket text distanced the First World War as past, making it a historical memory instead of a present reality, while the American G&D cover diminished the soldier into a toy. In contrast, the 1947 Swedish cover (fig. 9.6) gives us a Rilla in khaki, a Red Cross pinned on her service jacket.[60] Her elegant blonde beauty contrasts with the lurid blood-red of the background and the dark figure of the soldier behind her, in combat uniform with tin hat and bared bayonet. The single broken tree silhouetted in the background represents the devastated landscape of war, while we remain uncertain if the soldier, who frowns with heavy

brows, is protecting Rilla or threatening her. The two figures are parallel, both following the tracks of war, though Rilla is in the light and
the soldier in the red haze. Both gaze to the right, towards war, with
the red of Rilla's cross connecting her to blood, which the overwhelming blood-red in the background symbolizes.[61] The brutality of
war is uncovered here.

Such covers directly connect Montgomery's text to the Second
World War, and to the Scandinavian Winter War and Continuation
War, rather than to the First World War: even though the destroyed
tree reminds us of Frank Hurley's First World War photographs,[62]
many more women were in uniform in these later wars. War is not
past, but present, this cover suggests, and it is brutal and vicious. But
this depiction of war still features an active soldier and an inactive
woman, who, following Potter's adage, gazes into the distance. Nonetheless, she is undoubtedly gazing directly at war, and at the blood it
spills, rather than towards romance.

In contrast to many other covers, this Swedish edition serves much
the same role as Walter Blythe's final poem, "The Aftermath," which
Montgomery wrote and placed near the end of her posthumously
published book *The Blythes Are Quoted*.[63] "The Aftermath" relates
Walter's horror about the experience of bayonetting a young German
soldier, and *The Blythes Are Quoted* undercuts the illusion of the myth
of romantic sacrifice in which Rilla Blythe, now Rilla Ford, a mother
with a son at war, still believes.[64] In this book, Rilla carries Walter's
"heart and hope" with her as a way to endure the suspense of the Second World War.[65] Only Anne Blythe, who has read Walter's poem and
realizes the impact killing has had on her son, and war veteran Jem,
who was with Walter in the trenches, understand the actual horror of
war: it is not victory or defeat, but the profound horror of the change
that killing causes in the sons and brothers who must perform this
act.[66] Perhaps this is why the Swedish cover is so startling – because
we cannot tell whether this soldier is a friend or an enemy, is Ken or
Walter or an unknown German. He is an unknown soldier with a
bared bayonet, running to kill. In this sense, he brings to mind Walter's words in *Rilla*: "War isn't a khaki uniform or a drill parade ... I
... see the blood and filth and misery of it all. And a bayonet charge!

If I could face the other things I could never face that. It turns me sick to think of it – sicker even to think of giving it than receiving it – to think of thrusting a bayonet through another man."[67] Ironically, the soldier on this cover is running to perform that very action.

What becomes clear in looking at these covers is that, even when war is present, Rilla is given limited roles to play. Troublingly, on the majority of covers, Rilla does "gaze vacantly into space."[68] She offers herself up to our gaze and, with few exceptions, becomes an object for our contemplation. If we read Montgomery's text only through these images of Rilla, she becomes static and fixed. The active, energetic Rilla who runs the Junior Red Cross, rescues a baby in a soup tureen, keeps her brother from despair, suffers and grieves, laughs and matures, is considered "bossy,"[69] and takes over as chatelaine of Ingleside when her mother fails, has been banished, subsumed by this limited depiction of what artists and publishers allow her to become. The complexity of her emotions and of Montgomery's war has been sacrificed for the safe image of romance. And the universality of this image becomes even more troubling. Not only the Canadian covers, but most covers, regardless of time or culture, speak to the limited roles that women are allowed during wartime and the continued marginalization of women's war work.

A Forgotten War?

The covers published through the 1940s do remind us that a war took place; letters, soldiers, and wartime romance are depicted, albeit glamorized, in images of Rilla. Yet by the 1960s and 1970s, when both the First and the Second World Wars were relegated to history,[70] war vanishes from the covers, replaced by decontextualized romantic or domestic images. As early as 1958, as a British Harrap cover (fig. 9.7) shows, war has been banished from illustrations.[71] Rilla, decontextualized from any signs of war, gazes upwards; she is surrounded by flowers, but gazes above them, clearly at the lover who brought the flowers, though he is out of the frame. Her position is below him, and he thus claims power over her. Not only is romance primary, but

9.7
Cover, *Rilla of Ingleside*,
Harrap (UK), 1958.

women have become subordinate to men, without the need for the staunchness or strength of the 1947 Cavendish edition, and so presumably – for this illustrator, at least – they resume their appropriate place in the world.

The 1970s faced the rise of feminism and female power; in a sense, as Pearl James notes about images of women at work in the First World War,[72] some images of women in the 1970s showed an anxiety about traditional gender roles and their shifting boundaries. But the 1973 Canadian Favourites edition firmly places Rilla in a traditional female role.[73] Like the powerful Rilla on the 1947 Cavendish Library edition, the 1973 edition shows Rilla high against the landscape, a letter in her hand. But in contrast to the 1947 edition, the full-length impressionistic portrait makes the 1973 Rilla an object of contemplation instead of one of power. Her rounded shoulders and slight stoop indicate subordination instead of strength, and her expressionless gaze holds no meaning. The white and light blue of her figure – her blouse, her apron, her hand – overwhelm the letter she holds, which is also white, and which fades into insignificance. In fact, the flowers in her other hand attract more attention. The apron she wears ties her to home and domesticity, and is, in some ways, the most salient object in the image. Rilla appears to have little connection to the lovely landscape behind her – even her bouquet droops in her un-energetic hand. This cover, appearing at a time when feminism and freedom were once again on the rise, is a curious statement about women's role, not just in wartime, but any time. Although Rilla is outside, her apron places her inside a house; although surrounded by the beauty of the landscape, her shadow leads away from it. War has no place in this picture; it is lost in the image of Rilla taking a break from her usual domestic chores to perform another routine task: fetching the mail.

Although conflicts such as Vietnam, a contested war, continued to take place, by 1965 Canada's accepted military role was one of peace-keeping under the auspices of the United Nations.[74] Montgomery's authorial status, too, had changed: according to Carole Gerson, Montgomery's popular novels were "demoted by the rigorous mid-century modernists who ... attempted to purge the Canadian canon of writing they regarded as sentimental, popular, or feminine."[75] In libraries and bookstores, Montgomery's novels were, for the most part, relegated to the children's section.[76] The combination of the drive to peace and the narrowing of Montgomery's presumed audience led to reinforcing girls' and women's traditional gender roles without the context of war on the visual narratives of the covers. This trend ex-tended beyond North America: for instance, the 1962 Finnish cover comically depicts Rilla trying to wash her baby, a domestic role with no war in sight.[77]

By the 1980s and 1990s, war has been displaced by desire, glam-orized and dominant: on both a Spanish 1990s cover and the Cana-dian 1985 Seal Bantam paperback edition,[78] Rilla and Kenneth are shown as lovers in evening clothes, indistinguishable from the narra-tive depicted on any modern romance novel. Rilla now leans on a lover as the element that will lead modern-day readers into the text.

The year 2014 represented the hundredth anniversary of the open-ing of the First World War, with a rising academic and popular in-tensity in Canada and internationally focused on commemoration. In

2010, with the centenary approaching, the restored original text of
Rilla of Ingleside was republished, having been mostly unavailable in
North America for approximately forty years. This edition included
text that had been cut from the original 1921 edition, much of it from
the early chapters about the approach of war and the characters' responses to it. The cover (fig. 9.8) shows an inset portrait of a young
Rilla, plainly dressed, seated at a desk, reading or writing a letter, with
a pot of ink beside her.[79] Though the room itself is dark, the open
window lightens the scene, providing hope in a time of darkness. The
inset portrait is surrounded by handwriting; a careful examination
shows that it is a quotation taken from Montgomery's own words
about *Rilla of Ingleside*, which are also printed on the back cover. In
part, it reads: "In my latest story, 'Rilla of Ingleside,' I have tried, as
far as in me lies, to depict the fine and splendid way in which the girls
of Canada reacted to the Great War – their bravery, patience, and self-
sacrifice." Rilla does not hold her letter "pressed to her bosom," but
is actively reading it. It could be written to or from a brother or a
lover, but its purpose is to establish words as a strong connection between Rilla and those overseas, bringing the absent soldiers into her
world. Words become power, with Rilla an active writing participant,
as the inkpot beside her symbolizes. Montgomery's words about her
intentions for the book reinforce the power of writing and firmly place
Rilla in the context of war, as an active heroine who will cope with its
grief and its complex play of absence and presence.

During the centenary year itself, two publishing companies an-
nounced new editions of Montgomery's works, including *Rilla of Ingleside*: both demonstrate the continuation of limiting women's roles
in wartime but are also troublingly conjoined to the juvenilization of
war and of women in it. The cover of the British Virago Press edition
depicts a paradise of pastel colours, with Rilla gazing (as usual) into
the distance.[80] She is nestled into the landscape, which enfolds her – the
pink flowers around her, the tree branch in blossom above her – and this
beauty frames her even as she gazes towards a seemingly limitless hori-
zon. This cover shows Prince Edward Island as what Epperly calls "an
enchanted place." "Beauty and magic," as she observes about the physical beauty of the Island, "fairly leap from the sky and earth and sea."[81]

9.8
Cover, *Rilla of Ingleside*,
Viking Canada, 2010,
illustrated by Vince McIndoe.

We could say the same about a second cover, from Canadian publisher Tundra: another enchanted scene, which depicts a very young couple in a boat, surrounded by the natural beauty of sea and sky at night, with a glorious explosion of lights in the background signalling their rapture.[82] And yet, where is Montgomery's war? Virago actually kick-started the reclaiming of women's war writing in 1978, when it reprinted Vera Brittain's *Testament of Youth*, now considered a classic war text. Since that time, Virago has also made available many lost women's texts from the First World War. Why, then, is the war absent from its depiction of Rilla? And, charming as Tundra's cover is, Rilla has become cartoon-like, a modality that is furthest from realism. The covers of these latest versions will most definitely attract readers, yet they shield those potential buyers – probably children or young adults – from Montgomery's content and from the war itself.

The covers promise an Edenic paradise that utterly contradicts Montgomery's war-torn, complex, and troubling text.

In "Women and War," I wrote that, unlike many other women's texts from the First World War era, Montgomery's *Rilla* "does not need recovering; it has been with us, read, and in print since the War. Montgomery thus holds a unique place in women's war literature and in Canadian war literature: she is perhaps the only English-speaking woman and the only Canadian author, male or female, to have written a contemporary war book that has maintained its place in popular culture since the War. She has also given us a uniquely Canadian version of war myths, focused on women and community, in place of male-combatant, British-based myths."[83] But the depictions of Rilla, especially the ones published during the centenary of the opening shots of the First World War, demonstrate once again that a book that contributed to shaping Canada's "image" of the war has been demoted to the children's shelves of bookstores and libraries, with women demoted to unrealistic juvenile romantics. The war itself has been forgotten, its grief, its sacrifices, and its impact on the twentieth century obliterated.

What, then, do the covers show about the role of women in wartime, and of Montgomery's Rilla in particular? When war is present or immediately past, some artists and publishers do acknowledge its impact on national attitudes and cultures. For instance, the 1924 H&S cover speaks to Britain's sense of grief and loss; the 1947 Canadian edition echoes the Second World War's depiction of women as strong and resilient; and the 1947 Swedish cover, depicting Rilla in uniform gazing at the blood-red haze of war, salutes women's active role in recent Scandinavian wars. Yet these covers, tailored to local cultures and national attitudes, are rarities. For the most part, a century of images of Rilla demonstrates a remarkably uniform categorization of women in wartime as passive sweethearts who focus only on romance, coming wifehood, or potential motherhood. Rilla is rarely shown as active; she becomes, instead, a pretty and feminine object for us to contemplate. Not surprisingly, given the anxiety about women taking on non-traditional work and roles during wartime, such covers in immediate postwar periods emphasize a return to stability after the chaos of war. Unfortunately, they also erase the grief and suffering women underwent during the war years, as well as ignoring the expanded spheres of war work and other labour that women undertook in the absence of men.

Such a limited sense of women's roles in wartime is indeed troubling, especially given the complexity of Montgomery's war novel and her emphasis on an entire community caught up in the First World War. The women of the community do leave their homes and do take on new roles, especially Rilla, who hones her organizational abilities, develops maturity through grief, and expands her knowledge of the world and of humanity because of the war. What Montgomery's text shows us, and what the covers do not, is the transformation that war made in ordinary people's lives, women, men, and children alike: "all were [indeed] mobilized" and impacted.[84] To decontextualize Rilla from Montgomery's war is to limit all women caught up in similar conflicts, to downplay the depth of emotion that they experienced and the very real work they undertook.

Today, the world is still at war, with conflicts and terrorist attacks reported almost daily, and with refugees fleeing their destroyed or threatened homes, just as they did during the First World War. Montgomery's *Rilla* has much to teach us about the ambiguities, the heroism, and the ugliness common to any war: her work remains as relevant today as it was in 1921. The disturbing universality of the romanticized cover images across time shows the entrenchment of myths about women's limited roles in wartime and an equally disturbing reduction of Montgomery's text and heroine. Her novel contradicts male battle-based myths of war, giving us an alternative reading by showing us active women such as Rilla Blythe. Rilla, like most other women in the book, refuses to remain in the passive voice; she actively transforms her wartime world. Through Montgomery's *Rilla of Ingleside*, the women of the First World War generation not only speak and refuse to be silenced; they act upon their world, with power, intensity, and energy.

NOTES

1 Kress and van Leeuwen, *Reading Images*, 4.
2 For a more in-depth explanation of book covers, publishers, audiences, and visual theory, see McKenzie, "Writing in Pictures."
3 McKenzie, "Women at War," 327.
4 Vance, *Death So Noble*, 10.
5 Brittain, *Testament of Youth*. Virago's 1978 reprint led to a resurgence of interest in Brittain and her writings; *Testament of Youth* has not been out of print since then.
6 Higonnet, "All Quiet," 220–1.
7 Ibid.
8 Watson, *Fighting Different Wars*, 9–10.
9 M.L. Kirk, cover of *Rilla of Ingleside* by L.M. Montgomery (Toronto: McClelland & Stewart, 1921).
10 Vance, *Death So Noble*, 10.
11 McKenzie, "Women at War," 327–31.
12 Ibid., 338–45.
13 American Marie Louise Kirk illustrated the covers of more than fifty children's books, including the covers of Montgomery's *Anne's House of Dreams*, *Rainbow Valley*, *Rilla of Ingleside*, and the *Emily* trilogy. McKenzie, "Writing in Pictures," 113.
14 [A Captivating, Sunny Story], *New York Times Book Review and Magazine*, in Lefebvre, *Montgomery Reader* 3: 226. Noticeably, this review also observes that "the reader of either sex will love" *Rilla*.
15 The distinctive red maple leaf flag of Canada was adopted only in 1965, replacing the red ensign, which was the flag in Montgomery's day.
16 Vance studies "contemporaries' *sense* of the past," arguing that "Canadians remembered their first world war in terms that sometimes bore little resemblance to its actualities." *Death So Noble*, 4. His work focuses on how Canadians commemorated the war in the 1920s and 1930s. McKenzie examines Montgomery's feminizing of masculine war myths in "Women at War."
17 Cover of *Rilla of Ingleside* (London: Hodder & Stoughton, 1924).
18 Acton, "Writing and Waiting," 55.
19 Potter, *Boys in Khaki*, 91.
20 Ibid.; Hynes, *A War Imagined*, 12.
21 Ouditt, *Fighting Forces*, 89.

22 Edwards, "L.M. Montgomery's *Rilla*," 166.

23 Ibid.

24 Acton, *Grief in Wartime*, 18.

25 Potter, *Boys in Khaki*, 73.

26 Cover of *Rilla of Ingleside* (Toronto: McClelland & Stewart, 1947), Cavendish Library edition.

27 The Second World War's most famous woman's image is probably Rosie the Riveter, whose sexuality is only enhanced by her muscular arms and active stance in factory work. Dirt and grime are subsumed; lipstick and an attractive figure are gained through such active war work. Such outright sexuality was certainly more subdued in First World War images, replaced with the soldier's sweetheart, the romantic image depicted on numerous posters, postcards, and book covers, such as *Rilla of Ingleside*.

28 Cavendish Library edition of *Rilla*, inside jacket text.

29 Acton intersperses readings of magazine and other images in *Grief in Wartime*, as does Potter in *Boys in Khaki*. Becker's *Voir la Grande Guerre* examines the ways in which images, film, art, and objects depict the First World War during and afterwards. My PhD dissertation, "Witnesses to War," devotes a chapter to the gendered ways in which men and women were depicted in popular images.

30 E.J. Kealey, "Women of Britain Say 'GO!'" UK Parliamentary Recruiting Committee poster, May 1915.

31 Harry R. Hopps, "Destroy This Mad Brute: ENLIST," U.S. Army poster, ca. 1917.

32 Fred Spear, "Enlist," poster printed by Sackett & Wilhelms Corporation, New York, ca. 1915.

33 John Hassall, Belgian Canal Boat Fund poster, ca. 1915.

34 E. Henderson's poster, "Waste Not – Want Not. Prepare for Winter. Save Perishable Foods by Preserving *Now*," Canada Food Board (Ottawa), ca. 1917 depicts a white-haired woman showing a jar of canned goods to a younger woman in front of a table heaped with colourful produce and attractive-looking canned goods in glass jars. Older women's experience in the kitchen became valued as kitchen economy and preserving became valuable skills that contributed to the war effort.

35 Montgomery, *Rilla*, 63.

36 Ibid.

37 Ibid., 107.

38 Ibid., 156.

39 Jem and Jerry, for instance, learn this lesson after they arrive in the trenches.

40 Ibid., 160.

41 Ibid., 155.

42 Grayzel, *Women's Identities*, 2.

43 Cover of *Rilla of Ingleside* (New York: Grosset & Dunlap, 1938).

44 Rilla had just turned fifteen when the war began and was Canadian, not American.

45 Cover of *Rilla of Ingleside* (Sydney: Angus & Robertson, 1956).

46 Epperly, *Fragrance of Sweet-Grass*, 115.

47 Ibid.

48 Edwards and Litster, "End of Canadian Innocence," 32.

49 Acton, *Grief in Wartime*, 23, 38.

50 Montgomery, *Rilla*, 239.

51 Ibid., 121.

52 Ibid., 220.

53 Ibid., 242.

54 Ibid., 295.

55 Ibid., 128–9.

56 Tector, "A Righteous War," 75.

57 Montgomery, *Rilla*, 136, 244.

58 Grayzel, *Women's Identities*, 11.

59 Cover of *Rilla of Ingleside* (Australia: n.p., n.d.).

60 Cover of *Lilla Marilla* (Swedish) (N.p.: Gleerups, 1947).

61 M.L. Kirk's original cover also used red, but not the blood red of the 1947 cover. Kirk used flame red for Rilla's coat and the maple leaves on the trees and ground. Context creates meaning out of colour: on Kirk's cover, violence and threat are absent. On the Scandinavian cover, the soldier and Rilla's Red Cross brooch make war and wounds present.

62 For instance, see Frank Hurley's iconic photo, *The Shell Shattered Areas of Chateau Wood*, taken in 1917, available online from the State Library of New South Wales, at www.sl.nsw.gov.au.

63 Montgomery, *Blythes*, 509–10.

64 Interestingly, Rilla appears to contradict her attitude in the previous

book; Walter has told her, before enlisting, about his horror of killing other men, and has done so in graphic detail. In *The Blythes Are Quoted*, she appears to refute this knowledge.

65 Ibid., 477.

66 Ibid., 510.

67 Montgomery, *Rilla*, 62.

68 Potter, *Boys in Khaki*, 73.

69 Montgomery, *Rilla*, 325.

70 The threat of atomic war, mentioned on the jacket copy of the 1947 American edition, led to a backlash against war and conflict in the 1950s and 1960s. America's war in Vietnam in the 1960s and early 1970s, as is commonly known, was a contested war, openly and widely protested within and outside the United States.

71 Cover of *Rilla of Ingleside* (London: George G. Harrap, 1958).

72 James, introduction, 2–3.

73 Cover of *Rilla of Ingleside* (Toronto: McClelland & Stewart, 1973), Canadian Favourites edition.

74 Canada, "Permanent Mission of Canada to the United Nations," Date Modified 5 April 2011, http://www.canadainternational.gc.ca/prmny-mponu/canada_un-canada_onu/positions-orientations/peace-paix/peace-operations-paix.aspx?lang=eng.

75 Gerson, "*Anne of Green Gables* Goes to University," 18.

76 In my own hometown library in the mid-1970s, I originally discovered a few of Montgomery's novels in the adult fiction section, only to find the rest shelved in the children's section.

77 Maija Karma, cover of *Kotikunnaan Rilla* (Finnish) (Helsinki: WSOY, 1962).

78 Cover of *Rilla la de Ingleside* (Spanish) (n.p., Circulo de Lectores [Book Club edition], 1996); cover of *Rilla of Ingleside* (Toronto: Seal Bantam, 1985).

79 Cover of *Rilla of Ingleside* (Toronto: Viking Canada, 2010).

80 Cover of *Rilla of Ingleside* (London: Virago, 2014), Virago Modern Classics.

81 Epperly, *Fragrance of Sweet-Grass*, 31.

82 Elly MacKay, cover of *Rilla of Ingleside* (Toronto: Tundra, 2014).

83 McKenzie, "Women and War," 344.

84 Winter and Baggett, *The Great War*, 12.

CHAPTER 10

Emily's Quest: L.M. Montgomery's Green Alternative to Despair and War?

Elizabeth Epperly

What is *Emily's Quest* (1927) – the novel and the pursuit? Why did Montgomery leave out the First World War in the telling of Emily's story?[1] Is the apparently happy ending a farce;[2] a believable uniting of love, career, and equal partnership;[3] or is it what Elizabeth Waterston calls an "ambiguous epilogue," readable as both young love's dream and also "dark grey irony"?[4] Struggling with how ecocritical and neuroscientific theories affect my understanding of Montgomery's complex conceptions of nature and human perception, I now read this seeming ambiguity as the novel's point and a triumph for Montgomery the writer as well as for Emily the character. To be faithful to her own code of providing a happy ending and at the same time to be believably truthful about a writer's challenge to withstand despair, Montgomery may leave out the war, but she does not leave out suffering and grief. In her own life, she could not erase little Hugh's death or Frede's, her husband's mental illness, or the war, but she could put them into her house of life in such a way that they could be preserved in relationship with the healing land. Owning the Disappointed House, metaphorically, is vital.

The Disappointed House features throughout the Emily trilogy, a series long considered autobiographical in many of its details depicting a talented female's abiding passions for home and writing. In the first two books, *Emily of New Moon* (1923) and *Emily Climbs* (1925), when Emily is a child and adolescent, the nearby unfinished Clifford house – unfinished because the bride for whom it was being built jilted the groom before the house was completed – is charmingly mysterious.

It is a place that calls especially to Emily's imagination and sense of story (she names it), sensitive as she is to every natural setting and to the personalities of all houses and rooms. The Disappointed House even provides a place for hopeful young writer Emily and budding artist Teddy to dream about their possible future life together, when they will buy and finish the Clifford house and fulfil its dreams as well. In the third Emily book, when writer Emily is an adult and is questioning the importance of writing in relation to the rest of her life, the Disappointed House and its setting take on a distinctly darker metaphorical role. *Emily's Quest* is Montgomery's only sustained portrait of an adult full-time writer, and its concerns and narrative strategies invite comparison with the personal preoccupations and choices Montgomery, as a woman writer, may have faced. Choosing to leave out the war in the telling of Emily's story, Montgomery concentrates instead on what the writer can do with (other) apparently irremediable loss.

I suggest *Emily's Quest* is Montgomery's literary manifesto, and key to *it* is the Disappointed House. Dwelling with the Disappointed House affirms and enacts Montgomery's and Emily's articulated experience of nature as home. From my perspective, Montgomery's manifesto is conveyed through densely patterned, multi-sensory descriptions of "dwelling," an ecopoetic concept I adapt from Jonathan Bate.

"Dwelling" is a process and a state of being as well as a place; in Montgomery it involves a "union of the senses" and a "sense of union," phrases commonly used to describe synaesthesia, the involuntary multi-modal response to experience.[5] In 2009, I suggested that Montgomery may have been synaesthetic, enjoying heightened responses to several senses and possibly experiencing them simultaneously through sight. Her response to colour, in particular, seems to have registered on more than one sense simultaneously. Whether or not she was herself synaesthetic, she created images that enable readers to experience, through metaphor, colours, shapes, textures, tastes, fragrances, movement, and space.[6] All three *Emily* books – like all Montgomery's books and yet differently – are filled with passionate nature descriptions that rely on synaesthetic metaphor. In "Embodied Landscape Aesthetics in *Anne of Green Gables*," Irene Gammel says

Montgomery's is an "embodied landscape aesthetic in which experiencing nature is not about simply looking at nature with distanced aesthetic appreciation; rather, it is an invitation to let go and become involved in an ecological relationship that is aesthetic, dynamic, and multi-sensuous."[7] I could not agree more. Gammel goes on to say that central to her essay is her focus on "the subject's *engagement* of and *immersive* involvement in nature."[8] I think these concepts of "engagement" and "immersive involvement" are exactly the point; in fact, I think it is impossible to appreciate what Montgomery is saying about life and writing, particularly in the *Emily* books so explicitly about writing, if we do not also take up these processes of engagement and immersion. Unlike Gammel, I find Montgomery's quality of engagement and immersion firmly rooted in a Romanticism Jonathan Bate has helped me to understand differently.

In *The Song of the Earth*, like his earlier *Romantic Ecology*, Bate establishes the importance of reading the poetry of the Romantics, and Wordsworth in particular, in terms of environmental engagement and mutual interaction. He explains that, as the two roots of the word suggest – *oikos*, meaning "dwelling" and *poesis*, meaning "making" – the term *ecopoesis* describes a poetry that unifies the human and the earthly, the making of poetic space for dwelling that embodies, as Rilke says, "a purely earthly, deeply earthly, blissfully earthly consciousness."[9] Ecopoesis is diametrically opposed to the picturesque, to any suggested Cartesian separation between mind and body, a split that presupposes a division between human life and non-human life. Bate puts this succinctly: "Where the picturesque looks, the ecopoetic connects."[10] The mind/body split is not only a mistake and a limiting of human potential, but it has dire consequences for the environment. A mind/body split, dualism, encourages feelings of and expectations for dominance and mastery rather than partnership. The kind of conscious communing Wordsworth depicts and Bate describes is akin to the "partnership model" for the balancing of powers in gender relations that Riane Eisler outlined in the 1980s and upon which Carolyn Merchant has built a "partnership ethic" concerning human responsibility and the environment.[11] Montgomery anticipates these more recent theoretical developments by showing synaesthetic nature descriptions as mirroring the growing consciousness of a woman who also writes.

The ecopoetic offers readers a way to enter directly into a connection with nature and be reminded of their connection. Dwelling becomes home, and dwelling encourages the recognition of other homes. Interestingly, Bate uses Wordsworth's "Tintern Abbey" as a primary example of ecopoesis; in it, he says Wordsworth is not providing a "*view* in the manner of the picturesque, but an exploration of the inter-relatedness of perception and creation, a meditation on the *networks* which link mental and environmental space."[12] "Tintern Abbey" is particularly appropriate for a reading of Montgomery's literary manifesto.

In the poem, Wordsworth describes himself five years before, when he first visited the Wye River Valley and experienced the "aching joys" and "dizzy raptures" that belong to unconscious seeing. This is a perfect description of the responses of the child Emily and to some extent those of the adolescent in high school. Consciousness of suffering and "[t]he still, sad music of humanity" alter the "dizzy rapture" and "appetite"; in their place, "I have felt / A presence ..."

> Whose dwelling is the light of setting suns,
> And the round ocean, and the living air,
> And the blue sky, and in the mind of man,
> A motion and a spirit, that impels
> All thinking things, all objects of all thought,
> And rolls through all things.[13]

The line from "Tintern Abbey" that Montgomery quotes in *Emily's Quest* comes a little later in the poem, when Wordsworth addresses his sister Dorothy. He prays that when his sister has outgrown the "wild ecstasies" akin to his "dizzy rapture," when her mind has "matured / Into a sober pleasure," that it will be "a mansion for all lovely forms, / Thy memory be as a dwelling-place / For all sweet sounds and harmonies."[14] He knows this dwelling is possible for her because "Nature never did betray / The heart that loved her."[15] In other words, "Tintern Abbey" describes the blessing of experiencing consciously the powerful positive connection and interaction between human being and environment.

Montgomery has Emily quote Wordsworth's line at a crucial place in her life of writing and self-understanding. Emily has recovered from the grief of breaking off with Dean, Teddy has come and gone again – apparently without giving Emily any sign of his love – and Emily has written her new novel, *The Moral of the Rose,* and it has been rejected several times. The diary entries chronicling this part of Emily's life are right out of Montgomery's Cavendish journals, with alternating nature rhapsodies and white nights of doubt.[16] Emily is confused about where her life is going, and even though she can still experience the "flash" – her moment of "supernal" knowing – and between times she can experience connections with beauty, she is starting to wonder if she can will herself to optimism. Emily walks out in April, and sea, hills, and trees call to her as their sister: "Looking at them the flash came – my old supernal moment that has come so sadly seldom these past dreary months ... But at least it came to me this morning and I felt my immortality. After all, freedom is a matter of the soul. 'Nature never did betray the heart that loved her.' She has always a gift of healing for us if we come humbly to her."[17]

In May, Emily turns twenty-four and finds out that her *Moral of the Rose* has been accepted for publication. In July, Teddy comes home. When he whistles, she does not go to him, but rather sits so that he can see her not coming, and thus satisfies her vanity and pride. Has she learned nature's lessons humbly, as she somewhat proudly claimed to her journal? She has not. She is not yet the mature woman she will be by the end of the book. Emily may have reached a peak along the Alpine Path as a writer, but as a woman, as a human being, she is on a plateau. Why does Emily not go to Teddy? She has just read the letter she wrote at fourteen to herself at twenty-four, and she has been dismayed – stung – to find in that letter Teddy and the Disappointed House so confidently featured. Angrily, stubbornly, she thinks she can do well without Teddy, without love, and she resists the call she said she would always answer. Emily has not yet experienced the suffering she must undergo to appreciate all that the Disappointed House means metaphorically in her life as writer and woman. To dwell apart, in mistaken pride, is a sure way to thwart nature's lessons of interdependence and connection. It is also a sure way for a writer to lose connection with the pulsing tides of nature that sustain art and life.

Immersion, engagement, embodiment: Emily disconnects from an embodied rapture and dismay when she chooses pride over Teddy.

Montgomery is not punishing Emily with the long years of unneces-
sary separation from Teddy, nor is she merely delaying their getting together. Instead, I suggest she is showing how even beauty, even for the
artist, cannot supply what is human and must be satisfied. Emily's lesson is echoed in Emerson's "random word" she thinks she is pursuing. Emerson and Montgomery have a different lesson to give Emily
the artist, the woman, the human being, who is choosing her dwelling.

In the years after Teddy's aborted wedding to Ilse, Emily is the
artist she thought she had wanted to be – not the author of *A Seller
of Dreams*, perhaps, but a famous, successful author, as was Montgomery after *Anne of Green Gables*. And she keeps writing, despite
loneliness and terrible "white nights" when she wonders why she ever
thought she could write or make a difference. Isolated, mostly by
choice, she writes and she turns to nature, as she has done all her life.
But something has changed.

> Alone? Ay, that was it. Always alone. Love – friendship gone for-
> ever. Nothing left but ambition. Emily settled herself resolutely
> down to work. Life ran again in its old accustomed grooves. Year
> after year the seasons walked by her door. Violet-sprinkled val-
> leys of spring – blossom-script of summer – minstrel-firs of au-
> tumn – pale fires of the Milky Way on winter nights – soft,
> new-mooned skies of April – gnomish beauty of dark Lom-
> bardies against a moonrise – deep of sea calling to deep of wind
> – lonely yellow leaves falling in October dusks – woven moon-
> light in the orchard. Oh, there was beauty in life still – always
> would be. Immortal, indestructible beauty beyond all the stain
> and blur of mortal passion. She had some very glorious hours of
> inspiration and achievement. But mere beauty which had once
> satisfied her soul could not wholly satisfy it now.[18]

As so many of the descriptive passages about loneliness and beauty
from the adult Emily's journal are taken right out of Montgomery's
diaries when she was living alone with her grandmother in Cavendish,
this acknowledgment of incompletion seems especially poignant and
instructive. A quick reading of the passage suggests Emily is open to
beauty but is too weary and lonely to feel it really often, as she once

did. A closer reading suggests something else: Emily's interaction with beauty is no longer a sustained engagement that is sometimes lifted to rapture, but is instead a flat sameness visited occasionally by transport. The recurring of sudden rapture is not a life-sustaining engagement. A life-sustaining engagement involves a dailiness that will include pain and loneliness as well as rapture. I think the passage suggests it is a mistake to regard beauty as a concept separate from daily embodied experience. It is a mistake to reverence the abstract and supposedly immutable at the expense of our humanness. Nature, while "immortal, indestructible" apparently incorruptible by the "stain and blur of mortal passion," cannot be continuously, rapturously beautiful for a normal human being, no matter how sensitive. The passage shifts emphasis and meaning, away from the poetic phrases – that may be separate from Emily's actual feelings – and back to Emily's embodied experience. The words "immortal" and "indestructible" suggest superior to this world and separate from it; the world, on the other hand, sounds like a smudge; its very passion is "stain and blur." Significantly, in the next sentence, this seemingly lofty, unassailable beauty is characterized as "mere beauty" and cannot satisfy a human being needing passionate engagement. Emily's need makes her split herself between thinking and feeling, labelling what she sees as "immortal" and "indestructible" but feeling it as inadequate, "mere beauty."

Life, vital life, demands engagement even when passion seems to blur and stain. What does this need for human engagement say about Emily and about Montgomery's self-portrait of the artist as woman? As I read it, Emily needed the time after Teddy's departure to realize what art means in relation to human life. Elizabeth Barrett Browning said in *Aurora Leigh*, "Art is much, but Love is more."[19] Emerson suggests the poet's experience of love must encompass all of life's moods, not just rapture. Dean first quotes Emerson's lines from "The Poet" to Emily in the first chapter of *Emily Climbs*:

The gods talk in the breath of the world,
They talk in the shaken pine,
And they fill the reach of the old seashore

With dialogue divine;
And the poet who overhears
One random word they say
Is the fated man of men
Whom the ages must obey.[20]

Emily, like Montgomery, is a lover of words, and it is not surprising that the idea of some "random word" overheard from a "dialogue divine" would give her the "flash" or provide frequent inspiration. She longs to transcend her human limitations to be able to translate some divine word. But Emerson's seven-page poem is a warning to the poet, rather than just a description of his powers. The poem sounds at the outset like Montgomery's "Alpine Path," though this poet is a he. It opens with "Right upward on the road of fame / With sounding steps the poet came"; and it goes on to describe the poet's breadth of vision and his delight in sharing the glory of firmaments. The quotation Montgomery uses appears some seventy lines into the poem, at the opening of Part 2. As the poem proceeds, we find that the poet cannot sustain his high trance, but sits dejected, waiting for a divine spark to renew his rapture. He even despairs because he cannot sustain the power to relate what he can perceive. A chorus of spirits eventually tells him that since he, as a mere man, is not an angel, he cannot sustain rapture all the time. He must be ready for the "word" when it comes, but he cannot bid it or hold it or suspend his life in anticipating it. He must accept his humanness in order to live fitly and consciously in the times between raptures.

This, to me, seems the lesson Emily needed to learn before she could marry Teddy. This is the lesson Montgomery learned through the fire of her thirteen years of apprenticeship and service with her grandmother in Cavendish and, I think, wanted to embrace freshly after war, grief, and madness assault her house of life. She must engage with the dailiness of living, trusting to a larger, inclusive pattern where "Nature never did betray the heart that loved her."

Emily had thought she understood this all-inclusive pattern of nature earlier in the story, when she was rapturously happy with Teddy. She had broken the engagement with Dean and had recovered her will and power to work. In this heightened state, she thinks she sees life clearly – she even echoes the lesson of Emerson's poem: "Friendship – love – joy of sense and joy of spirit – sorrow – loveliness – achievement – failure – longing – all were part of life and therefore interesting and desirable."[21] But her rapture over Teddy is, I suggest, as self-deluding here concerning art as is the dejection without rapture later concerning love. In love with Teddy and feeling loved in turn, she pulses with life, recklessly devaluing the art that is also in her blood. She thinks, "What did one book more or less matter in this great universe of life and passion? How pale and shadowy was any pictured life beside this throbbing, scintillant existence!"[22] Emily the artist and woman spends the novel learning to love life passionately even between the raptures of love, nature, or art.

The first four chapters of *Emily's Quest* contain Montgomery's writing credo and reveal her practice. Montgomery establishes almost immediately how writing is in Emily's flesh and blood because Emily is connected so intimately with nature's tides and dwellings.

In the first chapter, Montgomery introduces or reintroduces a large network of images: the Alpine Path, houses as people, the difference between the poetry and prose of life, the pursuit of Emerson's "random word," adolescence as the "enchanted portal" to adulthood, Emily's garden as Emily herself, Emily as a "chaser of rainbows." Montgomery makes it unmistakably clear that Emily is a speaking expression of the very nature she seeks to describe. In describing the flush on Emily's cheek, for example, Montgomery unites girl, flower, and rapture: "Faint stains of rose in her rounded cheeks that sometimes suddenly deepened to crimson. Very little could bring that transforming flush – a wind off the sea, a sudden glimpse of blue upland, a flame-red poppy, white sails going out of the harbour in the magic of morning, gulf-waters silver under the moon, a Wedgewood-blue columbine in the old orchard. Or a certain whistle in Lofty John's bush."[23] Emily blushes at beauty and she blushes when Teddy whistles for her. She is nature and feeling and thought incarnate: "She had the grace of running water. Something, too, of its sparkle and limpidity. A thought swayed her like a strong wind. An emotion shook her as a tempest shakes a rose."[24] And as though the text is not already loaded with emblems, Montgomery adds the rainbow. The narrator creates a new story from Emily's past: Emily the child started out one day in Maywood to see the "rainbow's end. Over long wet fields and hills she ran, hopeful, expectant. But as she ran the wonderful arch was faded – was dim – was gone. Emily was alone in an alien valley, not too sure in which direction lay home. For a moment her lips quivered, her eyes filled. Then she lifted her face and smiled gallantly at the empty sky. 'There will be other rainbows,' she said. Emily was a chaser of rainbows."[25]

What a perfect image for Emily, the writer – evanescent, iridescent, with archetypal, mythological, biblical, architectural, and scientific resonances. In *Emily's Quest* the rainbow is also used to link Emily and Teddy: "There was more of the rainbow-seeker in Teddy Kent, of the Tansy Patch ... He, too, knew – had known for years – the delight and allurement and despair and anguish of the rainbow quest."[26] This "rainbow quest" becomes almost immediately "rainbow gold" – the search not just for rainbows or even their ends but for the pot of gold at that end. When Teddy confides in Emily that he thinks Ilse believes Perry is more likely than Teddy to "bring home the bacon," Emily spins the suggested inadequacy into an artist's wealth: "But you are not going after bacon. You're going after rainbow gold."[27] Dean's unsuitability as Emily's partner should be very clear from Dean's inability to understand rainbow chasing. Instead he admonishes her not "to waste your best years yearning for the unattainable or striving to reach some height far beyond your grasp."[28] I cannot help but think of war and *Rainbow Valley* and the shattering loss involved in chivalric rainbow quest.

Also in the first four chapters is Mr Carpenter's death scene. It is vintage Montgomery, with its richly layered, multisensory images and analogies. He is a shrewd critic of literature and people, and he voices Montgomery's own defiance of the kind of modernism she did not endorse: "Live under your own hat. Don't be – led away – by those howls about realism. Remember – pine woods are just as real as – pigsties – and a darn sight pleasanter to be in."[29] As Ben Lefebvre has discussed concerning *A Tangled Web,* and as others point out in this volume, Montgomery is not saying she doesn't endorse realism of every kind, just not realism that insists on ugliness as the only view.[30] Mr Carpenter is a complex character whose insights are to be trusted.

He is broken, regarded by many as a failure and regarding himself as one. Yet his passion to detect the "random word" from a "dialogue divine" and his endorsement of Emily as one who experiences that "random word" mark him as emblematic of another kind of lesson. In *Emily's Quest*, careful patterning, I think, invites us to see Mr Carpenter broken *not* by failure but by his own inability to withstand his failures, like Emerson's "The Poet." Montgomery prepares the death scene so that we are immersed in and engaged with Emily and Mr Carpenter as they live out the inexorable laws of nature – Emily to embody experience and write and Mr Carpenter to critique Emily's writing and to obey nature's tides.

The paragraph describing Emily's vigil with Mr Carpenter contains in miniature the patterns of the book. In this synaesthetic imaging, Montgomery engages an understanding of a woman writer writing about perceiving:

> Mr. Carpenter closed his eyes and relapsed into silence. Emily sat quietly, her head a soft blur of darkness against the window that was beginning to whiten with dawn. The ghostly hands of a fitful wind played with her hair. The perfume of June lilies stole in from the bed under the open window – a haunting odour, sweeter than music, like all the lost perfumes of old, unutterably dear years. Far off, two beautiful, slender, black firs, of exactly the same height, came out against the silver dawn-lit sky like the twin spires of some Gothic cathedral rising out of a bank of silver mist. Just between them hung a dim old moon, as beautiful as the evening crescent. Their beauty was a comfort and stimulant to Emily under the stress of this strange vigil. Whatever passed – whatever came – beauty like this was eternal.[31]

From the outside, as with a picture, the passage provides a view – of Mr Carpenter lying silently and of young Emily, still close to the dawn of her life, pictured with a halo of light against the dawn sky. We also see and experience haptically two black firs of exactly the same height. These twin spires (the twinning itself is evocative) may suggest a Gothic cathedral, but not a traditional stationary one, not a fixed form so much as an emergence "rising out of a bank of silver mist." The use of the word *Gothic* is packed with associations; in addition to the spiritual and architectural, "Gothic" is connected to the "ghostly hands" and "fitful" wind on its own errands but taking the time to caress a familiar figure. The June-lily perfume has a touch of the Gothic, too – perhaps even suggesting Easter and resurrection as well as pagan rites of renewal, while also connecting what is "haunting" – "sweeter than music" – and full of memories of "old, unutterably dear years."[32] Have we shifted to nature's perspective or Mr Carpenter's or the narrator's in this almost painful yearning for old years and old sweetness – tasted not spoken, felt, more potent than the sound of music? Significantly, "a dim old moon" worn out like Mr Carpenter himself, appears in this setting as beautiful "as the evening crescent" – Emily's slender crescent of a new moon, but in reverse. Young and old, student and teacher, mystic and sage. The images unite the senses, fusing young life and old in a nature that can haunt, steal into a window, rise eerily majestic from silver mists and play fragrance as music on the body. And finally a voice that affirms immortality – not of Mr Carpenter nor of Emily but of what they experience and share: "Whatever passed – whatever came – beauty like this was eternal." Montgomery sounds the key notes of her manifesto, her determination to heal and to inspire with her pen. She is also creating an ecopoetic green space where the reader may engage directly with nature, where feeling and thought are as one.

Mr Carpenter haltingly welcomes death in the language of poetry and nature; he says: "Going out – beyond the dawn. Past the morning star."[33] Echoing the architectural metaphor of the spires, sensing the turn of the tide, he welcomes death by calling out: "'Open the door – open the door. Death must not be kept waiting.' Emily ran to the little door and set it wide. A strong wind of the grey sea rushed in." He remembers what he wanted to say to Emily about her "italics" and dies "with a little impish chuckle." The immediate scene closes, not with poetry, but with the comic misunderstanding and cliché of Aunt Louisa, telling people "Graceless old Mr. Carpenter had died laughing – saying something about Italians."[34] The larger scene again echoes the architectural. The narrator says Mr Carpenter's death ages Emily, matures her so that "she left 'some low-vaulted past' and emerged into some 'new temple' of the soul more spacious than all that had gone before."[35] In the Romantic imagery of "Tintern Abbey" Emily's mind has become "a mansion," a "dwelling-place / For all sweet sounds and harmonies."[36] Readers are invited to dwell with Emily.

In Montgomery novels, land and dwelling commune, and their communion becomes a place we may enter directly. This communion, like Bate's ecopoetic green space, involves a direct apprehension of several levels of understanding and feeling simultaneously. We are immersed, and we engage.[37] From her own reading, Montgomery was well schooled in the literary practice of investing the house with meaning, and her journals as well as photographs are full of personal comments about domestic interiors and exteriors. Her poetics naturally involve houses and homes that resonate purposefully in the text.

The Disappointed House unites the Gothic and the everyday. The house mysteriously calls to Emily from the first, and it evidently called to Dean, himself a would-be Rochester from *Jane Eyre*.[38] The Gothic, a dark strand of Romanticism, is deliberately woven into the *Emily* novels, marking the sharp difference between the original *Anne* books and the *Emily* series.[39] It is not just that Montgomery's vision is darker after the First World War; this darker Gothic quality is also influenced, as Kate Lawson explains, by the deep reading Montgomery was doing in psychology. Perhaps because she hoped to understand Ewan's apparently sudden mental breakdown and because she hoped to be able to contact Frede Campbell after Frede's death, Montgomery was reading about the subliminal and the unconscious and abnormal psychology.[40] Lawson reminds us that just after Montgomery got the call from Montreal that Frede was ill with flu, Montgomery had what she later realized was a prophetic dream: "I had arrived home. In my absence workmen seemed to have torn the whole inside of my house to pieces ... I felt broken-hearted ... My own room had narrowed down to a mere closet."[41] Montgomery knew her "house of life" had been gutted by Frede's death.[42]

Emily claimed the Disappointed House as her own when she was eleven: "Why had it never been finished? And it was meant to be such a pretty little house – a house you could love – a house where there would be nice chairs and cozy fires and bookcases and lovely, fat purry cats and unexpected corners; then and there she named it the Disappointed House."[43] On the first evening Emily and Dean look at the house together, Montgomery's description of its setting makes the house seem complete, as desirable as any "rainbow gold": "there was a sloping field before them, dotted with little, pointed firs, windy, grassy, lovable. And on top of it, surrounded by hill glamour and upland wizardry, with great sunset clouds heaped up over it, the house – *their* house. A house with the mystery of woods behind it and around it, except on the south side where the land fell away in a long hill looking down on the Blair Water, that was like a bowl of dull gold now, and across it to meadows of starry rest beyond."[44] And just a few paragraphs later, Emily "looked at the Disappointed House adoringly. Such a dear *thoughtful* little house … This house was ignorant and innocent like herself. Longing for happiness. It should have it. She and Dean would drive out the ghosts of things that never happened."[45] In my opinion, Emily is trying to make the Disappointed House something it is not. She and Dean would never be able to "drive out the ghosts" because those ghosts are also Emily. The ghosts, the secrets, of this house are also its life and its gift of life-giving. The ghosts in the Disappointed House suggest a Gothic eeriness also connected to Emily's psychic experiences – the power of the subliminal or unconscious mind that cannot be known or fully explained but must have its acknowledged place in any account of an artist's dwelling. The ghosts of things that never happened are compounded in the Disappointed House with Emily's fears and Dean's desires and jealousies.

The pattern of images reflects Emily's will and her secrets in conflict. Even apparent content registers disquiet: "Sometimes they sat on their sandstone steps listening to the melancholy loveliness of night-wind on the sea and watching the twilight creep up from the old valley and the shadows waver and flicker under the fir-trees and the Blair Water turning to a great grey pool tremulous with early stars."[46] The multisensory invitation here – sound and feel of the wind, movement of the twilight shadows, sight of the grey water reflecting stars – seems concentrated in "tremulous," a vivid, odd, apt word, I think, to suggest Emily's disturbance. The stars' light broken on the rippled surface of the water is not glimmering or sparkling – it is "tremulous," suggesting a quivering with what? Expectancy? Desire? The melancholy of the wind and the stealth of the shadows suggest fear. All the descriptions of place and dwelling are carefully loaded with evocative meaning. Nothing is exactly what it seems when Emily does not know herself.

After Emily breaks with Dean, he says, "Houses, like people, can't escape their doom, it seems."[47] Exactly. Emily tries to avoid looking at the Disappointed House: "I never go where I can see it. But I *do* see it for all that. Waiting there on its hill – waiting – dumb – blind."[48] Emily's faith in life is shaken even though the flash comes back to her. She says, "My dear little house! And it is never to be a home. I feel as I felt that evening years ago when I followed the rainbow and lost it. 'There will be other rainbows' I said then. But will there?"[49] Emily relearns there will always be other rainbows, and she comes to accept that they will always be the same – impossibly, disappointingly, intriguingly elusive. I assume that is what being a writer, a painter, a completely fulfilled human being with a perfectly complementary partner, an equal, means. The ideal is not achievable, but the pursuit of it is. The pilgrimage, the journey, matters. Ironically, Emily achieves the artistically necessary patience and understanding of life between raptures when she gives up on sharing Teddy's love and imagines herself a beneficent spirit and a ghost. Mrs Kent writes to tell her that she is dying and she asks Emily to tell Teddy, when she is dead, how she had steamed open and burned Teddy's proposal to Emily. Emily thinks it is too late to do that and imagines instead he can feel her as an "invisible benediction" "guarding him from ill."[50] Soon after, she hears the Disappointed House is going to be sold, and she who has avoided looking at it, now goes to visit it. Significantly, she does not turn away from its chill and disorder, its "rank weeds crowding around the long-unopened door." Instead "Emily stretched out her arms as if she wanted to put them around the house."[51]

The connection with nature, and the home for the imagination, is with nature in all its forms and moods, through seasons and losses and gains. The poet must learn to live completely, and not just when there is rapture. Without full immersion in and engagement with anguish and blank as well as joy, the writer is one who experiences only an idea of life. I think because Emily learns to embrace her Disappointed House, she can be a writer and be fully human; because she is fully human and an artist, she can live with her Disappointed House. Love, Montgomery's novel suggests, is embodied engagement of the deepest and most expansive kind. Montgomery is declaring in the most honest, powerful way possible, I think, that she as a writer had to come to terms with her house of loss and grief, and she did, over and over in her writing, "year after year" recognizing that the poetry of life is impossible to sustain or perceive all the time but that what matters is how she as artist, as woman, as human being, lives between those moments of creative rapture, keeping herself capable of them.

While it is certainly possible to read the ending of *Emily's Quest* as ambiguous, I think it may be even more helpful to read it as paradoxical. The ending is happy because it cannot possibly be an ending nor can it be happy. As I see it, *Emily's Quest* is about process, not arrival. Montgomery the writer believed in giving her readers happy endings; Montgomery the writer writing honestly about a writer, has been careful to suggest throughout that Emily's happiness depends on continuing engagement with a process, not sudden arrival at a state of being or place. A rainbow chaser must negotiate despair and dejection as natural, inevitable parts of chasing. For Emily to be happy at the end of the story, her happiness must contain unhappiness. Like Montgomery, Emily has had to learn that rapture – of whatever kind – is not enough to sustain life, but passionate engagement with nature in all its forms can be a practice and a dwelling. Montgomery promotes the immersion in place, the felt sense of engagement, because in her imagined, written world there is no damaging Cartesian dualism, no limiting mind/body split; we are invited to be one with the text and one with our world as this one. The Disappointed House is the part of all of us that must hold grief and pain; reading Montgomery may help us dwell with grief and pain differently.

Montgomery chose to leave the First World War out of Emily's story, and she focused instead on addressing our consuming human struggle with meaning and despair. Her descriptions are meant to engage readers in perceiving what writing also engaged her in creating:

that imaginative power builds through a connecting that is inspiringly accessible and always in process. We are not meant to hold rainbow gold, but to perceive and to pursue it, knowing disappointments always to be part of any meaningful dwelling.

NOTES

1 Montgomery gestures to the First World War in the opening sentence of *Emily Climbs*: "Emily Byrd Starr was alone in her room, in the old New Moon farmhouse at Blair Water, one stormy night in a February of the olden years before the world turned upside down" (9). Halfway through the book, she provides an actual date. Mrs MacIntyre identifies the year as 1903, two years after Queen Victoria's death; Emily is fifteen. The war is only eleven years away, and the novel goes "year after year" beyond Emily's twenty-fourth birthday. Featuring motorcars and flapper styles, the story seems to have leapt over the war and into the time of *The Blue Castle*. One could argue that the chronology of a fiction is flexible, and it clearly is, but that does not change the fact that Montgomery chose not to deal with war directly in the third *Emily* book.

2 See Rubio, "Subverting the Trite," and Campbell, "Wedding Bells and Death Knells."

3 Epperly, *Fragrance of Sweet-Grass*, 182–207; see Thompson, "That House Belongs to Me."

4 Waterston, *Magic Island*, 150.

5 This is the definition most commonly given to *synaesthesia* and was the subject of my paper in 2009 in Sweden, "L.M. Montgomery and the Colour of Home." See especially Cytowic, *The Man Who Tasted Shapes*; Cytowic and Eagleman, *Wednesday Is Indigo Blue*; Rich, "A Union of the Senses"; and Rich et al., "Neural Correlates."

6 In the 2009 paper, I explained, "I suspect that the visually gifted L.M. Montgomery may have been synaesthetic. I suspect she may have experienced colours and shapes not only in exquisite visual detail but also exquisitely through other senses, immeasurably enriching the imagery she created. Whether or not she was synaesthetic, I think Montgomery encourages a metaphorically synaesthetic reading of *Anne of*

Green Gables and later books. Visually, haptically, gustatorily, and aurally keenly aware, she created images that invite readers to experience a 'union of the senses' and 'a sense of union,' phrases used to describe synaesthesia. Experiencing the colours, shapes, textures, tastes, sounds, and fragrances all at once in the text is the metaphoric equivalent of the synaesthete's involuntary multi-modal responses to experience."

7 Gammel, "Embodied Landscape Aesthetic," 228.

8 Ibid., 232.

9 Bate, *Romantic Ecology*; Bate, *Song of the Earth*, 263, quotes from Rilke's *Letters of Rainer Maria Rilke*.

10 Bate, *Song of the Earth*, 145.

11 I referred to Riane Eisler's "partnership model" in *Fragrance of Sweet-Grass* (183) concerning Teddy. In *Reinventing Eden*, Merchant says, "A partnership ethic holds that the greatest good for the human and nonhuman communities is in their mutual living interdependence," 191.

12 Bate, *Song of the Earth*, 148.

13 Wordsworth, "Tintern Abbey," lines 94–103.

14 Ibid., lines 141–3.

15 Ibid., lines 123–4.

16 See, for example, Montgomery, *CJ* 2: 206–8, 3, 13, and 20 December 1908, which also include the quotation from Wordsworth.

17 Montgomery, *Emily's Quest*, 165.

18 Ibid., 228.

19 Browning, *Aurora Leigh*, book 9, line 656. For the importance of *Aurora Leigh* in *Emily's Quest*, see Epperly, *Fragrance of Sweet-Grass*, 191–6.

20 Montgomery, *Emily Climbs*, 17–18.

21 Montgomery, *Emily's Quest*, 115.

22 Ibid.

23 Ibid., 11.

24 Ibid.

25 Ibid., 11–12.

26 Ibid., 13.

27 Ibid., 14.

28 Ibid., 37.

29 Ibid., 24.

30 Lefebvre, "Pigsties and Sunsets."

31 Montgomery, *Emily's Quest*, 28.

32 I am grateful to Moira Devereaux, with whom I discussed this passage in March 2014. She said, "You've just described Easter – the resurrection – and the Christian idea of life eternal: halo, dawn, lilies, cathedral spires." She added, "There is something not Christian about it, too, as though Montgomery is also talking about the pagan celebration of the renewal of life on which the Christian one was modelled."

33 Montgomery, *Emily's Quest*, 29.

34 Ibid., 31.

35 Ibid.

36 Wordsworth, "Tintern Abbey," lines 141–3.

37 Drawing from Bachelard and Heidegger (as does Bate), Francesca Saggini and Anna Enrichetta Soccio declare that their edited collection is designed to investigate a long history of research into "issues related to the house and home imagery, examining its domestic dimension and the mental structures it invokes, as well as its potential to articulate spatially a writer's poetics and, more at large, the contemporaneous view of the world which [the writer] represents." "Introduction: The Paper Houses of English Literature," 1.

38 Epperly, *Fragrance of Sweet-Grass*, 163–4.

39 For an excellent discussion, see Miller, "Haunted Heroines."

40 Lawson's analysis of the psychological theories Montgomery had read by F.W.H. Myers is fascinating and persuasive. See "The Alien at Home."

41 Ibid., 164; Montgomery's journal entry, *SJ* 2: 288.

42 While I agree with Lawson's reading, in "The Disappointed House," of the Disappointed House as a deliberate marker in the novel for Emily's and Montgomery's losses and psychological gaps, and I admire her interpretation of the uncanny and the disturbances registered in the third *Emily* book in particular, I do not share her view that the novel's ending offers too little too late.

43 Montgomery, *Emily's Quest*, 75.

44 Ibid., 78.
45 Ibid., 79.
46 Ibid., 87.
47 Ibid., 104.
48 Ibid., 107.
49 Ibid., 108.
50 Ibid., 230.
51 Ibid., 231.

Bibliography

Archives

Library and Archives Canada, Ottawa

"Soldiers of the First World War, 1914–1918." CEF Database

Public Archives and Record Office, Charlottetown, PE

Cornwall WI fonds, PARO ACC 4700
Ladies Auxiliary Records fonds, PARO ACC 2990
Maple Leaf WI Travellers Rest fonds, PARO ACC 4761
Meadowbank WI fonds, PARO ACC 3466/HF74.192
New Annan fonds, PARO ACC 3472
Red Point WI fonds, PARO ACC 4403
Royal Edward Chapter fonds, IODE, PARO ACC 3471

University of Guelph Archival and Special Collections, Guelph, ON

L.M. Montgomery Collection, XZ1 MS A1000002

University of Saskatchewan Archives, Saskatoon

A.F.L. Kenderdine Papers. MG 87, vol. 3 f. 10

Books and Articles

Abrams, Gary William David. *Prince Albert: The First Century, 1866–1966.*
Saskatoon: Modern Press, 1966.

Acton, Carol. "Diverting the Gaze: The Unseen Gaze in Women's War
Writing." *College Literature* 31, no. 2 (2004): 53–79.

– *Grief in Wartime: Private Pain, Public Discourse.* New York: Palgrave
Macmillan, 2007.

– "Writing and Waiting: The First World War Correspondence between
Vera Brittain and Roland Leighton." *Gender and History* 11, no. 1
(1999): 54–83.

Acton, Carol, and Jane Potter. "'These Frightful Sights Would Wreak
Havoc with One's Brain': Subjective Experience, Trauma, and Resilience
in First World War Writings by Medical Personnel." *Literature and
Medicine* 31, no. 1 (2012): 61–85.

Aitken, Max [Lord Beaverbrook]. *Canada in Flanders.* Vol. 2 of *The
Official Story of the Canadian Expeditionary Force.* London: Hodder &
Stoughton, 1916.

Akamatsu, Yoshiko. "The Continuous Popularity of Red-Haired Anne in
Japan." In Ledwell and Mitchell, *Anne around the World*, 216–27.

Arras, Lens-Douai and the Battles of Artois. Clermont-Ferrand: Michelin
& Cie, 1919.

Ashenburg, Katherine. "Why Literature Written Out of the First World
War Is Some of the Last Century's Finest Writing." *Globe and Mail*, 18
July 2014. http://www.theglobeandmail.com/arts/books-and-media/why-
literature-written-out-of-the-first-world-war-is-some-of-the-last-centurys-
finest-writing/article19674494/?page=all. Accessed 19 August 2016.

Askey, Jennifer. *Good Girls, Good Germans: Girls' Education and Emotional Nationalism in Whilhelminian Germany.* Rochester, NY: Camden
House, 2013.

Asper, Barbara, Hannelore Kempin, and Bettina Münchmeyer-Schöneberg.
Wiedersehen mit Nesthäkchen: Else Ury aus heutiger Sicht. Berlin: Text
Verlag, 2007.

Aytoun, William Edmonstoune. "Edinburgh after Flodden." In Barry,
Doody, and Doody, *The Annotated Anne of Green Gables*, 467–9.

Babbington, Thomas [Lord MacAulay]. "Horatius." In *Lyra Heroica: A*

Book of Verse for Boys, edited by William Ernest Henley, 179–99. 1925. Reprint, Freeport, NY: Books for Libraries Press, 1970.

Baetz, Joel. "Anna's Monuments: The Work of Mourning, the Gender of Melancholia, and Canadian Women's War Writing." In *Home Ground and Foreign Territory: Essays on Early Canadian Literature*, edited by Janice Fiamengo. Ottawa: University of Ottawa Press, 2014. Kindle edition.

Barry, Wendy E., Margaret Anne Doody, and Mary E. Doody, eds. *The Annotated Anne of Green Gables*. New York: Oxford University Press, 1997.

Basavarajappa, K.G., and Bali Ram. "Section A: Population and Migration." http://www.statcan.gc.ca/pub/11-516-x/pdf/5500092-eng.pdf.

Bate, Jonathan. *Romantic Ecology: Wordsworth and the Environmental Tradition*. London: Routledge, 1991.

– *The Song of the Earth*. Cambridge, MA: Harvard University Press, 2000.

Becker, Annette. *Voir la Grande Guerre: Un autre récit 1914–1919*. Paris: Armand Colin, 2014.

Bode, Rita, and Lesley D. Clement, eds. *L.M. Montgomery's Rainbow Valleys: The Ontario Years, 1911–1942*. Montreal: McGill-Queen's University Press, 2015.

Bolger, Francis W.P. *The Years before "Anne."* Halifax: Nimbus Publishing, 1991.

Bothwell, Robert, Ian Drummond, and John English. *Canada, 1900–1945*. Toronto: University of Toronto Press, 1987.

Braudy, Leo. *From Chivalry to Terrorism: War and the Changing Nature of Masculinity*. New York: Vintage, 2005.

Braybon, Gail, and Penny Summerfield. *Out of the Cage: Women's Experiences in Two World Wars*. New York: Pandora Press, 1987.

Brittain, Vera. *Chronicle of Youth*. Glasgow: Fontana/Collins, 1982.

– *Testament of Youth*. London: Gollancz, 1933.

Browning, Elizabeth Barrett. "Aurora Leigh." In *Aurora Leigh and Other Poems*, edited by John Robert Glorney Bolton and Julia Bolton Holloway, 1–308. Suffolk, UK: Penguin Books, 1995.

Bürgschwentner, Joachim, Matthias Egger, and Gunda Barth-Scalmani, eds. *Other Fronts, Other Wars? First World War Studies on the Eve of the Centennial*. Leiden, Boston: Brill, 2014.

Buss, Helen M. *Mapping Our Selves: Canadian Women's Autobiography in English*. Montreal: McGill-Queen's University Press, 1993.

Butler, Kate Macdonald. "The Heartbreaking Truth about Anne's Creator." *Globe and Mail* (Toronto), 20 September 2008, F1, F6.

Campbell, Marie. "Wedding Bells and Death Knells." In Rubio, *Harvesting Thistles*, 137–45.

Campbell, Thomas. "The Battle of Hohenlinden." In Barry, Doody, and Doody, *The Annotated Anne of Green Gables*, 467.

– "On the Downfall of Poland." In Barry, Doody, and Doody, *The Annotated Anne of Green Gables*, 471–2.

Canada. Census and Statistics Office, Department of Trade and Immigration. *Fifth Census of Canada, 1911*. Vols. 1 and 2. Ottawa: King's Printer, 1912.

Canadian War Museum. "Young Adults – Age 15 and Up: Fiction." http://www.warmuseum.ca/firstworldwar/ressources/book-list/young-adults-age-15-and-up-fiction/. Accessed 19 August 2016.

Cavert, Mary Beth. "If Our Women Fail in Courage, Will Our Men Be Fearless Still." *Shining Scroll, Part 1* (2014): 2–12.

– "'To the Memory Of': Leaskdale and Loss in the Great War." In Bode and Clement, *L.M. Montgomery's Rainbow Valleys*, 35–53.

CBC. "The Great Canadian War Novels Everyone Must Read." 25 June 2014. http://www.cbc.ca/books/canadawrites/2014/06/the-great-canadian-war-novels-everyone-should-read.html. Accessed 19 August 2016.

Ceraldi, Gabrielle. "Utopia Awry: L.M. Montgomery's Emily Series and the Aftermath of the Great War." In *Message in a Bottle: The Literature of Small Islands; Proceedings from an International Conference, Charlottetown, Prince Edward Island, Canada, June 28–30, 1998*, edited by Laurie Brinklow, Frank Ledwell, and Jane Ledwell, 247–63. Charlottetown, PE: Institute of Island Studies, 2000.

Clarke, Nic. "'You Will Not Be Going to This War': The Rejected Volunteers of the First Contingent of the Canadian Expeditionary Force." *First World War Studies* 1, no. 2 (2010): 161–83.

Coates, Donna. "The Best Soldiers of All: Unsung Heroines in Canadian Women's Great War Fictions." *Canadian Literature* 151 (1996): 66–99.

Cole, Sarah. "Enchantment, Disenchantment, War, Literature." *PMLA: Special Topic: War* 124, no. 5 (2009): 1632–47.

Collins, Carolyn Strom. "An Occasional Story or Bit of Verse: A Brief
   Analysis of L.M. Montgomery's Stories and Poems Published during the
   Great War." *Shining Scroll, Part 1* (2014): 13–21.
Collins, James. *Rural Schools in Canada: Their Organization, Administra-
   tion and Supervision.* New York: Columbia University Press, 1913.
Connor, Ralph. *The Major.* Toronto: McClelland, Goodchild & Stewart,
   1917.
– *The Sky Pilot in No Man's Land.* Toronto: McClelland and Stewart,
   1919.
Cook, Tim. "Documenting War and Forging Reputations: Sir Max Aitken
   and the Canadian War Records Office in the First World War." *War in
   History* 10, no. 3 (2003): 265–95.
Creighton, Donald. *Dominion of the North: A History of Canada.* Toronto:
   Macmillan of Canada, 1957.
Cytowic, Richard E. *The Man Who Tasted Shapes: A Bizarre Medical
   Mystery Offers Revolutionary Insights into Emotions, Reasoning and
   Consciousness.* New York: G.P. Putnam's, 1993.
Cytowic, Richard E., and David M. Eagleman. *Wednesday Is Indigo Blue:
   Discovering the Brain of Synesthesia.* Cambridge, MA: MIT Press, 2009.
Daley, Hartwell. *Volunteers in Action: The Prince Edward Island Division
   Canadian Red Cross Society, 1907–1979.* Summerside, PE: PEI Division,
   Canadian Red Cross Society, 1981.
Das, Santanu, ed. *Race, Empire, and First World War Writing.* Cambridge:
   Cambridge University Press, 2011.
Devereux, Cecily. "Writing with a 'Definite Purpose': L.M. Montgomery,
   Nellie L. McClung and the Politics of Imperial Motherhood in Fiction for
   Children." *Canadian Children's Literature / Littérature canadienne pour
   la jeunesse* 99, no. 26 (2000): 6–22.
Dewar, Katherine. *Those Splendid Girls: The Heroic Service of Prince
   Edward Island Nurses in the Great War, 1914–1918.* Charlottetown, PE:
   Island Studies Press, 2014.
Donson, Andrew. "Models for Young Nationalists and Militarists: German
   Youth Literature in the First World War." *German Studies Review* 27,
   no. 3 (2004): 579–98.
– *Youth in the Fatherless Land: War Pedagogy, Nationalism, and Authority
   in Germany, 1914–1918.* Cambridge, MA: Harvard University Press, 2010.

Doody, Margaret. "L.M. Montgomery and the Significance of 'Classics,' Ancient and Modern." In Ledwell and Mitchell, *Anne around the World*, 83–91.

Doyle, Lucy Swanton. "Canadian Women Help the Empire: 'What Could Women Do in Time of War?'" *Everywoman's World*, November 1914, 32.

Drummond, Julia. Foreword to *A Story of the Canadian Red Cross Information Bureau during the Great War*, by Iona K. Carr. Nabu Public Domain Reprints, circa 1923.

Duley, Margot I. "The Unquiet Knitters of Newfoundland: From Mothers of the Regiment to Mothers of the Nation." In Glassford and Shaw, *A Sisterhood of Suffering and Service*, 51–74.

Durkin, Douglas Leader. *The Fighting Men of Canada*. Toronto: McClelland, Goodchild & Stewart, 1918.

– *The Magpie*. Toronto: Hodder & Stoughton, 1923.

Dyer, Geoff. *The Missing of the Somme*. London: Penguin, 1995.

Edwards, Owen Dudley. "L.M. Montgomery's *Rilla of Ingleside*: Intention, Inclusion, Implosion." In Lefebvre, *The L.M. Montgomery Reader*, 2: 163–77.

Edwards, Owen Dudley, and Jennifer H. Litster. "The End of Canadian Innocence: L.M. Montgomery and the First World War." In Gammel and Epperly, *L.M. Montgomery and Canadian Culture*, 31–46.

Epperly, Elizabeth. "Chivalry and Romance: L.M. Montgomery's Re-vision of the Great War in *Rainbow Valley*." In *Myth and Milieu: Atlantic Literature and Culture, 1918–1939*, edited by Gwendolyn Davies, 87–94. Fredericton, NB: Acadiensis Press, 1993.

– Foreword to *The Blythes Are Quoted*, edited by Benjamin Lefebvre, ix–xiv. Toronto: Penguin Canada, 2009.

– *The Fragrance of Sweet-Grass: L.M. Montgomery's Heroines and the Pursuit of Romance*. 1993. Reprint, Toronto: University of Toronto Press, 2014.

– "L.M. Montgomery and the Colour of Home." Paper presented at conference L.M. Montgomery: Writer of the World, Uppsala University, Sweden, 20–23 August 2009.

Falla, Frederick G. "Dauntless Canadian Woman Tells of Grim Experience While Painting the Nightmare Land of the Somme." *McClure Newspaper Syndicate*, 10 September 1922.

Fell, Alison S., and Christine E. Hallett, eds. *First World War Nursing: New Perspectives*. New York: Routledge, 2013.

Ferguson, Felicity. "Making the Muscular Briton." *Children's Literature in Education* 37, no. 3 (2006): 253–65.

Fiamengo. Janice. "'... The Refuge of My Sick Spirit ...': L.M. Montgomery and the Shadows of Depression." In *The Intimate Life of L.M. Montgomery*, edited by Irene Gammel, 170–86. Toronto: University of Toronto Press, 2005.

Findley, Timothy. *The Wars*. Toronto: Clark & Irwin, 1977.

Fishbane, Melanie J. "'My Pen Shall Heal, Not Hurt': Writing as Therapy in *Rilla of Ingleside* and *The Blythes Are Quoted*." In Bode and Clement, *L.M. Montgomery's Rainbow Valleys*, 131–44.

Fisher, Susan. *Boys and Girls in No Man's Land: English Canadian Children and the First World War*. Toronto: University of Toronto Press, 2011.

– "Canada and the Great War." In *The Cambridge History of Canadian Literature*, edited by Coral Ann Howells and Eva-Marie Kröller, 224–43. Cambridge: Cambridge University Press, 2009.

Fox, Anne L. "Else Ury, a Life in Hitler's Time." Berlin.de. December 2007. http://www.berlin.de/aktuell/ausgaben/2007/dezember/beitraege/artikel.223595.php. Accessed 15 April 2015.

Fussell, Paul. *The Great War and Modern Memory*. London: Oxford University Press, 1975.

Gallagher, Maureen O. "Young Germans in the World: Race, Gender, and Imperialism in Wilhelmine Youth Literature, 1870–1918." PhD diss., University of Massachusetts, Amherst, 2015.

Gammel, Irene. "Embodied Landscape Aesthetics in *Anne of Green Gables*." *The Lion and the Unicorn* 34, no. 2 (2010): 228–47.

– "Staging Personalities in Modernism and Realism." *The Cambridge History of Canadian Literature,* edited by Coral Ann Howells and Eva-Marie Kroller, 247–71. Cambridge: Cambridge University Press, 2009.

– ed. *Making Avonlea: L.M. Montgomery and Popular Culture*. Toronto: University of Toronto Press, 2002.

Gammel, Irene, and Elizabeth Epperly, eds. *L.M. Montgomery and Canadian Culture*. Toronto: University of Toronto Press, 1999.

Gammel, Irene, Andrew O'Malley, Huifeng Hu, and Ranbir K. Banwait.

"An Enchanting Girl: International Portraits of Anne's Cultural Trans-
fer." In *Anne's World: A New Century of Anne of Green Gables*, edited
by Irene Gammel and Benjamin Lefebvre, 166–91. Toronto: University
of Toronto Press, 2010.
Garner, Barbara Carman. "A Century of Critical Reflection on Anne of
Green Gables." In Ledwell and Mitchell, *Anne around the World*, 63–79.
Garvin, John, ed. *Canadian Poems of the Great War*. Toronto: McClelland
and Stewart, 1918.
Gerson, Carole. "*Anne of Green Gables* Goes to University." In Gammel,
Making Avonlea, 17–31.
– "'Dragged at Anne's Chariot Wheels': The Triangle of Author, Publisher,
and Fictional Character." In Gammel and Epperly, *L.M. Montgomery
and Canadian Culture*, 49–63.
– "L.M. Montgomery and the Conflictedness of a Woman Writer." In
Mitchell, *Storm and Dissonance*, 67–80.
Glassford, Sarah. "Bearing the Burdens of Their Elders: English-Canadian
Children's First World War Red Cross Work and Its Legacies." *Études
canadiennes / Canadian Studies* 80 (2016): 129–50.
– "'The Greatest Mother in the World': Carework and the Discourse of
Mothering in the Canadian Red Cross Society during the First World
War." *Journal of the Association for Research on Mothering* 10, no. 1
(2008): 219–32.
– "Marching as to War: The Canadian Red Cross Society, 1885–1939."
PhD diss., York University, 2007.
Glassford, Sarah, and Amy Shaw, eds. *A Sisterhood of Suffering and Serv-
ice: Women and Girls in Canada and Newfoundland during the First
World War*. Vancouver: UBC Press, 2012.
– "Introduction: Transformation in a Time of War." In Glassford and
Shaw, *A Sisterhood of Suffering and Service*, 1–23.
Gordon, Neta. *Catching the Torch: Contemporary Canadian Literary Re-
sponses to World War I*. Waterloo: Wilfrid Laurier University Press, 2014.
Grace, Sherrill. "The Great War and Contemporary Memory." In *Re-
Imagining the First World War: New Perspectives in Anglophone Litera-
ture and Culture*, edited by Anna Branach-Kallas and Nelly Strehlau,
2–23. Cambridge, UK: Cambridge Scholars, 2015.
– *Landscapes of War and Memory: The Two World Wars in Canadian*

Literature and the Arts, 1977–2007. Edmonton: University of Alberta Press, 2014.

Grassi, Laurie. "5 Must-Read Canadian Novels about the Great War." *Chatelaine*, 11 November 2014. http://www.chatelaine.com/living/ chatelaine-book-club/5-must-read-canadian-novels-about-the-great-war. Accessed 19 August 2016.

Grayzel, Susan R. *Women and the First World War*. London: Routledge, 2002.

– *Women's Identities at War: Gender, Motherhood, and Politics in Britain and France during the First World War*. Chapel Hill: University of North Carolina Press, 1999.

Grodzinski, John R. "The Use and Abuse of Battle: Vimy Ridge and the Great War over the History of the First World War." *Canadian Military Journal* 10, no. 1 (2009): 83–6.

Gwyn, Sandra. *Tapestry of War: A Private View of Canadians in the Great War*. Toronto: HarperCollins, 1992.

Hale, Katherine. *Grey Knitting and Other Poems*. Toronto: William Briggs, 1914. http://canadianpoetry.org/poets/Hale_Katherine/ grey_knitting_ and_other_poems.html#1. Accessed 15 March 2015.

Hamilton, Mary Riter. "An Artist Impressionist on the Battlefields of France." *Gold Stripe* 3 (1919): 11–12.

Harrison, Charles Yale. *Generals Die in Bed: A Story from the Trenches*. 1930. Reprint, Toronto: Annick, 2007.

Hearts of the World. Directed by D.W. Griffith. D.W. Griffith Productions, Famous Players–Lasky and British War Office Committee, 1918, DVD.

Hedges, Chris. *War Is a Force That Gives Us Meaning*. New York: Public Affairs, 2002.

Helmers, Marguerite. "A Visual Rhetoric of World War I Battlefield Art: C.R.W. Nevinson, Mary Riter Hamilton and Kenneth Burke's Scene." *Space Between: Literature and Culture, 1914–1945* 5, no. 1 (2009): 77–95.

Higonnet, Margaret. "All Quiet in No Woman's Land." In *Gendering War Talk*, edited by Miriam Cooke and Angela Woollacott, 205–25. Princeton, NJ: Princeton University Press, 1993.

– ed. *Lines of Fire: Women Writers of World War I*. New York: Plume, 1999.

Higonnet, Margaret, Jane Jenson, Sony Michel, and Margaret Collins Weitz, eds. *Behind the Lines: Gender and the Two World Wars*. New Haven, CT: Yale University Press, 1987.

Hill, Colin. "Generic Experiment and Confusion in Early Canadian Novels of the Great War." *Studies in Canadian Literature* 34, no. 2 (2009): 58–76.

Hoare, J.E. "The Muse in Khaki." *University Magazine* 14, no. 3 (April 1915): 194–202.

Hoffenberg, Peter. "Landscape, Memory and the Australian War Experience, 1915–18." *Journal of Contemporary History* 36, no. 1 (2001): 111–31. http://bit.ly/1q6ZgDf.

James, Pearl. Introduction to *Picture This! World War I Posters and Visual Culture*. Edited by Pearl James, 2–3. Lincoln: University of Nebraska Press, 2009.

Kay, Carolyn. "War Pedagogy in the German Primary School Classroom during the First World War." *War and Society* 33, no. 1 (2014): 3–11.

Kazantzis, Judith. Preface to *Scars upon My Heart: Women's Poetry and Verse of the First World War*, edited by Catherine Reilly, xv–xxiv. London: Virago, 1981.

Kechnie, Margaret C. *Organizing Rural Women: The Federated Women's Institutes of Ontario, 1897–1919*. Montreal: McGill-Queen's University Press, 2003.

Keen, Paul. "'So –, So – Commonplace': Romancing the Local in *Anne of Green Gables* and *Aurora Leigh*." In Ledwell and Mitchell, *Anne around the World*, 92–105.

Kennedy, Margaret. "Lampman and the Canadian Thermopylae: 'At the Long Sault: May, 1660.'" *Canadian Poetry* 1 (1977): 54–9.

Keshen, Jeff. "All the News That Was Fit to Print: Ernest J. Chambers and Information Control in Canada, 1914–1919." *Canadian Historical Review* 73, no. 3 (1992): 315–44.

Kilpatrick, T.B. "The War and the Christian Church." *Report for the General Assembly's Commission on the War and Spiritual Life of the Church*. Toronto: Presbyterian Church in Canada, 1917.

Kinnear, Mary. "'Do You Want Your Daughter to Marry a Farmer?' Women's Work on the Farm, 1922." In *Canadian Papers in Rural History*. Vol. 6, edited by Donald H. Akenson, 137–53. Gananoque, ON: Langdale Press, 1988.

Klinck, Carl, ed. *Literary History of Canada: Canadian Literature in English*. Toronto: University of Toronto Press, 1965, 1973.

Kress, Gunther, and Theo van Leeuwen. *Reading Images: The Grammar of Visual Design*. 2nd ed. London: Routledge, 2006.

Lawson, Kate. "The Alien at Home." *Gothic Studies* 4, no. 2 (2002): 155–66.

– "The Disappointed House: Trance, Loss and the Uncanny in L.M. Montgomery's Emily Trilogy." *Children's Literature Review* 91 (2004): 71–90.

Leacock, Stephen. "The War Mania of Mr Jinks and Mr Blinks." In *Moonbeams from the Larger Lunacy*. Toronto: S.B. Gundy, 1915.

Ledwell, Jane, and Jean Mitchell, eds. *Anne around the World: L.M. Montgomery and Her Classic*. Montreal: McGill-Queen's University Press, 2013.

Lefebvre, Benjamin. Afterword to *The Blythes Are Quoted* by L.M. Montgomery, edited by Benjamin Lefebvre, 511–20. Toronto: Penguin Canada, 2009.

– "Pigsties and Sunsets: L.M. Montgomery, *A Tangled Web* and a Modernism of Her Own." *English Studies in Canada* 31, no. 4 (2005): 123–46.

– "'That Abominable War!' *The Blythes Are Quoted* and Thoughts on L.M. Montgomery's Late Style." In Mitchell, *Storm and Dissonance*, 109–30.

– "Walter's Closet." *Canadian Children's Literature* 25, no. 2 (1999): 7–20.

– ed. *The L.M. Montgomery Reader*. Volume 1. *A Life in Print*. Toronto: University of Toronto Press, 2013.

– ed. *The L.M. Montgomery Reader*. Volume 2. *A Critical Heritage*. Toronto: University of Toronto Press, 2014.

– ed. *The L.M. Montgomery Reader*. Volume 3. *A Legacy in Review*. Toronto: University of Toronto Press, 2015.

– ed. "Montgomery Ad 2: *Anne of Windy Poplars*." L.M. Montgomery Online. http://lmmonline.org/blog/2014/11/25/montgomery-ad-2-anne-of-windy-poplars/. Accessed 25 November 2014.

Lefebvre, Benjamin, and Andrea McKenzie. Introduction to *Rilla of Ingleside* by L.M. Montgomery, edited by Benjamin Lefebvre and Andrea McKenzie, ix–xix. Toronto: Viking, 2010.

Lunn, Joe. *Memoirs of the Maelstrom: A Senegalese Oral History of the First World War*. Portsmouth, NH: Heinemann, 1999.

MacDonald, Edward. *If You're Stronghearted: Prince Edward Island in the Twentieth Century*. Charlottetown: Prince Edward Museum and Heritage Foundation, 2000.

MacDonald, Heidi. "Reflections of the Great Depression in L.M. Montgomery's Life and Her *Pat* Books." In Mitchell, *Storm and Dissonance*, 142–58.

MacGregor, Stafford. "Mars La Tour, or The Maiden's Vow." In Barry, Doody, and Doody, *The Annotated Anne of Green Gables*, 481–2.

Macleod Moore, Mary. *The Maple Leaf's Red Cross: The War Story of the Canadian Red Cross Overseas*. London: Skeffington & Son, 1919.

Macphail, Sir Andrew. *Official History of the Canadian Forces in the Great War, 1914–1919: The Medical Services*. Ottawa: King's Printer, 1925.

Mann, Susan. *Margaret Macdonald: Imperial Daughter*. Montreal: McGill-Queen's University Press, 2005.

Martin, Chris. "The Right Course, the Best Course, the Only Course: Voluntary Recruitment in the Newfoundland Regiment, 1914–1918." *Newfoundland and Labrador Studies* 24, no. 1 (2009): 55–89.

"Mary Riter Hamilton: An Artist Impressionist on the Battlefields of France." *Gold Stripe* 3 (1919): 11–12.

McCabe, Kevin. Introduction to *The Poetry of Lucy Maud Montgomery*, edited by John Ferns and Kevin McCabe, 2–19. Markham, ON: Fitzhenry and Whiteside, 1987.

McCrae, John. "In Flanders Fields." In *In Flanders Fields and Other Poems*, 1. Toronto: Ryerson Press, 1920.

McKenzie, Andrea. "Witnesses to War: Discourse and Community in the Correspondence of Vera Brittain, Roland Leighton, Edward Brittain, Geoffrey Thurlow and Victor Richardson." PhD diss., University of Waterloo, 2000.

– "Women at War: L.M. Montgomery, the Great War and Canadian Cultural Memory." In Lefebvre, *The L.M. Montgomery Reader*, 2: 325–49.

– "Writing in Pictures: International Images of Emily." In Gammel, *Making Avonlea*, 99–113.

Merchant, Carolyn. *Reinventing Eden: The Fate of Nature in Western Culture*. New York: Routledge, 2003.

Miller, James Collins. *Rural Schools in Canada: Their Organization, Administration, and Supervision*. New York: Teachers College, Columbia

University, 1913. Internet Archive.org, https://archive.org/details/
schoolsinruralcaoomillrich. Accessed 15 August 2016.

Miller, Kathleen Ann. "Haunted Heroines: The Gothic Imagination and the
Female Bildungsroman of Jane Austen, Charlotte Brontë, and L.M.
Montgomery." *The Lion and the Unicorn* 34, no. 2 (2010): 125–47.

Mitchell, Jean. "Civilizing *Anne*: Missionaries of the South Seas, Cavendish
Evangelicalism, and the Crafting of *Anne of Green Gables.*" In Ledwell
and Mitchell, *Anne around the World,* 147–63.

– Introduction to Mitchell, *Storm and Dissonance,* 1–21.

– ed. *Storm and Dissonance: L.M. Montgomery and Conflict.* Newcastle,
UK: Cambridge Scholars Publishing, 2008.

Montgomery, L.M. *After Green Gables: L.M. Montgomery's Letters to
Ephraim Weber, 1916–1941,* edited by Hildi Froese Tiessen and Paul
Gerard Tiessen. Toronto: University of Toronto Press, 2006.

– *Anne of Green Gables.* 1908. Edited by Cecily Devereux. Reprint, Peter-
borough, ON: Broadview, 2004.

– *Anne's House of Dreams.* 1917. Reprint, Toronto: Seal, 1983.

– *Anne of Ingleside.* 1939. Reprint, Toronto: Seal, 1983.

– *Anne of the Island.* 1915. Reprint, Toronto: Seal, 1987.

– *Anne of Windy Poplars.* 1936. Reprint, Toronto: Seal, 1983.

– *The Blythes Are Quoted.* Edited by Benjamin Lefebvre. Toronto: Viking
Canada, 2009.

– *The Complete Journals of L.M. Montgomery: The PEI Years.* Edited by
Mary Henley Rubio and Elizabeth Hillman Waterston. 2 vols. Don Mills,
ON: Oxford University Press, 2012–13.

– *Emily Climbs.* Toronto: McClelland and Stewart, 1925.

– *Emily of New Moon.* Toronto: McClelland and Stewart, 1923.

– *Emily's Quest.* Toronto: McClelland and Stewart, 1927.

– "How I Became a Writer." *Manitoba Free Press* (Winnipeg, MB), 3
December 1921, Christmas Book Section: 3.

– *Jane of Lantern Hill.* 1937. Reprint, New York: Bantam, 1989.

– *Mistress Pat.* 1935. Reprint, New York: Bantam, 1989.

– *My Dear Mr. M: Letters to G.B. MacMillan,* edited by Francis W.P. Bolger
and Elizabeth Epperly. Toronto: McGraw–Hill Ryerson, 1980.

– *Rainbow Valley.* 1919. Reprint, New York: Bantam, 1985.

– *Rilla of Ingleside.* Edited by Benjamin Lefebvre and Andrea McKenzie.
Toronto: Viking Canada, 2010.

– *The Road to Yesterday*. Toronto: McGraw-Hill Ryerson, 1974.
– *The Selected Journals of L.M. Montgomery*. Edited by Mary Rubio and
  Elizabeth Waterston. 5 vols. Toronto: Oxford University Press, 1985–
  2004.
– *A Tangled Web*. 1931. Reprint, New York: Bantam, 1989.
– *The Watchman and Other Poems*. Toronto: McClelland, Stewart and
  Goodchild, 1916.
Morrow, John H. *The Great War: An Imperial History*. New York: Rout-
  ledge, 2004.
Morton, Desmond. *Fight or Pay: Soldiers' Families in the Great War*.
  Vancouver: UBC Press, 2004.
Munro, Alice. Afterword to *Emily of New Moon* by L.M. Montgomery,
  357–61. Toronto: McClelland and Stewart New Canadian Library, 1989.
Nicholson, G.W.L. *Canada's Nursing Sisters*. Toronto: Hakkert, 1975.
Norman, Allison. "'In Defense of the Empire': The Six Nations of the
  Grand River and the Great War." In Glassford and Shaw, A *Sisterhood
  of Suffering and Service*, 29–50.
Norton, Caroline. "Bingen on the Rhine." In Barry, Doody, and Doody,
  The Annotated Anne of Green Gables, 470–1.
Novak, Dagmar. *Dubious Glory: The Two World Wars and the Canadian
  Novel*. New York: P. Lang, 2000.
Ouditt, Sharon. *Fighting Forces, Writing Women: Identity and Ideology in
  the First World War*. London: Routledge, 1994.
Owen, Wilfred. "Strange Meeting." In Silkin, *The Penguin Book of First
  World War Poetry*, 191.
Palmer, Andrew, and Sally Minogue. "Memorial Poems and the Poetics of
  Memorializing." *Journal of Modern Literature* 34, no. 1 (2010): 162–81.
Palmer, Svetlana, and Sarah Wallis, eds. *Intimate Voices from the First
  World War*. London: Simon & Schuster, 2003.
Paul, Lissa, Rosemary Ross Johnston, and Emma Short, eds. *Children's
  Literature and Culture of the First World War*. New York: Routledge,
  2016.
Parrott, Edward. *The Children's Story of the War*. Vol. 4. Toronto: Nelson,
  1915.
Peabody, George. *School Days: The One-Room Schools of Maritime
  Canada*. Fredericton, NB: Goose Lane, 1992.
Potter, Jane. *Boys in Khaki, Girls in Print: Women's Literary Responses to
  the Great War, 1914–1918*. London: Routledge, 1994.

Potter, Jane, and Carol Acton. *Working in a World of Hurt: Trauma and Resilience in the Narratives of Medical Personnel in Warzones*. Manchester: Manchester University Press, 2015.

Quiney, Linda. "'Bravely and Loyally They Answered the Call': St. John Ambulance, the Red Cross, and the Patriotic Service of Canadian Women During the Great War." *History of Intellectual Culture* 5, no. 1 (2005): 1–19.

– "'We Must Not Neglect Our Duty': Enlisting Women Undergraduates for the Red Cross during the Great War." In *Cultures, Communities, and Conflict: Histories of Canadian Universities and War*, edited by Lisa Panavotidis and Paul Stortz, 71–94. Toronto: University of Toronto Press, 2012.

Redmann, Jennifer. "Doing Her Bit: German and Anglo-American Girls' Literature of the First World War." *Girlhood Studies* 4, no. 1 (2011): 10–29.

– "Nostalgia and Optimism in Else Ury's Nesthäkchen Books for Young Girls in the Weimar Republic." *German Quarterly* 79, no. 4 (2006): 465–83.

Reznick, Jeffrey S. *Healing the Nation: Soldiers and the Culture of Caregiving in Britain during the Great War*. Manchester: Manchester University Press, 2004.

Rich, Anina. "A Union of the Senses or a Sense of Union." *Cortex* 42, no. 3 (2006): 444–9.

Rich, Anina N., Mark A. Williams, Aina Puce, Ari Syngeniotis, Matthew A. Howard, Francis McGlone, and Jason B. Mattingley. "Neural Correlates of Imagined and Synaesthetic Colours." *Neuropsychologia* 44, no. 14 (2006): 2918–25.

Roberts, Charles G.D. *Canada in Flanders*. Vol. 3. London: Hodder & Stoughton, 1918.

Roper, Michael. "Between Manliness and Masculinity: The 'War Generation' and the Psychology of Fear in Britain, 1914–1950." *Journal of British Studies* 44 (2005): 343–62.

– *The Secret Battle: Emotional Survival in the Great War*. Manchester: Manchester University Press, 2009.

Rothwell, Erika. "Knitting Up the World: L.M. Montgomery and Maternal Feminism in Canada." In Gammel and Epperly, *L.M. Montgomery and Canadian Culture*, 133–44.

Royal Readers. Vols. 1–6. Royal School Series. London: Thomas Nelson,

1877. Internet Archive.org, https://archive.org/details/royalreaders00
publgoog. Accessed 15 August 2016.

Rubio, Mary. "Introduction: Harvesting Thistles in Montgomery's Textual
Garden." In Rubio, *Harvesting Thistles*, 1–13.

– "L.M. Montgomery: Scottish-Presbyterian Agency in Canadian Culture."
In Gammel and Epperly, *L.M. Montgomery and Canadian Culture*,
89–105.

– *Lucy Maud Montgomery: The Gift of Wings*. Toronto: Doubleday, 2008.

– "Subverting the Trite: L.M. Montgomery's 'Room of Her Own.'" In
Lefebvre, *The L.M. Montgomery Reader*, 2: 109–48.

Rubio, Mary, ed. *Harvesting Thistles: The Textual Garden of L.M. Montgomery. Essays on Her Novels and Journals*. Guelph, ON: Canadian Children's Press, 1994.

Russell, Ruth Weber, D.W. Russell, and Rea Wilmhurst. *Lucy Maud Montgomery: A Preliminary Bibliography*. Waterloo: University of Waterloo
Library, 1986.

Rutherdale, Robert. *Hometown Horizons: Local Responses to Canada's
Great War*. Vancouver: UBC Press, 2004.

Saggini, Francesca, and Anna Enrichetta Soccio. "Introduction: The Paper
Houses of English Literature." In *The Houses of Fiction as the House of
Life: Representations of the House from Richardson to Woolf*, edited by
Francesca Saggini and Anna Enrichetta Soccio, 1–9. Newcastle upon
Tyne, UK: Cambridge Scholars Publishing, 2012.

Samigorganroodi, Gholamreza. "Teaching and Reading *Anne of Green
Gables* in Iran, the Land of Omar Khayyam." In Ledwell and Mitchell,
Anne around the World, 181–91.

Sangster, Joan. "Mobilizing Women for War." In *Canada and the First
World War*, edited by David Mackenzie, 157–93. Toronto: University of
Toronto Press, 2005.

Sassoon, Siegfried. "Glory of Women." *Poems of the Great War, 1914–
1918*, 105. London: Penguin, 1998.

– "The Rank Stench of Those Bodies Haunts Me Still." In Silkin, *The Penguin Book of First World War Poetry*, 119.

Scates, Bruce. "The Unknown Sock Knitter: Voluntary Work, Emotional
Labour, Bereavement and the Great War." *Labour History* 81 (2002):
39–40.

Service, Robert. *Rhymes of a Red Cross Man*. Toronto: W. Briggs, 1916.

– *Songs of a Sourdough*. Toronto: W. Briggs, 1909.

Sharpe, C.A. "Enlistment in the Canadian Expeditionary Force, 1914–1918: A Regional Analysis." *Journal of Canadian Studies* 18, no. 3 (1983): 15–29.

Shaw, Amy J. *Crisis of Conscience: Conscientious Objection in Canada during the First World War*. Vancouver: UBC Press, 2009.

Shaw, Bernard. *Heartbreak House, Great Catherine, and Playlets of the War*. London: Constable & Co., 1919.

Sheard, Virna. *Carry On!* Toronto: Warwick Bros. & Rutter, 1917.

Sheehan, Nancy M. "Junior Red Cross in the Schools: An International Movement, a Voluntary Agency, and Curriculum Change." *Curriculum Inquiry* 17, no. 3 (1987): 247–66.

Silkin, Jon, ed. *The Penguin Book of First World War Poetry*. London: Penguin, 1996.

Smith, Angela K. *The Second Battlefield: Women, Modernism and the First World War*. Manchester: Manchester University Press, 2000.

Stead, Robert J.C. *The Cow Puncher*. Toronto: Musson Book Company, 1918.

– *Dennison Grant: A Novel of To-Day*. Toronto: Musson Book Company, 1920.

– *Grain*. Toronto: McClelland and Stewart, 1926.

– *Kitchener, and Other Poems*. Toronto: Musson Book Company, 1917.

Steffler, Margaret. "'Being a Christian' and a Presbyterian in Leaskdale." In Bode and Clement, *L.M. Montgomery's Rainbow Valleys*, 54–73.

Street, Kori. "Patriotic, Not Permanent: Attitudes about Women's Making Bombs and Being Bankers." In Glassford and Shaw, *A Sisterhood of Suffering and Service*, 148–70.

Tector, Amy. "A Righteous War? L.M. Montgomery's Depiction of the First World War in *Rilla of Ingleside*." *Canadian Literature* 179 (2003): 72–86.

"They Drown the Conversation." *Bulletin* [Canadian Red Cross], October 1916, 6–7.

Thompson, Eric. "Canadian Fiction of the Great War." *Canadian Literature* 91 (winter 1981): 81–96.

Thompson, Rebecca J. "'That House Belongs to Me': The Appropriation of Space, Place, and Heritage in L.M. Montgomery's *Emily* Trilogy." MA thesis, Seton Hall University, 2012.

Thompson, William V. "The Shadow on the House of Dreams: Montgomery's Re-visioning of Anne." In Bode and Clement, *L.M. Montgomery's Rainbow Valleys*, 113–30.

Thomson, Denise. "National Sorrow, National Pride: Commemoration of War in Canada, 1918–1945." *Journal of Canadian Studies* 30, no. 4 (1995/96): 5–27. http://bit.ly/1q6ZcTP.

Tiessen, Paul. "Opposing Pacifism: L.M. Montgomery and the Trouble with Ephraim Weber." In Mitchell, *Storm and Dissonance*, 131–41.

"Trench, Vimy Ridge." *Gold Stripe* 3 (1919): 178.

Urquhart, Jane. Afterword to *Emily Climbs* by L.M. Montgomery, 330–4. Toronto: McClelland and Stewart New Canadian Library, 1989.

Ury, Else. *Nesthäkchen und der Weltkrieg*. Berlin: Meidinger, n.d. [1916].

Vance, Jonathan F. *Death So Noble: Memory, Meaning, and the First World War*. Vancouver: UBC Press, 1997.

Verhey, Jeffrey. *The Spirit of 1914: Militarism, Myth, and Mobilization in Germany*. Cambridge: Cambridge University Press, 2000.

Vice, Samantha. "Beauty, Mourning and the Commemoration of Evil." *Midwest Studies in Philosophy* 36, no. 1 (2012): 142–62.

Wachowicz, Barbara. "L.M. Montgomery: At Home in Poland." *Canadian Children's Literature / Littérature canadienne pour la jeunesse* 46 (1987): 7–36.

Waterson, Elizabeth. *Magic Island: The Fictions of L.M. Montgomery*. Toronto: Oxford University Press, 2008.

Watson, Janet S.K. *Fighting Different Wars: Experience, Memory, and the First World War in Britain*. Cambridge: Cambridge University Press, 2004.

Webb, Peter. "'A Righteous Cause': War Propaganda and Canadian Fiction, 1915–1921." *British Journal of Canadian Studies* 24, no. 1 (2011): 31–48.

White, Gavin. "The Religious Thought of L.M. Montgomery." In Rubio, *Harvesting Thistles*, 84–8.

Wilde, Terry. "Freshettes, Farmerettes and Feminine Fortitude at the University of Toronto during the First World War." In Glassford and Shaw, *A Sisterhood of Suffering and Service*, 75–98.

Wilkending, Gisela. "Mädchen-Kriegsromane im Ersten Weltkreig." In *Geschichte der Mädchenlektüre: Mädchenliteratur und die gesellschaft-*

liche Situation der Frauen von 18 Jahrhundert bis zur Gegenwart, edited by Dagmar Grenz and Gisela Wilkending, 151–72. Weinheim: Juventa, 1997.

Willson, H. Beckles. *Redemption: A Novel.* New York: Putnam, 1924.

Winter, Jay. *Sites of Memory, Sites of Mourning: The Great War in European Cultural History.* Cambridge: Cambridge University Press, 1995.

Winter, Jay, and Blaine Baggett. *The Great War and the Shaping of the Twentieth Century.* New York: Penguin Studio, 1996.

Wordsworth, William. "Lines Composed a Few Miles above Tintern Abbey." In *Wordsworth: Selected Poems*, edited by Walford Davies, 19–42. Letchworth, UK: J.M. Dent & Sons, 1975.

Young, Alan. "L.M. Montgomery's *Rilla of Ingleside* (1920): Romance and the Experience of War." In *Myth and Milieu: Atlantic Literature and Culture 1918–1939*, edited by Gwendolyn Davies, 95–122. Fredericton, NB: Acadiensis, 1993.

– "'We Throw the Torch': Canadian Memorials of the Great War and the Mythology of Heroic Sacrifice." *Journal of Canadian Studies / Revue d'études canadiennes* 24, no. 4 (winter 1989–90): 5–28.

Contributors

ANDREA MCKENZIE is associate professor with the Writing Department and the Graduate Program in History at York University. With Benjamin Lefebvre, she co-edited the restored text of L.M. Montgomery's *Rilla of Ingleside* (2010), and has also contributed chapters about L.M. Montgomery's works to *The L.M. Montgomery Reader*, volume 2, *A Critical Heritage*; *Textual Transformations in Children's Literature*; *Storm and Dissonance*; and *Making Avonlea*. She edited and introduced *War-Torn Exchanges: The Lives and Letters of Nursing Sisters Laura Holland and Mildred Forbes* (2016), and has published works on women's and children's war narratives in venues such as *The Lion and the Unicorn* and *Other Fronts, Other Wars?* (2014). A professional writer for over twenty-five years, McKenzie has previously held positions at New York University and MIT.

JANE LEDWELL is a poet, writer, and editor from Prince Edward Island and a recipient of the Prince Edward Island Award for Distinguished Contribution to the Literary Arts. She currently works as executive director of the PEI Advisory Council on the Status of Women and previously worked with the Institute of Island Studies and taught English at the University of Prince Edward Island. She holds an MPhil from the University of Waikato, New Zealand. With Jean Mitchell, she co-edited *Anne around the World: L.M. Montgomery and Her Classic* (2013); she contributed to *Storm and*

Dissonance: L.M. Montgomery and Conflict (2008) and co-edited
Message in a Bottle: The Literature of Small Islands (2000). She
has published two books of poems, *Last Tomato* (2005) and *Bird
Calls* (2016).

JONATHAN F. VANCE is Distinguished University Professor and
J.B. Smallman Chair in the Department of History at Western University, where he teaches Canadian and military history and social
memory. A native of Waterdown, Ontario, he holds degrees from
McMaster, Queen's, and York University. He is the author of many
books and articles, including *Death So Noble: Memory, Meaning,
and the First World War* (1997), *A Gallant Company: The True Story
of "The Great Escape"* (2003), and *Building Canada: People and
Projects That Shaped the Nation* (2006). His most recent books are
*Unlikely Soldiers: How Two Canadians Fought the Secret War
against Nazi Occupation* (2008), *A History of Canadian Culture*
(2009), and *Maple Leaf Empire: Canada, Britain and Two World
Wars* (2011).

IRENE GAMMEL holds a Canada Research Chair in Modern
Literature and Culture at Ryerson University in Toronto, where she
is professor of English and also directs the Modern Literature and
Culture Research Centre. She is the author of many articles and
books on L.M. Montgomery including *Looking for Anne* (2008).
She has also edited several volumes on Montgomery, including
Anne's World: A New Century of "Anne of Green Gables" (2011)
and *The Intimate Life of L.M. Montgomery* (2005). She is at work
on a book on Canadian battlefield artist Mary Riter Hamilton.

E. HOLLY PIKE is associate professor of English at Grenfell Cam-
pus, Memorial University of Newfoundland. She has published on
L.M. Montgomery in *Harvesting Thistles: The Textual Garden of
L.M. Montgomery*; *L.M. Montgomery and Canadian Culture*; *Mak-
ing Avonlea: L.M. Montgomery and Popular Culture*; *Storm and
Dissonance: L.M. Montgomery and Conflict*; *One Hundred Years of
Anne with an "e": The Centennial Study of Anne of Green Gables*;
and the philosophy journal *Animus*.

SUSAN FISHER, professor emerita at the University of the Fraser Valley, earned her doctorate in comparative literature and has published on a range of topics in Japanese and Canadian literature. She was acting editor of *Canadian Literature* from 2002 to 2004. Her book, *Boys and Girls in No Man's Land: English-Canadian Children and the First World War*, was awarded the 2011 Canada Prize in the Humanities.

LAURA M. ROBINSON is professor and dean of the School of Arts and Social Sciences, Grenfell Campus, Memorial University of Newfoundland. She has published articles about Canadian children's literature, Canadian women writers, and *The L Word*, in addition to many articles on L.M. Montgomery's work. She is the curator of the highly successful exhibit *The Canadian Home Front: L.M. Montgomery's Reflections on War*, which has toured in France and locations in Canada. Her current project examines Montgomery's depiction of friendship and sexuality.

SARAH GLASSFORD has a PhD in history from York University; she is co-editor, with Amy Shaw, of *A Sisterhood of Suffering and Service: Women and Girls of Canada and Newfoundland during the First World War* (2012). She welcomed this chance to combine her scholarly interest in women's and children's wartime voluntary work with her lifelong enjoyment of L.M. Montgomery's fiction.

MAUREEN O. GALLAGHER holds a PhD in German studies from the University of Massachusetts, Amherst. Her dissertation is entitled "Young Germans in the World: Race, Gender, and Imperialism in Wilhelmine Youth Literature, 1870–1919." Her research approaches the field of German studies from comparative, interdisciplinary, and transnational approaches; her research areas include migrant and minority literatures, race and German society, and children's and young adult literature.

CAROLINE E. JONES, PhD, is an editor, writer, and scholar work-ing in Austin, Texas. Her primary research interests are depictions of sexuality in children's and young adult literature, dystopias, and, of course, L.M. Montgomery. She has presented at each L.M. Montgomery Institute conference since 2008 and has contributed chapters in *Anne around the World* (2013) and *L.M. Montgomery's Rainbow Valleys: The Ontario Years, 1911–1942* (2015).

ELIZABETH ROLLINS EPPERLY, founder of the L.M. Mont-gomery Institute, professor emerita, and former president of the University of Prince Edward Island, is a life-long Montgomery reader and author or editor of numerous studies of Montgomery. She was guest curator for the Confederation Centre Art Gallery exhibition "This *Anne* Place: *Anne of Green Gables* as Idea, Book, and Musical" (May–September 2014). Her 1992 *Fragrance of Sweet-Grass* was reissued in 2014 with a new preface.

Index